# Diabetes

## Diagnosis, classification and treatment

# Diabetes

## Diagnosis, classification and treatment

Chapters from the Oxford Textbook of Endocrinology and Diabetes First Edition

Edited by

**John A.H. Wass**

*Professor of Endocrinology, University of Oxford;*
*Consultant Physician, Radcliffe Infirmary;*
*Consultant Physician, Nuffield Orthopaedic Centre, Oxford*

and

**Stephen M. Shalet**

*Professor of Endocrinology, Christie Hospital, Manchester;*
*Professor of Medicine, University of Manchester*

Diabetes section edited by

**Edwin Gale** and **Stephanie A. Amiel**

OXFORD
UNIVERSITY PRESS

# OXFORD
## UNIVERSITY PRESS

Great Clarendon Street, Oxford OX2 6DP

Oxford University Press is a department of the University of Oxford.
It furthers the University's objective of excellence in research,
scholarship, and education by publishing worldwide in

Oxford  New York

Auckland  Cape Town  Dar es Salaam  Hong Kong  Karachi
Kuala Lumpur  Madrid  Melbourne  Mexico City  Nairobi
New Delhi  Shanghai  Taipei  Toronto
With offices in
Argentina  Austria  Brazil  Chile  Czech Republic  France  Greece
Guatemala  Hungary  Italy  Japan  Poland  Portugal  Singapore
South Korea  Switzerland  Thailand  Turkey  Ukraine  Vietnam
and an associated company in Berlin

Oxford is a registered trade mark of Oxford University Press
in the UK and in certain other countries

Published in the United States
by Oxford University Press Inc., New York

British Library Cataloguing in Publication Data

Data available

Library of Congress Cataloging in Publication Data

Typeset in Minion by Newgen Imaging Systems (P) Ltd., Chennai, India
Printed in the UK
on acid-free paper by Ashford Colour Press, Ltd.

ISBN 978–0–19–954424–0

10 9 8 7 6 5 4 3 2 1

# Contents

# List of contributors

**Amiel, Stephanie A** Department of Diabetes, Endocrinology and Internal Medicine, Guy's, King's, and St Thomas's School of Medicine, King's College, London, UK

**Atkinson, Mark** Department of Pathology, University of Florida, Gainesvile, Florida, USA

**Courten, Maximilian de** Medical Officer, Non-communicable Diseases, Office of the WHO Representative for the South Pacific, Suva, Fiji Islands

**Gale, Edwin** Department of Diabetes, Medical School Unit, Southmead Hospital, Bristol, UK

**Groop, Leif** Department of Endocrinology, University of Lund, Malmö General Hospital, Malmö, Sweden

**Hales, C Nicholas** Professor of Clinical Biochemistry, University of Cambridge, Addenbrooke's Hospital, Department of Clinical Biochemistry, Cambridge, UK

**Hattersley, Andrew T** Professor of Molecular Medicine, Department of Diabetes and Vascular Medicine, University of Exeter, Exeter, UK

**Matthews, David R** Chairman of the Oxford Centre, The Oxford Centre for Diabetes, Endocrinology and Metabolism, Oxford Radcliffe Hospitals, The Radcliffe Infirmary, Oxford, UK

**Nerup, Jørn** Steno Diabetes Center, Denmark

**O'Rahilly, Stephen** Professor of Metabolic Medicine, University of Cambridge, Addenbrooke's Hospital, Cambridge

**Owen, Katharine** Clinical Research Fellow, Department of Diabetes and Vascular Medicine, University of Exeter, Exeter, UK

**Pociot, Flemming** Steno Diabetes Center, Denmark

**Shah, Baiju** Postgraduate Trainee, University of Toronto, Department of Medicine, Toronto, Canada

**Williams, Joanne** International Diabetes Institute, Caulfield, Victoria, Australia

**Zinman, Bernard** Director, Leadership Sinai Centre for Diabetes; Professor of Medicine, University of Toronto, Mount Sinai Hospital, Toronto, Ontario, Canada

# 1 Diagnosis and classification of diabetes mellitus

*Paul Zimmet, Joanne Williams, and Maximilian de Courten*

## Definition of diabetes

Diabetes mellitus is a group of metabolic diseases characterized by hyperglycaemia resulting from defects in insulin secretion, insulin action, or both. The chronic hyperglycaemia of diabetes is associated with long-term damage, dysfunction and failure of various organs especially the eyes, kidneys, nerves, heart and blood vessels.[1]

## History

Acknowledgement that diabetes is not a single disorder has been attributed to two Indian physicians – Charaka and Sushruta (600 AD). They recognized two forms of the disease, although most of the descriptions in the early literature probably relate to what today is known as type 1 (insulin-dependent) diabetes. Sushruta is also credited with the first observation that diabetes was associated with 'honeyed urine'. Throughout history such renowned scientists and physicians as Galen, Avicenna, Paracelsus, and Maimonides have made reference to diabetes.[2] Maimonides (1135–1204), who was both a physician and Talmudic scholar, observed on his travels that diabetes was seldom seen in 'cold' Europe but was frequently encountered in 'warm' Africa. During the 18th and 19th centuries a less symptomatic variety of the disorder was noted. It was identified by heavy glycosuria, often detected in later life and commonly associated with overweight rather than the previously-described wasting. In the current classification this would be regarded as type 2 diabetes.

It was observed in ancient China that ants were attracted to the urine of people with diabetes. Thomas Willis (London, 1621–1675) noted that diabetic urine tasted 'wondrous sweet' and in 1766 another Englishman, Matthew Dobson, observed that diabetic serum tasted sweet. He demonstrated the presence of sugar in diabetic urine by chemistry and chemical tests such as Fehling's were developed by the 1840s. Benedict's urine test (1911) was the mainstay for assessing control of diabetes for decades, although a blood sugar test was introduced in 1919 by the work of Folin and Wu.

As a consequence of the 1870 Siege of Paris, during the Franco-Prussian war, a French physician named Bouchardat noted the beneficial effects of food shortages on patients with diabetes. Glycosuria and ketonuria decreased or disappeared, as did the major symptoms and signs. Almost twenty years later the development of the theory of the pancreatic diabetes emerged when the results of an important study 'Diabetes Mellitus After Extirpation of the Pancreas' was published by Josef von Mering and Oskar Minkowski in 1889. The discovery was the result of a wager between Minkowski and von Mering, that a dog could not survive without a pancreas. The dog survived the experiment but kept urinating on the laboratory floor. Minkowski tested the dog's urine for glucose, as his mentor Bernard Naunyn had instructed him to do this for patients with polyuria, and found a high glucose content. This discovery inspired the work relating to the isolation of insulin for use in the therapy of diabetes, for which Banting and Best won the Nobel Prize in 1921.

In 1936, Harold Himsworth[3] proposed that there were at least two clinical types of diabetes, insulin-sensitive and insulin-insensitive. He suggested that insulin-sensitive diabetic patients were insulin deficient and required exogenous insulin to survive, while the other group did not require insulin. This observation was based on clinical observation alone, as there were then no assays for the measurement of insulin. An Australian scientist, Joseph Bornstein, was responsible for developing the first bioassay for insulin.[4] Bornstein's results were confirmed a decade later and Yalow was subsequently awarded the Nobel Prize for her development with Berson of a radioimmunoassay for insulin. Thereafter, there was widespread acceptance that there were at least two major forms of diabetes. As these appeared to be separated according to the age of onset, they were labelled 'juvenile-onset' and 'maturity-onset' diabetes. These were later assigned the names, insulin-dependent diabetes mellitus (IDDM) and non-insulin dependent diabetes mellitus (NIDDM), and most recently, type 1 and type 2 diabetes mellitus.

## Diabetes classification

Although different forms of diabetes have been recognized for over 2000 years,[5] the apparent diversity in the aetiology of the two major types made the development of a definitive classification difficult. The diagnostic criteria for diabetes have changed on a number of occasions over recent decades,[6] with both the World Health Organization (WHO) and the American Diabetes Association (ADA) reviewing and revising them. Without clear classification it is not easy to take a systematic epidemiological approach to clinical research and develop evidence based recommendations for the treatment and prevention of diabetes. In 1964, the WHO convened an Expert Committee on Diabetes Mellitus, which attempted to provide a universal classification on the diabetes syndrome. However, it was not until 1980 that the WHO Expert Committee offered a classification which was accepted internationally and even then controversy continued. Minor changes to the classification took place in 1985[7] based on both clinical and aetiological characteristics and these were widely accepted for the next decade. The 1985 WHO Study Group classification (1985) included a number of clinical classes, of which the major two were IDDM or type 1 diabetes and NIDDM or type 2 diabetes. Other important classes were described, including malnutrition-related diabetes (MRDM), the condition of impaired glucose tolerance (IGT) and gestational diabetes mellitus (GDM).

Over the next decade, data from genetic, epidemiological and aetiological studies accumulated and understanding of the aetiology and pathogenesis of the diabetes syndromes improved. In 1995, the American Diabetes Association sponsored an expert group to review the literature and determine whether changes to the classification were necessary. The WHO convened a Consultation in December 1996 to consider the issues and examine the available data. Its provisional report was published in 1998[8] with the document being finalized a year later.[9]

The new classification is based on stages of glucose tolerance status, with a complimentary sub-classification according to aetiological type (Fig. 1). Hyperglycaemia can be subcategorized regardless of the underlying cause by staging into:

- *Insulin requiring for survival* (corresponds to the former IDDM).
- *Insulin requiring for control* – that is, for metabolic control, not for survival (corresponds to the former insulin treated NIDDM).

- *Not insulin requiring*, that is, treatment by non-pharmacological methods or drugs other than insulin (corresponds to NIDDM on diet alone/or coupled with oral agents).

## Impaired Glucose Tolerance (IGT) and impaired fasting glycaemia (IFG)

IGT was previously a separate class. It is now categorized as a stage in the natural history of disordered carbohydrate metabolism. IGT is coupled with 'impaired fasting glycaemia' (6.1–7.0 mmol/l), which can be defined where glucose tolerance testing has not been performed. The two terms are not synonymous and the two conditions may have different implications.

The ADA[1] and WHO[9] recommended the following changes to the previously established criteria for the diagnosis of hyperglycaemic states:

- The fasting plasma glucose (FPG) threshold for diagnosis of diabetes is lowered from 7.8 to 7.0 mmol/l.
- Impaired fasting glycaemia (FPG 6.1–6.9 mmol/l) is introduced as a new category of intermediate glucose metabolism (named impaired fasting glucose by the ADA).

## The different types of diabetes (Box 1)

Type 1 diabetes mellitus is defined clinically as being insulin deficient and therefore ketosis-prone. It is due to the destruction of the pancreatic β cells. In most cases, this destruction is autoimmune (type 1a), with evidence of immunological activity directed against the β-cell – for example, antibodies directed against islet cells (ICA);

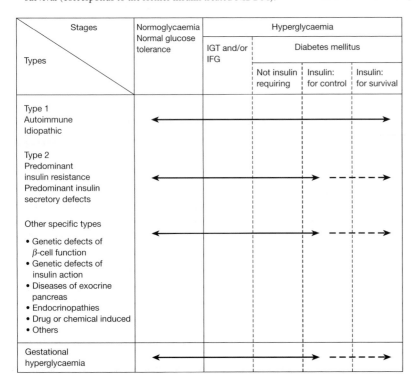

| Stages / Types | Normoglycaemia Normal glucose tolerance | Hyperglycaemia | | | |
|---|---|---|---|---|---|
| | | IGT and/or IFG | Diabetes mellitus | | |
| | | | Not insulin requiring | Insulin: for control | Insulin: for survival |
| Type 1 Autoimmune Idiopathic | | | | | |
| Type 2 Predominant insulin resistance Predominant insulin secretory defects | | | | | |
| Other specific types • Genetic defects of β-cell function • Genetic defects of insulin action • Diseases of exocrine pancreas • Endocrinopathies • Drug or chemical induced • Others | | | | | |
| Gestational hyperglycaemia | | | | | |

**Fig. 1** Clinical stages and aetiological classification of abnormalities of glucose metabolism. The arrows indicate that an individual may move between stages, and the broken arrows indicate that rarely, people in a category that would not by definition require insulin for survival may move into such an insulin need, for example, ketoacidosis precipitated by infection in a type 2 patient. Adapted from *Definition, Diagnosis and Classification of Diabetes Mellitus and its Complications – Part 1: Diagnosis and Classification of Diabetes Mellitus.* Geneva: World Health Organization, 1999.

- ◆ Type 1 diabetes mellitus: $\beta$ cell destruction → insulin deficiency, ketosis prone
  - ■ Type 1A: Proven autoimmune aetiology
  - ■ Type 1B: No demonstrable autoimmunity
- ◆ Type 2 diabetes mellitus: Variable degree of insulin resistance and insulin deficiency. Not ketosis prone
- ◆ Other specific types:
  - ■ Genetic causes of impaired $\beta$-cell function for example, Maturity Onset diabetes of Youth (MODY); mitochondrial DNA 3243 mutations
  - ■ Genetic defects in insulin action for example, Type A insulin resistance, leprachaunism, Rabson-Mendenhall syndrome; Lipoatrophy
  - ■ Secondary to pancreatic disease for example, cystic fibrosis, thalassaemia, haemochromatosis, $\alpha1$ antitrypsin deficiency, chronic or relapsing pancreatitis, congenital absence of islets or pancreas
  - ■ Secondary to other endocrine diseases for example, Cushing's, acromegaly
  - ■ Secondary to drugs or toxins for example, glucocorticoids, thiazides, asparaginase
  - ■ Secondary to infection for example, congenital rubella
  - ■ Other forms of immune disorder for example, polyglandular syndromes, APECED, Stiff Man
  - ■ Rare genetic disorders for example, Down's, Klinefelter's, Prader-Willi, Turners, Wolframs, Laurence-Moon-Biedl, myotonic dystrophy, ataxia telangectasia, porphyria
- ◆ Gestational diabetes: Any form of glucose intolerance first diagnosed in pregnancy

Adapted from Reference (8) and reproduced from Clinical Paediatric Endocrinology, eds. Charles Brook and Peter Hindmarch, by kind permission of the publishers, Blackwell Science Ltd.

or constituents of the $\beta$ cell such as glutamic acid (GAD) or IA-2, a tyrosine kinase constituent of the membrane of the insulin secretory granule. Evidence of such autoimmune activation can precede hyperglycaemia by several years, but the presence of the autoantibodies is diagnostic of the type 1 process. Later, subtle loss of $\beta$-cell mass can be detected by failure of the rapid initial response of insulin to an intravenous glucose bolus, until so much $\beta$ cell function is lost that spontaneous hyperglycaemia occurs. In a significant minority of people with insulin deficient, ketosis prone, type 1 diabetes, there is no evidence of autoimmune activation. This apparently non-autoimmune type 1 b diabetes is more common in Black people.

The class of type 2 diabetes mellitus probably includes a number of different aetiologies and is likely to shrink as understanding of the different diabetic syndromes grows. Type 2 diabetes results from a combination of insulin resistance and insulin deficiency, each in different degree in different cases. The normal response to insulin

resistance is hyperinsulinaemia and a degree of insulin deficiency is implicit in the presence of hyperglycaemia. However, the residual insulin secretion is enough to prevent lipolysis and ketogenesis, so these patients are not truly insulin dependent. Many may progress to require insulin to achieve optimal glycaemic control however, as the disease is progressive. A small number of patients with apparent type 2 disease may progress to absolute insulin deficiency rapidly (over a few years) and, on testing, have evidence of anti-islet autoimmunity. These patients have true type 1, albeit late in onset and slower in progression than the norm. They are typically non-obese at presentation. The condition of impaired glucose tolerance, which predisposes to type 2 diabetes, is a condition where insulin resistance accompanies normoglycaemia at the expense of hyperinsulinaemia.

Other specific types of diabetes include single gene defects causing insulin resistance or insulin secretory failure, often with very specific phenotypes to help identify them; diabetes secondary to pancreatic disease or damage by toxins, drugs or viruses; diabetes secondary to other endocrine disorders or drugs. Gestational diabetes is glucose intolerance or diabetes first diagnosed in pregnancy and is an indicator of high risk of later type 2 disease.

## Impaired Glucose Tolerance

The IGT category includes people whose oral glucose tolerance test (OGTT) result is beyond the boundaries of normality by WHO criteria (Table 1). IGT may represent a stage in the natural history of diabetes, as people with it are at higher risk for diabetes than the general population.[10] People with IGT have a heightened risk of macrovascular disease[10] and IGT is associated with other known CVD risk factors including hypertension, dyslipidaemia and central obesity.[9] The diagnosis of IGT therefore may have important prognostic implications, particularly in otherwise healthy and ambulatory individuals. The prognostic implications of the new category of impaired fasting glucose, diagnosed without recourse to an oral glucose tolerance test, is not yet clear.

## Current criteria for diagnosis ADA/WHO

### New diagnostic criteria for diabetes (see Box 1)

The ADA considered that diagnosis can generally be made on fasting plasma glucose alone, however, the WHO group supported the retention of the OGTT unless circumstances prevent it from being performed. The criteria used to classify individuals will obviously have an impact on incidence and prevalence rates. Retrospective comparisons of the two diagnostic criteria are being published throughout the world[11-13] as the debate on classification continues. The overall impression is that the OGTT should be retained for the diagnosis of diabetes when necessary. Table 2 demonstrates how the different criteria would classify patients with different blood glucose levels. There is complete agreement in classifying those individuals at either extreme, however, for those with a fasting plasma glucose (FPG) of between 6.1 and 7.8 mmol/l and a 2 h glucose between 7.8 and 11.1 mmol/l classification relies on the criteria being followed. For clinical purposes, the recording of an unequivocally high plasma glucose (greater than 11 mol/l) in the presence of characteristic

**Table 1** Values for diagnosis* of diabetes and other categories of hyperglycaemia

| | Glucose concentration (mmol/l) | | | |
| | Plasma | | Whole blood | |
| | Venous | Capillary | Venous | Capillary |
|---|---|---|---|---|
| Diabetes mellitus | | | | |
|   Fasting *or* | ⩾7.0 | ⩾ 7.0 | ⩾6.1 | ⩾6.1 |
|   2-h post glucose load | ⩾11.1 | ⩾12.2 | ⩾10.0 | ⩾11.1 |
| Impaired Glucose Tolerance | | | | |
|   Fasting concentration *and* | <7.0 | <7.0 | <6.1 | <6.1 |
|   2-h post glucose load | ⩾7.8 and <11.1 | ⩾8.9 and <12.2 | ⩾6.7 and <10.0 | ⩾7.8 and <11.1 |
| Impaired Fasting Glucose | | | | |
|   Fasting | ⩾6.1 and < 7.0 | ⩾6.1 and <7.0 | ⩾5.6 and < 6.1 | ⩾5.6 and <6.1 |
|   2-h (if measured) | <7.8 | <8.9 | <6.7 | <7.8 |

\* Note that diabetes can only be diagnosed in an individual when these diagnostic values are confirmed on another day.

**Table 2** Comparison of different glucose cut-off levels for diabetes criteria used by WHO – 1985, ADA – 1997 and WHO – 1999

| Fasting plasma glucose (mmol/l) | 2-hour plasma glucose (mmol/l) | | |
| | <7.8 | 7.8–11.1 | ⩾11.1 |
|---|---|---|---|
| <6.1 | N | IGT | D |
| | N | IGT | D |
| | N | IGT | D |
| 6.1–7.0 | N | IGT | D |
| | IFG | IFG+IGT | D |
| | IFG | IFG+IGT | D |
| 7.0–7.8 | N | IGT | D |
| | D | D | D |
| | D | D | D |
| ⩾7.8 | D | D | D |
| | D | D | D |
| | D | D | D |

symptoms obviates the need for more specific testing. Because there is at least one person in every cell of Table 1, the different cutoff levels used in the different criteria will necessarily identify different people.

The implications for an individual of a diagnosis of diabetes should not be underestimated. The diagnosis needs to be secure and the number of false positive results limited. Given the day to day variability of blood glucose measurements, it is recommended that diabetes be only diagnosed when two abnormal values have been found on separate days, except in the presence of appropriate symptoms and signs. It should be noted however, that in all the studies relating blood glucose to risk of retinopathy, on which the diagnostic thresholds are heavily based, only a single OGTT was performed.

Another significant detail is that all the evidence on which diagnostic thresholds are based is for venous plasma glucose. The thresholds given for other sample types (whole blood) have been calculated to be equivalent to the plasma values, however, formal comparisons in large populations have not been made and these values may not be as reliable as the plasma thresholds.

# Different diagnostic tests available

Where the issues for the present are to determine the optimal tests and criteria for epidemiological research and for clinical practice, in the future the selection of optimal tests (including HbA1c) and optimizing diagnostic levels with respect to costs and benefits will become important.

## What is the best test for diabetes?

A diagnostic test is used to confirm the presence or absence of a condition/disease for which the patient has demographic features or symptoms, whereas, screening tests are used to identify unrecognized disease. Screening is generally associated with chronic illness and is usually initiated by an agency providing care, while a patient with a complaint normally prompts diagnostic testing. The diagnosis of diabetes differs from the detection of most other diseases as often the same testing procedure is used for screening as for diagnosing the disease.

## The diagnostic test

There are various biochemical tests available to examine the presence of hyperglycaemia and the strengths and weaknesses of each are often dependent on whether they are being used for diagnosis or screening.

### Oral glucose tolerance test

The oral glucose tolerance test (OGTT) is the accepted standard for the diagnosis of diabetes. It involves the administration of 75 g anhydrous glucose to a person who has been on a diet containing at least 250 g carbohydrate per day over the previous three days and who has then fasted overnight prior to the test. Plasma glucose is measured before and 2 h after the consumption of the glucose drink. It is time consuming and inconvenient, and therefore unsuitable for widespread use amongst all people with risk factors for diabetes. Paired OGTTs performed 2–6 weeks apart have shown that amongst people who are diagnosed as having diabetes on an initial OGTT, 95 per cent of values in the second OGTT lie within ±20 per cent of the initial fasting glucose and ±36 per cent of the initial 2 h glucose.[12]

An initial screening test is required to select those people who need to have an OGTT. Either a random or fasting blood glucose can be used as the initial screening test in people who have been identified as being at risk of type 2 diabetes.[9]

### Fasting plasma glucose measurement

The properties of fasting plasma glucose (at a threshold of greater than or equal to 6.1 mmol/l) as a screening tool for diabetes has recently been reported in a number of studies using the new diagnostic thresholds for diabetes (Table 3). With only one exception, in each of these studies (Table 3), the OGTT was performed on the whole population, irrespective of an individual's fasting glucose. From these data, the median sensitivity was 81 per cent, and the median specificity was 92 per cent.

Since the introduction of the new lower diagnostic threshold of 7.0 mmol/l for fasting plasma, it has been suggested that the OGTT can be virtually dispensed with and the fasting glucose alone can be used to both diagnose and exclude diabetes.[1] However, a number of recent studies have shown that this approach would result in the misclassification of a significant proportion of people with diabetes (according to the 2 h level).[13,15–22] It is likely that all of these people are at risk of diabetes related complications (that is, are genuinely diabetic), and therefore the OGTT is necessary to exclude diabetes in anyone with a positive screening blood test. Approximately 35 per cent of all people with newly diagnosed diabetes still have a normal fasting glucose and 15–20 per cent have a normal 2 h value.

Notwithstanding these criticisms as a diagnostic test, the fasting blood glucose provides a simple and reliable method of screening for diabetes. The majority of all those with undiagnosed diabetes will have a diagnostic fasting blood glucose (FPG greater than or equal to 7.0 mmol/l). However, in the context of opportunistic screening, using the fasting glucose as the first screening test will mean an additional visit, following the identification of risk factors, which is likely to result in a significant non-attendance rate. This would not usually apply to a random test, which can be done immediately.

**Table 3** The performance of a fasting plasma glucose of more than or equal to 6.1 mmol/l as a screen for diabetes as defined by the OGTT

|  | n | Sensitivity | Specificity |
|---|---|---|---|
| Population based |  |  |  |
| Harris 1997[15] | 2844 | 81 | 90 |
| De Vegt 1998[16] | 2378 | 88 | 88 |
| Wahl 1998[17] | 4515 | 71 | 87 |
| Ko 1998[13] | 1513 | 58 | 98 |
| Chang 1998*[18] | 5303 | 73 | 93 |
| Gimeno 1998[19] | 647 | 87 | 92 |
| Shaw 1999[20] | 3528 | 78 | 97 |
| Referral based |  |  |  |
| Wiener 1998[21] | 401 | 91 | 75 |
| Gomez-Perez 1998**[22] | 1706 | 65 | 92 |

Diabetes is defined using the OGTT (FPG ⩾7.0 mmol/l or 2 hPG ⩾11.1 mmol/l) in the same way in all the studies.

* FPG 6.0 mmol/l used as cutoff, instead of 6.1 mmol/l.

** Only included subjects with FPG 3.3–8.9 mmol/l. That is, true sensitivity would be higher.

Median sensitivity — 81 per cent.

Median specificity — 92 per cent.

### Random blood glucose measurements

Only two studies have examined the properties of random blood glucose (measured by reflectance meter in both studies) as a screening tool for diabetes (Box 2). Unlike other studies in which a random glucose has been compared to the OGTT, these two studies are the only ones in which the OGTT was performed in the whole population irrespective of the random glucose value. On the basis of these two studies, in order to achieve a sensitivity of 80–90 per cent, the specificity of a random glucose is likely to be significantly lower than that of fasting glucose. Furthermore, WHO 1985 criteria (in which the fasting plasma threshold was 7.8 mmol/l) were used as the gold standard in both studies, but if current criteria were applied, performance of the test is likely to be slightly worse. People who are diabetic only on the new, lower fasting value (and who have a non-diabetic 2 h value) are more likely to have normal random blood glucose values.

### Blood glucose meters

Blood glucose meters have often been used as part of screening programmes for diabetes and the two studies summarized in Table 3 showed that a random glucose measured by reflectance meter had a reasonable sensitivity and specificity for diabetes. However, the precision of these meters is limited and the final diagnosis of diabetes must always rely on laboratory measurements. Even for the initial screening test, laboratory testing is always preferred and meters should only be considered if they are the only way of providing a screening service to a given population or individual. If meters are used, the imprecision, and possibility of a false negative result, should be considered in the interpretation of the results.

**Box 2 The performance of a random whole blood glucose as a screen for diabetes**

- ◆ Engelgau et al. 1995
  - ■ At sensitivity of 90 per cent*: median specificity 48–52 per cent (according to age group)
  - ■ At specificity of 90 per cent: median sensitivity 49–52 per cent
  - ■ Optimal
    - • median sensitivity 73–76 per cent
    - • median specificity 76–78 per cent
- ◆ Qiao et al. 1995
  - ■ Cutoff 5.8 mmol/l
    - • sensitivity 63 per cent
    - • specificity 85 per cent**
  - ■ Cutoff 5.2 mmol/l
    - • sensitivity 78 per cent
    - • specificity 62 per cent**

* The cut-off value of random whole blood glucose for a sensitivity of 90 per cent was 4.4–6.7, depending on age and post-prandial period.

** Sensitivities and specificities were worse in women than men at all thresholds.

The validity of these studies also needs to be considered in the light of two subsequent studies[23,24] examining the accuracy of a variety of blood glucose meters (as used by trained personnel). The later studies found only 35–83 per cent of readings using blood samples from people with diabetes were within ± 10 per cent of the adjusted laboratory plasma glucose values.

## HbA1c as screening and diagnostic test

HbA1c is attractive as both a screening and diagnostic test, because it is simple, requires no preparation of the patient and directly relates to treatment targets. Furthermore its relationship to retinopathy in population studies[1] is as close as that of blood glucose. However, the measurement of HbA1c is not yet standardized around the world and so it is not currently possible to produce diagnostic thresholds that would be valid in all laboratories.

## Urine glucose measurement

Urine glucose measurement, though cheap and convenient, has inadequate sensitivity,[24] and therefore, the choice of an initial screening test lies between fasting and random blood glucose.

## Assessment of diabetes related symptoms

Symptoms of hyperglycaemia (such as thirst and polyuria) have a poor sensitivity and specificity for diabetes.[25] Therefore, it is not recommended that symptoms form part of the screening process, although diabetes should be sought in someone presenting with symptoms of hyperglycaemia.

## Two-step blood screening approach

Recommendations are that two different glucose testing procedures on two different occasions should be used for determining diabetes status. This allows a number of opportunities for variation in diagnostic procedures and it is therefore important to establish diagnostic protocols. Currently there are insufficient data to determine the ideal lower limit for the initial screening test (fasting or random glucose) that would indicate the requirement for an OGTT as the diagnostic test. The ADA Expert Working Group judged that high sensitivity was essential in an initial screening test and, using the available data, attempted to select thresholds, which might approximate to a sensitivity of 90 per cent. These thresholds, however, remain arbitrary to a certain extent.

The clinical diagnosis of diabetes is often prompted by symptoms such as polyuria and polydipsia, recurrent infections, unexplained weight loss and, in severe cases, drowsiness and coma with high levels of glycosuria usually present. In such cases a single blood glucose determination in excess of the diagnostic values indicated in Fig. 2 (black zone) establishes the diagnosis. Figure 2 also defines levels of blood glucose below which a diagnosis of diabetes is unlikely in non-pregnant individuals. These criteria are unchanged from the 1985 WHO report.[8] For clinical purposes, an OGTT to establish diagnostic status need only be considered if casual blood glucose values lie in the uncertain range (that is, between the levels that establish or exclude diabetes) and fasting blood glucose levels are below those which establish the diagnosis of diabetes.

Until further evidence can be established for selection of optimal tests, procedures and diagnostic levels with respect to long-term complications of diabetes, diagnostic step by step procedures including

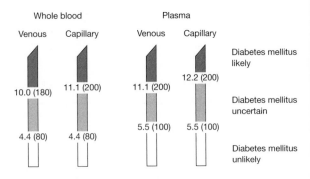

**Fig. 2** Index of suspicion for diabetes based on random blood glucose readings. Adapted from *Definition, Diagnosis and Classification of Diabetes Mellitus and its Complications – Part 1: Diagnosis and Classification of Diabetes Mellitus.* Geneva: World Health Organization, 1999.

re-testing intervals are only recommendations from the collated literature. The optimal tests, procedures and diagnostic levels may need to be adjusted according to the ethnic composition of specific populations and the available resources within the given health system. In Australia, the following recommendations have recently being put forward for endorsement by Commonwealth Department of Health and Family Services (Fig. 3)[26]:

- Fasting blood glucose should be the initial screening test, but a random sample is acceptable if there are concerns about compliance with an additional visit [9],
- An OGTT should be performed in all people with a fasting plasma glucose of 5.5–6.9 mmol/l (whole blood 4.4–6.0), or random plasma glucose of 5.5–11.0 mmol/l (whole blood 4.4–10.0 (11.1 if capillary)). Values below these thresholds effectively exclude diabetes,
- Laboratory testing (rather than reflectance meter) is preferable for the screening test,
- Laboratory testing is mandatory for the diagnostic test,
- The diagnosis of diabetes requires two positive laboratory blood tests (any of fasting, random or 2 h) on separate days in the absence of serious acute illness. When marked hyperglycaemia is coupled with acute metabolic decompensation, a second test is not required (WHO).

### Is screening for or diagnosing asymptomatic type 2 diabetes worthwhile?

Underlying the quest for diagnosis of a pathological condition is the notion that, once identified, suitable treatment can be undertaken to stop the disease progressing if not to cure it. Benefit of the intervention should outweigh any risk and justify both the treatment and also the detection/diagnosis of the condition. In case of a large part of the diabetic population, the lack of symptoms in the initial phase of the disease raises the question of whether diagnosing during the asymptomatic phase is appropriate. Before this can be decided it is necessary to determine if knowing their diabetes status influences management options amongst asymptomatic people. The underlying assumption is that identifying and treating diabetes at a stage before clinical presentation will reduce the risk of and morbidity from long term complications.

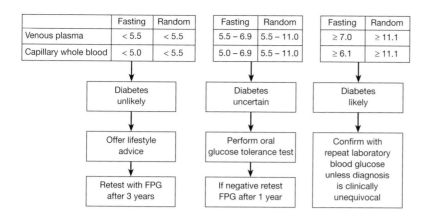

|  | Fasting | Random |
|---|---|---|
| Venous plasma | < 5.5 | < 5.5 |
| Capillary whole blood | < 5.0 | < 5.5 |

Diabetes unlikely

Offer lifestyle advice

Retest with FPG after 3 years

|  | Fasting | Random |
|---|---|---|
|  | 5.5 – 6.9 | 5.5 – 11.0 |
|  | 5.0 – 6.9 | 5.5 – 11.0 |

Diabetes uncertain

Perform oral glucose tolerance test

If negative retest FPG after 1 year

|  | Fasting | Random |
|---|---|---|
|  | ≥ 7.0 | ≥ 11.1 |
|  | ≥ 6.1 | ≥ 11.1 |

Diabetes likely

Confirm with repeat laboratory blood glucose unless diagnosis is clinically unequivocal

**Fig. 3** Suggested scheme for screening and diagnosing diabetes in an Australian population. Adapted from Welborn TA, Reid CM, Marriott G. Australian Diabetes Screening Study: impaired glucose tolerence and non-insulin-dependent diabetes mellitus. *Metabolism*, 1997; **46** (12 suppl. 1): 35–9.

Screening for a disease can only be justified if that disease represents an important health problem; is prevalent enough (within the total or a specific target population) to make screening cost effective; has a relatively long asymptomatic phase; and interventions are available which have a proven beneficial effect on clinically meaningful outcomes. Furthermore, the test for the disease must be safe, acceptable to the target population, and have adequate sensitivity and specificity. Ideally any screening programme should be assessed in controlled trials measuring health outcomes and costs in screened and unscreened populations. In the absence of such information, screening may be thought to be worthwhile if all or most of the above requirements are fulfilled.

No studies have compared outcomes in screened and unscreened populations, but two studies have approached this using computer modelling. In one study,[27] the cost per quality-adjusted life-year (QALY) gained by screening was calculated. Risks of complications were derived from a variety of epidemiological studies, and the impact of treatment on microvascular complications was calculated from DCCT data. Macrovascular complications were not considered. The cost/QALY (US$56,649 per QALY gained) was judged to be acceptable (that is, comparable to that for screening for other diseases), and lowest in young people from high risk ethnic groups (African American). In the other study,[28] the health difference (measured in QALYs) between a screened and an unscreened population was calculated and the negative impact of screening was included. DCCT data were used to calculate the reduction of microvascular complications, while it was assumed that treatment for diabetes would have a similar impact on macrovascular disease as does treatment for hypertension and hyperlipidaemia. Screening led to a benefit (159 versus 167 QALYs lost – no statistical test was provided to test for the significance of the difference), which increased with increasing age, and mainly resulted from reduced cardiovascular risk.

In type 2 diabetes, diabetic complications are common at the time of clinical diagnosis, and less frequent among people diagnosed during screening surveys. Diabetic retinopathy is the most specific of the diabetic complications, since neuropathy, nephropathy and macrovascular disease all occur in the non-diabetic population. Retinopathy is found in 7.4–37 per cent of people at the time of clinical diagnosis, and 1.5–18.8 per cent of people diagnosed with diabetes during screening surveys.[29,30] The prevalence of retinopathy increases in a linear fashion with increasing diabetes duration. Using the data from two populations of people with clinically

diagnosed diabetes (Australian and American), and by extrapolating the line backwards until a prevalence of zero is reached, it has been calculated that type 2 diabetes begins 4–7 years before the time of clinical diagnosis.[31]

Hyperglycaemia is an important cardiovascular risk factor. In a metaregression analysis[28] of 20 prospective studies (only two of which included women), the relationship between baseline blood glucose and cardiovascular events during 1,193,231 person-years of follow-up was assessed. The risk of developing cardiovascular disease increased with increasing glucose (fasting, 1 h, 2 h and casual), was apparent across the range of glucose and was highest for those in the diabetic range. Compared to a fasting glucose of 4.2 mmol/l, the relative risk (95 per cent confidence intervals) of cardiovascular events for a fasting glucose of 6.1 mmol/l was 1.33 (1.06–1.67) and for a 2 h glucose of 7.8 mmol/l was 1.58(1.19–2.10). In five out of 14 studies reporting other risk factors, the effect of glucose was independent of those other risk factors. The UK prospective diabetic study group (UKPDS)[30] has shown that aggressive glucose and blood pressure lowering therapy in newly diagnosed (after clinical presentation) diabetic people reduces the risk of long term complications.

Definitive studies comparing long term outcomes in screened and unscreened populations have not been performed for diabetes. Nevertheless, there is a now a large body of evidence showing that type 2 diabetes begins several years before clinical presentation, and that aggressive treatment of diabetes can significantly improve outcomes. Furthermore, since diabetes (and high levels of non-diabetic blood glucose values) increases the risk of cardiovascular disease, the knowledge of an individual's blood glucose is important, as it should influence the management of other cardiovascular risk factors.

Type 2 diabetes affects approximately 2.1 per cent of the world population,[32] but an estimated 50 per cent of these individuals are undiagnosed and largely asymptomatic. Diabetes, both diagnosed and undiagnosed, is a major independent risk factor for cardiovascular disease, blindness, renal failure and lower limb amputation and screening or case finding (early diagnosis) amongst asymptomatic individuals is the only way of uncovering their disease. Over 70 per cent of these people have readily identifiable risk factors, and, at least in developed countries such as Australia, over 90 per cent of them visit a doctor (predominantly general practitioners) each year.[33] Opportunistic screening in general practice therefore represents an excellent opportunity to identify individuals with undiagnosed diabetes.

*Size of the diabetes problem world-wide*

Type 2 diabetes affects large numbers of people from a wide range of ethnic groups and at all social and economic levels throughout the world. At least 120 million people today suffer from type 2 diabetes but by 2010 AD, 220 million people are projected to have the disease.[34] Diabetes is amongst the five leading causes of death in most countries[35] yet mortality statistics greatly underestimate the true diabetes related mortality, as diabetes is frequently underreported on death certificates.[35,36] Therefore, diabetes is often ignored in setting public health priorities. Quite apart from the health impact, the economic cost of diabetes and its complications are enormous for health care and loss of productivity to society.[35]

The extraordinarily high prevalence of type 2 diabetes reported over 20 years ago in the Pima Indians[36] and the Micronesian Nauruans in the Pacific[37] and then later in other Pacific and Asian island populations[38] highlighted the potential for a future diabetes epidemic. This scenario proved to be correct and type 2 diabetes has now reached epidemic proportions in many developing nations,[34] as well as in disadvantaged minorities in the developed countries. Examples of the latter include Australian Aboriginals and Torres Strait Islanders, Native, African- and Mexican-Americans, and migrant Asian Indians as well as populations in some of the Middle East Arab states.

There is every reason to expect that the epidemic of type 2 diabetes will continue to escalate over the next decade.[34] Inevitably, diabetes and its complications will emerge as one of the major threats to future public health resources throughout the world at a huge economic and social cost, particularly in developing countries.

Against this global epidemic, changes proposed for the classification and diagnostic criteria for diabetes become very important not only for individual epidemiological studies but also for global comparisons of incidence and prevalence. Therefore, the recommendations of the 1997 American Diabetes Association (ADA) report[1] and the 1999 provisional World Health Organization recommendations[9] will have important implications. The outcomes of the changes should be better management of diabetes both due to earlier diagnosis and better classification of cases for more appropriate therapy.

## Diabetes prevalence

What difference will these changes make to the prevalence of diabetes and to the individuals identified as having diabetes? Since the ADA has now recommended using only the new fasting criterion, while the 1985 WHO guidelines were heavily dependent on the 2 h value of the OGTT, it is this change from the OGTT to FPG alone that requires analysis. A number of studies have now been published comparing the old and new criteria. These are summarized in Table 4, and reveal that the changes may have a rather variable impact. Compared to the old OGTT-based criteria, and excluding people already known to have diabetes, the new fasting criterion identifies between 65 per cent fewer (Mexico) and 42 per cent more (Newcastle) people as having newly diagnosed diabetes, depending on the population studied. Since in most populations, a significant proportion (at least 50 per cent in developed nations, but lower in developing nations) of all those with diabetes are already known to have the disease, the impact of these changes on the total prevalence will be somewhat less than these figures indicate, though how much less is unknown.

Furthermore, even when the total prevalence is similar by the two methods, the individuals identified by screening may be different. The percentage of individuals classified as having diabetes by the new FPG cutoff who also have diabetes on the old criteria varies from only 41 per cent (DECODE) to 91 per cent (Japanese-Brazilians, Hong Kong). It is not clear what drives this variation in the degree of classification disagreement, but in the DECODE study of 16 different European populations,[39] obese diabetic individuals were more likely to satisfy the fasting criterion and non-obese diabetic individuals the 2 h criterion. It is possible that ethnicity is also important, but there are not yet enough data to assess this. This change in the individuals that are identified raises the further question of whether changing to the new fasting threshold will alter the phenotype of diabetes, or the associations between risk factors, such as obesity, and the subsequent development of diabetes. These issues are currently unresolved, although NHANES III shows that the mean HbA1c is higher in the group diagnosed by the new fasting criterion than in the group diagnosed by the 1985 WHO OGTT criteria.[15]

The association of hyperglycaemia and cardiovascular disease is a crucial one on which to test the validity of the new criteria. The Hoorn Study has shown that people with a FPG over 6.9 mmol/l (that is, diabetic), but a non-diabetic 2hPG have an abnormal cardiovascular risk profile[14] and data from two large cohorts of men with a non-diabetic 2 h glucose value at baseline showed an increased 20 year mortality when the baseline FPG was above 7.0 mmol/l.[43] Similarly, evidence would now indicate that people whose only abnormality is in the post glucose load state have elevated blood pressure and lipids[14] and a higher cardiovascular mortality than their non-diabetic counterparts.[44] Thus, isolated abnormalities in either the fasting or the post-load state have important associations with cardiovascular disease. While lowering of the fasting threshold will help to identify one group, abandonment of the OGTT may prevent or delay diagnosis in the other group. Cardiovascular risk, however, demonstrates again the arbitrary nature of glucose cut-points. Blood glucose represents a continuous cardiovascular risk factor extending well into the normal range and interacts with other risk factors.

Will the new criteria influence the total number of people in whom diabetes is diagnosed (rather than the prevalences estimated by epidemiological studies) and will this reduce morbidity and mortality? The simple lowering of the fasting threshold alone should increase the number of people who are classified as having diabetes. However, when lowering of the threshold is combined with a switch from using the OGTT to just using the FPG, it can be seen from Table 4 that the overall effect can be either to increase or decrease the prevalence as determined by epidemiological studies.

In routine clinical practice, the OGTT is rarely used, and in this setting the number of people diagnosed should increase as a result of lowering the fasting threshold. However, the degree to which it will increase is unclear, and probably depends more on increasing the number of people screened (by whichever diagnostic test) than it does on altering the parameters of the screening test. The proportion of diabetes that is undiagnosed is directly influenced by the diagnostic test and the thresholds used. NHANES III data show that using 1985 WHO criteria this proportion was 44 per cent, but was only 35 per cent using the new fasting criterion.[44] Thus, future diagnoses rates will need to be analysed and interpreted with caution.

No study has specifically addressed the effects on mortality or morbidity of type 2 diabetes of early diagnosis but a computer

**Table 4** Numbers of people identified as having diabetes in different studies, according to diagnostic classification

| | ADA fasting criterion* | | WHO (1985) criteria | |
|---|---|---|---|---|
| | n | per cent with 2 hPG = 11.1 mmol/l | n | per cent with FPG = 7.0 mmol/l |
| Population based | | | | |
| Hoorn†[16] | 120 | 61 | 118 | 62 |
| NHANES III†[15] | 4100000 | 77 | 6000000 | 53 |
| Taiwan†[18] | 220 | 79 | 453 | 39 |
| Japanese-Brazilians†[19] | 124 | 91 | 131 | 86 |
| DECODE‡[39] | 1044 | 41 | 904 | 48 |
| S Hemisphere†[40] | 1298 | 70 | 1319 | 68 |
| Newcastle (UK)‡[41] | 136 | 48 | 96 | 69 |
| Referral based | | | | |
| Hong Kong†[13] | 394 | 91 | 627 | 57 |
| Mexico†[22] | 78 | 85 | 222 | 30 |
| Manchester (UK)‡[42] | 166 | 84 | 178 | 78 |

Data are numbers and per cent.

\* FPG = 7.0 mmol/l irrespective of 2 hPG.

† WHO diagnosis based on FPG = 7.8 or 2 hPG = 11.1mmol/l.

‡ WHO diagnosis based on 2 hPG = 11.1 mmol/l alone.

simulation showed opportunistic screening for diabetes was cost effective.[27] Furthermore, the UKPDS has recently shown that intensive glucose lowering therapy reduces the risk of microvascular disease[46] and that in obese diabetic patients, metformin reduces mortality and myocardial infarction.[47]

A major question that arises from the ADA recommendations[1] is how does the value of IFG compare with IGT for predicting future type 2 diabetes. Screening by the ADA criteria for IFG alone would identify fewer people who subsequently progress to type 2 diabetes than would the OGTT recommended by the WHO.[9] Shaw and colleagues demonstrated the higher sensitivity of IGT over IFG for predicting progression to type 2 diabetes.[20] If data from other populations confirm this, screening programmes aimed at identifying people at risk of diabetes would lose by relying on fasting values alone. Thus, whilst the new category of IFG may broaden and improve our description of states of intermediate glucose metabolism, it should be seen as complementary to rather than a replacement for IGT.

# The impact of new diagnostic criteria for diabetes on different population prevalence

We studied data collated from nine different populations based in the Southern Hemisphere, in which a 75 g oral glucose tolerance test was performed to compare diabetes prevalence derived from fasting values only with the prevalence derived from 2 h values only.[40] Diabetes was diagnosed as known diabetes mellitus (KDM) if participants were on oral hypoglycaemic drugs or insulin. These participants had only a FPG measured, while all other participants had an OGTT. In order to compare prevalence estimates according to the ADA (1997) and WHO (1999) guidelines, diabetes was determined in all non-KDM subjects according to both FPG = 7.0 mmol/l, irrespective of 2hPG and 2hPG = 11.1 mmol/l, irrespective of FPG).

To examine the extent to which individuals are classified differently by the two approaches, all newly diagnosed diabetic subjects were further classified as 'ADA only' (FPG ≥ 7.0 mmol/l and 2hPG < 11.1 mmol/l), 'WHO only' (FPG < 7.0 mmol/l and 2hPG = 11.1 mmol/l) or 'Both' (FPG = 7.0 mmol/l and 2hPG = 11.1 mmol/l).

Amongst the 20 624 participants in the nine surveys, 1036 had previously diagnosed diabetes and 1714 had newly diagnosed diabetes, according to either fasting or 2 h glucose. The differences in prevalence within each population resulting from changing the diagnostic criteria, ranged from +30 per cent to −19 per cent (relative difference) and +4.1 percentage points to −2.8 percentage points (absolute difference). BMI was the most important determinant of disagreement in classification. Thirty one per cent of those individuals who were diabetic on the fasting value were not diabetic on the 2 h value, and 32 per cent of those with diabetes on the 2 h value were not diabetic on the fasting value.

The prevalence of diabetes according to the different diagnostic criteria is shown for each survey in Table 5. In three populations, the total prevalence was significantly higher when using the new ADA criteria, in three populations it was significantly lower, and in the remaining three, there were no significant changes.

Changing the diagnostic criteria is likely to have variable, and sometimes quite large, effects on the prevalence of diabetes in different populations. The fasting criterion identifies different people as being diabetic from those identified by the 2 h criterion.

The data presented in this analysis show a complex effect resulting from a change in the diagnostic thresholds for diabetes. The ADA anticipated that changing to the FPG threshold would lead to a slight reduction in the prevalence of diabetes as determined by epidemiological surveys[1] and this was supported by data from the USA from (14.3–12.3 per cent).[15] Our own analyses find a variable effect, with some populations increasing the number of individuals with diabetes, and others showing a fall. This variability is in keeping with similar variability seen in the DECODE study of different European populations,[39] and other single population reports.

**Table 5** Prevalence of diabetes according to the criteria on which diabetes is diagnosed

| Survey site | n | Prevalence KDM (%) | Prevalence ADA criteria* (%) | Prevalence WHO criteria[†] (%) | Change in prevalence (95 %) | |
|---|---|---|---|---|---|---|
| Nauru | 1423 | 14.3 | 31.3 | 27.1[‡] | +4.1 | (+2.9 to +5.4) |
| Western Samoa | 1777 | 5.7 | 14.9 | 11.5[‡] | +3.4 | (+2.5 to +4.4) |
| Rodrigues | 1530 | 3.9 | 10.8 | 9.3[‡] | +1.6 | (+0.6 to +2.6) |
| New Caledonia and Wallis Islands | 1404 | 4.6 | 7.8 | 7.5 | +0.3 | (−0.4 to +1.0) |
| Cook Islands | 2179 | 3.6 | 7.1 | 7.1 | 0.0 | (−0.5 to +0.6) |
| Fiji | 3046 | 3.8 | 8.8 | 8.8 | 0.0 | (−0.7 to +0.7) |
| Kiribati | 2864 | 1.2 | 5.0 | 6.2[‡] | −1.2 | (−1.9 to −0.5) |
| Mauritius | 4990 | 5.5 | 10.9 | 12.8[‡] | −1.9 | (−2.5 to −1.3) |
| PNG | 1411 | 7.3 | 17.2 | 19.9[‡] | −2.8 | (−4.0 to −1.6) |
| Overall | 20624 | 5.0 | 11.3 | 11.4 | −0.1 | (−0.4 to +0.2) |

KDM – subjects with known (previously diagnosed) diabetes.

* KDM plus diabetes diagnosed by FPG = 7.0 mmol/l.

[†] KDM plus diabetes diagnosed by 2 hPG = 11.1 mmol/l.

[‡] $p < 0.01$ vs ADA prevalence.

Obesity seems to be a important factor in determining on which criterion diabetes is diagnosed. This is apparent from the finding that the two studies (Nauru and Western Samoa) with the highest mean population BMI also had the highest proportion of diabetic subjects with FPG ⩾ 7.0 mmol/l. A similar trend was seen in the European study.[41] However, this finding is not consistent amongst the populations, so it is not possible to predict the effects of changing to a particular set of diagnostic criteria on the prevalence of diabetes in that population.

The influence of age is also not clear. Older people are more likely in our analyses to be 'WHO only' than younger people. This is in keeping with recent findings in older Americans, in whom 14.8 per cent were diabetic on the 1985 WHO criteria, but only 7.7 per cent according to the ADA fasting criteria,[17] and data from the Rancho Bernardo study showing that in the elderly 60 per cent of those with undiagnosed diabetes are only diabetic on the 2 h and not the fasting value.[48] In the DECODE study, of the five data sets focussing on the elderly, WHO diabetes was more common than ADA diabetes in three, and less common in two.

Irrespective of changes in the overall prevalence, the classification of individuals was markedly different with the two methods. There was more overlap between the methods in this study than in the European populations, which is probably due to greater obesity leading to a higher proportion of subjects being diabetic on both criteria in our study, but there were still 24 per cent of all diabetic subjects who were 'WHO only', and a further 23 per cent who were 'ADA only'.

The influence of potential reclassification of subjects with previously diagnosed diabetes (KDM) cannot be accurately assessed from such studies, though ultimately it is likely to be important. It is probable that KDM individuals represent greater abnormalities of glucose, as many of them would have been symptomatic at diagnosis. Thus most of them would probably be diabetic on both criteria.

Assuming that most KDM subjects are diabetic on both criteria, then for the total diabetic population, the degree of agreement would be higher if KDM subjects were included in such analyses.

A degree of caution should be maintained in extrapolating the results of an epidemiological study to the individual subjects, since for an individual, hyperglycaemia needs to be confirmed on another day to diagnose diabetes.

In conclusion, changing over from performing the OGTT to using the FPG more than or equal to 7.0 mmol/l cut-off alone can have variable, unpredictable and sometimes quite large effects on both the number of people, and the specific individuals classified as having diabetes. Furthermore, diabetic individuals defined by the new FPG level, as a group, will be more obese than those identified by the 2hPG level. Therefore, a major change of diagnostic practice should have very clear justification from a variety of studies confirming its validity in terms of pathophysiological processes, risk of diabetic complications, and screening strategies.

# References

1.  **American Diabetes Association**. Report of the expert committee on the diagnosis and classification of diabetes mellitus. *Diabetes Care*, 1997; **20**: 1183–97.

2.  **Zimmet P**. The Challenge of Diabetes – Diagnosis, Classification, 'Cocacolonization', and the Diabetes Epidemic. In: Fischer EP, Moller G (eds). *The Medical Challenge Complex Traits*. Munchen: Piper, 1997; 55–110.

3.  **Himsworth HP**. Diabetes mellitus: its differentiation into insulin-sensitive and insulin insensitive types. *Lancet*, 1936; **1**: 117–20.

4.  **Bornstein J, Lawrence RD**. Plasma insulin in human diabetes mellitus. *British Medical Journal*, 1951; **2**: 1541–4.

5.  **Major RM**. *A History of Medicine*. Oxford: Blackwell, 1954; 67.

6.  **Zimmet P**. Diabetes epidemiology as a tool to trigger diabetes research. (Peter Bennett Lecture). *Diabetologia*, 1999; **42**: 499–518.

7. **World Health Organization**. *Diabetes Mellitus: Report of a WHO Study Group*. WHO Tech Rep Ser No. 727, Geneva, 1985.

8. **Alberti KGMM, Zimmet PZ**. Definition, diagnosis and classification of diabetes mellitus and its complications. Part 1: diagnosis and classification of diabetes mellitus. Provisional report of a WHO Consultation. *Diabetic Medicine*, 1998; **15**: 539–53.

9. **World Health Organization**. *Definition, Diagnosis and Classification of Diabetes Mellitus and its Complications – Part 1: Diagnosis and Classification of Diabetes Mellitus*. Geneva: WHO, 1999.

10. **Harris MI, Zimmet P**. Classification of diabetes mellitus and other catergories of glucose intolerance. In: Alberti KGMM, DeFronzo RA, Keen H, Zimmet P, eds. *International Textbook of Diabetes Mellitus*. John Wiley and Sons Ltd. 1992; 3–18.

11. **Balkau B, Eschwege E, Tichet J, Marre M, D.E.S.I.R Study Group.** Proposed criteria for the diagnosis of diabetes: Evidence from a French epidemiological study (D.E.S.I.R). *Diabetes and Metabolism*, 1997; **23**: 428–34.

12. **Cordido F, Muniz J, Rodriguez IL, Beiras AC**. New diagnostic criteria for diabetes and mortality in older adults. *Lancet*, 1999; **353**(9146): 69–70.

13. **Ko GTC, Woo J, Chan JCN, Cockram CS**. Use of the 1997 American Diabetes Association diagnostic criteria for diabetes in a Hong Kong Chinese population. *Diabetes Care*, 1998; **21**: 2094–7.

14. **Mooy JM, Gootenhuis PA, de Vries H, Kostense PJ, Popp-Snijders C, Bouter LM, Heine RJ**. Intra-individual variation of glucose, specific insulin and proinsulin concentrations measured by two oral glucose tolerance tests in general Caucasian population: the Hoorn Study. *Diabetologia*, 1996; **39**: 298–305.

15. **Harris MI, Eastman RC, Cowie CC, Flegal KM, Eberhardt MS**. Comparison of diabetes diagnostic categories in the US population according to 1997 American Diabetes Association and 1980–85 World Health Organization diagnostic criteria. *Diabetes Care*, 1997; **20**: 1859–62.

16. **de Vegt F, Dekker JM, Stehouwer CD, Nijpels G, Bouter LM, Heine RJ**. The 1997 American Diabetes Association criteria versus the 1985 World Health Organization criteria for the diagnosis of abnormal glucose tolerance: poor agreement in the Hoorn Study. *Diabetes Care*, 1998; **21**(10): 1686–90.

17. **Wahl PW, Savage PJ, Psaty BM, Orchard TJ, Robbins JA, Tracy RP**. Diabetes in older adults: comparison of 1997 American Diabetes Association classification of diabetes mellitus with 1985 WHO classification. *Lancet*, 1998; **352**: 1012–15.

18. **Chang CJ, Wui JS, Lu FH, Lee HL, Yang YC, Wen MJ**. Fasting plasma glucose in screening for diabetes in the Taiwanese population. *Diabetes Care*, 1998; **21**: 1856–60.

19. **Gimeno SG, Ferreira SR, Franco LJ, Iunes M**. Comparison of glucose tolerance categories according to World Health Organization and American Diabetes Association diagnostic criteria in a population-based study in Brazil. The Japanese-Brazilian Diabetes Study Group. *Diabetes Care*, 1998; **21**(11): 1889–92.

20. **Shaw JE, Zimmet PZ, de Courten M, Dowse GK, Chitson P, Gareeboo H, Hemraj F, Fareeed D, Tuomilehto J, Alberti KGMM**. Impaired fasting glucose or impaired glucose tolerance: what best predicts future diabetes? *Diabetes Care*, 1999; **22**: 399–402.

21. **Wiener K, Roberts NB**: The relative merits of haemoglobin A1c and fasting plasma glucose as first-line diagnostic tests for diabetes mellitus in non-pregnant subjects. *Diabetic Medicine*, 1998; **15**: 558–63.

22. **Gomez-Perez FJ, Aguilar-Salinas CA, Lopez-Alvarenga JC, Perez-Jauregui J, Guillen-Pineda LE, Rull JA**. Lack of agreement between the World Health Organization category of impaired glucose tolerance and the American Diabetes Association category of impaired fasting glucose. *Diabetes Care*, 1998; **21**(11): 1886–8.

23. **Poirier JY, Le Prieur N, Campion L, Guilhem I, Allannic H, Maugendre D**. Clinical and statistical evaluation of self-monitoring blood glucose meters. *Diabetes Care*, 1998; **21**(11): 1919–24.

24. **Chan JC, Wong RY, Cheung CK, Lam P, Chow CC, Yeung VT, Kan EC, Loo KM, Mong MY, Cockram CS**. Accuracy, precision and user-acceptability of self blood glucose monitoring machines. *Diabetes Research & Clinical Practical*, 1997; **36**(2): 91–104.

25. **Davies MJ, Williams DR, Metcalfe J, Day JL**. Community screening for non-insulin-dependent diabetes mellitus: self-testing for post-prandial glycosuria [see comments]. *Quarterly Journal of Medicine*, 1993; **86**(10): 677–84.

26. **Welborn TA, Reid CM, Marriott G**. Australian Diabetes Screening Study: impaired glucose tolerance and non-insulin-dependent diabetes mellitus. *Metabolism*, 1997; **46**(12 Suppl 1): 35–9.

27. **CDC Diabetes Cost-Effectiveness Study Group**. The Cost-effectiveness of Screening for type 2 Diabetes. *Journal of the American Medical Association*, 1998; **280**: 1757–63.

28. **Goyder E, Irwig L**. Screening for type 2 diabetes: a decision analysis approach. NSW Health Department 1998.

29. **Harris MI, Klein R, Welborn TA, Knuiman MW**. Onset of NIDDM occurs at least 4–7 years before clinical diagnosis. *Diabetes Care*, 1992; **15**(7): 815–9.

30. **UK Prospective Diabetes Study Group**. Tight blood pressure control and risk of macrovascular and microvascular complications in type 2 diabetes. (UKPDS 38) *British Medical Journal*, 1998; **317**(7160): 703–13.

31. **Coutinho M, Gerstein HC, Wang Y, Yusuf S**. The relationship between glucose and incident cardiovascular events. A metaregression analysis of published data from 20 studies of 95,783 individuals followed for 12.4 years. *Diabetes Care*, 1999; **22**(2): 233–40.

32. **Amos AF, McCarty DM, Zimmet P**. The rising global burden of diabetes and its complications: estimates and projections to the year 2010. *Diabetic Medicine*, 1997; **14** (Suppl 5): S1–S85.

33. **Australian Bureau of Statistics**. *National Health Survey: Diabetes*. Catalogue No 4364.0, ABS, Canberra 1997a.

34. **McCarty D, Zimmet P**. *Diabetes 1994 to 2010: Global Estimates and Projections*. Melbourne: International Diabetes Institute, 1994.

35. *Diabetes Atlas 2000*. Brussels: International Diabetes Federation, 2001.

36. **Knowler W, Bennett P, Hamman RF, Miller M**. Diabetes incidence and prevalence in Pima Indians: a 19-fold greater incidence than in Rochester, Minnesota. *American Journal of Epidemiology*, 1978; **108**: 497–505.

37. **Dowse GK, Zimmet PZ, Finch CF, Collins VR**. Decline in incidence of epidemic glucose intolerance in Nauruans: implications for the 'thrifty genotype'. *American Journal of Epidemiology*, 1991; **133**: 1093–1104.

38. **Dowse GK, Spark RA, Mavo B, Hodge AM**. Extraordinary prevalence of non-insulin-dependent diabetes mellitus and bimodal plasma glucose distribution in the Wanigela people of Papua New Guinea. *Medical Journal of Australia*, 1994; **160**: 767–74.

39. **DECODE Study Group**. Will new diagnostic criteria for diabetes mellitus change phenotype of patients with diabetes? Reanalysis of European epidemiological data. *British Medical Journal*, 1998; **317**: 371–5.

40. **Shaw JE, de Courten M, Boyko EJ, Zimmet PZ**. The impact on different populations of new diagnostic criteria for diabetes. *Diabetes Care*, 1999; **22**: 762–66.

41. **Unwin N, Alberti KGMM, Bhopal R, Harland J, Watson W, White M**. Comparison of the current WHO and new ADA criteria for the diagnosis of diabetes mellitus in three ethnic groups in the UK. *Diabetic Medicine*, 1998; **15**: 554–7.

42. **Riste L, Khan F, Cruickshank K**. High prevalence of type 2 diabetes in all ethnic groups, including Europeans, in a British inner city: relative poverty, history, inactivity, or 21st century Europe? *Diabetes Care*, 2001; **24**: 1377–8.

43. **Balkau B, Shipley M, Jarrett RJ, Pyorala K, Pyorala M, Forhan A, Eschwege E.** High blood glucose concentration is a risk factor for mortality in middle-aged nondiabetic men. *Diabetes Care*, 1998; **21**: 360–7.

44.  **Barrett-Connor E, Ferrarra A.** Isolated postchallenge hyperglycemia and the risk of fatal cardiovascular disease in older women and men. *Diabetes Care*, 1998; **21**: 1236–9.

45.  **Harris MI, Flegal KM, Cowie CC, Eberhardt MS, Goldstein DE, Little RR, Wiedmeyer H-M, Byrd-Holt DD.** Prevalence of diabetes, impaired fasting glucose and impaired glucose tolerance in U.S. adults. *Diabetes Care*, 1998; **21**: 518–24.

46.  **UK Prospective Diabetes Study Group.** Intensive blood glucose control with sulphonylureas or insulin compared with conventional treatment and risk of complications in patients with type 2 diabetes (UKPDS 33). *Lancet*, 1998; **352**: 837–53.

47.  **UK Prospective Diabetes Study Group.** Effect of intensive blood glucose control with metformin on complications in overweight patients with type 2 diabetes (UKPDS 34). *Lancet*, 1998; **352**: 854–65.

48.  **Barett-Connor E, Ferrara A.** Isolated post challenge hyperglycaemia and the risk of fatal cardiovascular disease in older men and women. The Rancho Bernado Study. *Diabetes Care*, 1998; **21**: 1236–9.

## 2.1 Genetics of type 1 (insulin-dependent) diabetes mellitus

*Flemming Pociot and Jørn Nerup*

## Introduction

Diabetes mellitus represents a heterogeneous group of disorders. Some distinct diabetic phenotypes can be characterized in terms of specific aetiology and/or pathogenesis, but in many cases overlapping phenotypes make aetiological and pathogenetical classification difficult.

Type 1 diabetes (insulin-dependent diabetes mellitus) is characterized by absolute insulin deficiency, abrupt onset of symptoms, proneness to ketosis and dependency on exogenous insulin to sustain life. It is the most common form of diabetes among children and young adults in populations of Caucasoid origin. The prevalence of type 1 diabetes in most Caucasoid populations is approximately 0.4 per cent, whereas the incidence varies significantly.

Type 1 diabetes is the result of pancreatic β-cell destruction. The development of the disease requires a genetic predisposition and interaction with environmental triggers that activate pathogenetic mechanisms leading to progressive loss of pancreatic islet β-cells. Although these β-cell destructive processes are associated with a variety of immune phenomena, the immunological mechanisms directly involved in β-cell killing have not yet been fully clarified in man.

Migration studies and twin studies have provided evidence that non-genetically determined factors are important in causing type 1 diabetes. Such studies have demonstrated rapid changes in diabetes incidence within one generation upon migration. All diabetic twin studies to date indicate a higher concordance rate for type 1 diabetes in monozygotic (MZ) than in dizygotic (DZ) twins. Most studies of MZ twins have shown that the majority of co-twins of patients with type 1 diabetes remain non-diabetic, although recent data suggest a cumulative proband-wise risk from birth to age 35 of 70 per cent.[1]

## Genetics of type 1 diabetes

Type 1 diabetes does not follow a clear Mendelian pattern of inheritance. Type 1 diabetes may be influenced by multiple genes that act in concert to cause disease. Such a genetic aetiology is called polygenic, or complex inheritance. Multifactorial inheritance is an extension of polygenic inheritance, where additional, nongenetic (environmental) factors may also be involved. Hence, type 1 diabetes is classified as a multifactorial disease although it is not precisely known how many genetic loci are involved or how they interact with environmental factors. These polygenes are referred to as susceptibility genes which only act to modify the risk for disease. As individual susceptibility genes they are neither necessary nor sufficient for development of the disease, that is, some gene variant carriers may never develop the disease while some non-carriers may have the disease. This lack of definite correlation between genotype and phenotype is a major complicating factor in mapping and cloning genes for type 1 diabetes and other common multifactorial diseases.

In the 1970s, association and affected-sib pair linkage studies established the role of human leukocyte antigen (HLA) genes in type 1 diabetes predisposition (the HLA contribution to disease is referred to as *IDDM1*).[2] HLA also demonstrated type 1 diabetes and type 2 diabetes (non insulin-dependent diabetes mellitus) to be distinct disease entities, since type 2 diabetes generally does not show an association with HLA, although certain subsets may demonstrate some association. The differences in rates of type 1 diabetes disease concordance in siblings who share two, one or zero parental HLA haplotypes with the concordance rate in monozygotic twins, the risk in relatives, and the population prevalence implicates the existence of additional non-HLA genetic factors (Table 1).

The increased type 1 diabetes risk in siblings over population prevalence ($\lambda_s$) is 15 (lifetime sib risk = 6 per cent/population frequency = 0.4 per cent). This value of $\lambda_s$ is comparable to that of other autoimmune polygenic diseases such as multiple sclerosis and

**Table 1** Empirical risks of type 1 diabetes

|  | Concordance rate (%) |
| --- | --- |
| General population | 0.4 |
| Average risk for siblings | 6 |
| HLA-identical siblings | 12–15 |
| Children of one parent with type 1 diabetes | 2–7 |
| Children of two parents with type 1 diabetes | 5–20 |
| Monozygotic twins | 30–70 |

systemic lupus erythematosus. However, it is much lower than $\lambda_s$ of monogenic disorders caused by rare highly penetrant gene mutations. In general, the lower the $\lambda_s$, the more difficult it will be to identify, that is clone, the genes involved. It will also be difficult to prove which of the possibly many polymorphisms in an type 1 diabetes-associated chromosomal segment that are of aetiological importance. In addition, it is possible that the clustering of type 1 diabetes in families is due to shared environmental factors, for example viral infections, cow's milk protein, and certain other nutritional factors.

Dissection of the genetics of type 1 diabetes has been carried out by candidate-gene analysis and whole-genome screening approaches. Candidate genes have been derived either from obvious physiological/biochemical information or from the fact that the gene is expressed in affected tissue, pancreatic islets, or has a function known to be affected in the disorder. Over the last 4–5 years extensive efforts have been invested in order to genetically map chromosomal regions demonstrating evidence of linkage to type 1 diabetes by a whole-genome approach. The materials used for such studies are large numbers of type 1 diabetes multiplex families, that is families with at least two affected offspring. The method of choice, using current technology, for genotyping in whole-genome searches is the use of simple sequence length polymorphisms, sometimes referred to as microsatellites. The most common method for analysing data from whole-genome screenings is based on affected sib-pair analysis where observed sharing of alleles is compared to expected sharing. Four complete genome scans[3–6] and several partial ones have now been reported.[7–12] These studies together suggested that close to 20 genomic intervals with variable degrees of linkage evidence might be underlying type 1 diabetes.

For all these loci, including the HLA (IDDM1), the aetiological mutation(s) in sensu strictu has not been identified. Even in the·HLA region several genes seem to be involved (see below). IDDM2 corresponds to the insulin gene (INS) region on chromosome 11p15.5.[13] Most of the other regions comprise regions of 2–20 centimorgan (cM) in size, corresponding roughly to 2–20 Mb, which may contain several hundred genes.

# The genes
## HLA-encoded susceptibility to type 1 diabetes

The best evidence for a genetic component in the susceptibility to type 1 diabetes comes from studies of the HLA region. The HLA region is a cluster of genes located within the major histocompatibility complex (MHC) on chromosome 6p21. According to structural and functional characteristics, the many genes in this region have been classified into three families, classes I, II and III.

Class I genes include HLA-A, -B, -C, as well as the class I-like genes E, F, G, and H. Class II genes are divided into the main sub-regions DR, DQ, DN/DO, and DP. Other genes in this region are the large multifunctional protease (LMP) and transporter associated with antigen processing (TAP) genes. The class III region comprises a great number of genes encoding products with a variety of functions, example complement components, tumour necrosis factor (TNF)-$\alpha$ and -$\beta$, and heat shock protein (HSP) 70.

The function of HLA molecules is to bind antigenic peptides, of foreign or endogenous origin, processed by antigen-presenting cells, and present them to T-lymphocytes. Class I molecules display mainly antigenic peptide fragments of intracellularly generated foreign protein antigens in a form that CD8 + T cells can recognize. Peptides displayed by class II molecules – mainly peptide fragments derived from intracellular degradation of foreign protein antigens – are presented to CD4 + T-cells. Their recognition by CD4 + T cells leads to activation of Th-cells and to the initiation of the immune response. The HLA molecular structure, the binding of antigenic peptide, and antigen presentation are not only crucial for the regulation of the immune response in the periphery, but also for the selection of T-cell repertoire during the fetal development in the thymus. Both positive and negative selection of T-cell clones and hence the building of the immunological repertoire require HLA molecule expression and adequate peptide presentation in thymus.

## HLA associations with type 1 diabetes

The statistically strongest genetic association with type 1 diabetes is conferred by class II gene alleles. One of these, DQB1*0302, represents the predominant, but not the only, class II allele associated with type 1 diabetes in Caucasoid populations. Although numerous studies have emphasized the primary role of DQ in the predisposition to type 1 diabetes, the involvement of DR is likely.[14,15] Thus, analysis of the linkage between DQ and DR alleles on haplotypes which carry DQB1*0302 genes, demonstrated that the frequencies of only certain DR4-associated DRB1 alleles are increased among type 1 diabetes patients. The strong linkage disequilibrium of the HLA region makes it difficult to determine whether the DQ or the DR locus, or indeed other non-class II genes, are the principal type 1 diabetes-associated loci on certain haplotypes. The population frequencies of HLA gene alleles as well as their combinations differ greatly between various ethnic groups. This is due to evolutionary recombination events which have 're-sorted' specific HLA alleles among different human lineage's and resulted in different type 1 diabetes-associated genotypes by breaking up the linkage disequilibrium among class II genes present in a single ethnic group. Table 2 lists the various haplotypes that have been implicated in contributing to type 1 diabetes susceptibility in different ethnic groups.

Interestingly, a strong negative association with type 1 diabetes of certain haplotypes is observed (Table 2). DR2 haplotypes are negatively associated with type 1 diabetes in most populations, and are protective of type 1 diabetes even in heterozygotes who carry a disease-susceptibility haplotype like DRB1*04-DQB1*0302. There are several different DR2 positive haplotypes and only the DRB1*1501-DQB1*0602 combination is negatively associated with type 1 diabetes. Other haplotypes, including DR5 and DR6 haplotypes, may confer reduced susceptibility.

## The correlation of specific amino acid residues with HLA-DQ/DR encoded susceptibility to type 1 diabetes

The fact that several different class II alleles and combinations of alleles may be associated with type 1 diabetes can be reconciled in a hypothesis that these alleles have something in common that is central to disease susceptibility, for example specific amino acid substitutions. Indeed, certain amino acids in the DQ and DR$\beta$ chains

**Table 2** Type 1 diabetes-associated HLA class II molecules and haplotypes. Relative risk (RR) are for the combined DQ-DR haplotype

| DQ molecules | DR-haplotypes | Population | RR |
|---|---|---|---|
| Positive associations (Susceptibility haplotypes) | | | |
| A1*0301-B1*0302 | DRB1*04 | Multiple | 2.5–9.5 |
| A1*0501-B1*0201 | DRB1*301 | Multiple | 2.5–5.0 |
| A1*0501-B1*0302 | DRB1*301/DRB1*04 | Multiple | 12.0–32.0 |
| A1*0301-B1*0201 | DRB1*301/DRB1*04 | Multiple | |
| A1*0301-B1*0402 | DRB1*04/DRB1*801 | Caucasians | 4.0–15.0 |
| A1*0301-B1*0201 | DRB1*701 | Blacks | 8.0–13.0 |
| A1*0301-B1*0201 | DRB1*901 | Blacks | 5.5 |
| A1*0301-B1*0401 | DRB1*04 | Japanese | 3.5–4.5 |
| A1*0301-B1*0303 | DRB1*901 | Japanese | 2.0–4.5 |
| Negative associations (Protective haplotypes) | | | |
| A1*0102-B1*0602 | DRB1*1501 | Multiple | 0.03–0.2 |
| A1*0103-B1*0603 | DRB1*1301 | Multiple | 0.05–0.25 |
| A1*0301-B1*0301 | DRB1*04 | Multiple | 0.2–0.5 |
| A1*0501-B1*0301 | DRB1*1101 | Multiple | 0.05–0.5 |

correlate with disease susceptibility/resistance, and these amino acids are known to be critical for the function of the class II molecule in peptide binding and T cell recognition.[16] For example, aspartic acid (Asp) at position 57 of the DQβ chain is encoded by DQB protective alleles while an alanine, valine or serine residue at the same position characterises predisposing alleles. Although it has been shown that Asp 57 has indeed a pronounced role in the function of class II molecules with respect to peptide binding, it cannot account for all the complexity of HLA and type 1 diabetes associations. To evaluate the role of specific residues of the DRβ chain one approach has been to compare the *DRB1*04* subtype alleles (Table 3). Clearly no single residue explains the type 1 diabetes associations of the respective alleles. Rather a combination of polymorphic residues in the DQα and DQβ chains and the DRβ chain may be influencing the conformation of the antigen-binding groove of the DQ/DR molecules and hence their role in risk determination.

## Non-HLA encoded susceptibility to type 1 diabetes

Which are the genes responsible for conferring the non-HLA encoded susceptibility to type 1 diabetes? As discussed above very little is known about this. In broad terms, such genes/loci/regions have been identified/analysed either by a candidate gene approach or by whole or partial genome screenings using affected sib pair (ASP) analysis. In Table 4 are listed type 1 diabetes susceptibility loci suggested by genome screenings. The symbols of these loci, approved by the Human Gene Nomenclature Committee, are *IDDM1–IDDM17* (www.gene.ucl.ac.uk/nomenclature). The symbols *IDDM9*, *IDDM14* and *IDDM16* have not been approved yet, even though these symbols have been reserved by researches based upon preliminary data suggesting evidence of linkage of new chromosomal regions to type 1 diabetes.

Although ASP analysis is a powerful tool to map major susceptibility genes, its power to map minor genes (that is, with relative risks less than 4) is very limited because several hundreds or even thousands of sib-pair families may be required. Such large numbers of families are difficult and expensive to collect and analyse. Linkage disequilibrium (LD) analysis, such as the transmission disequilibrium test (TDT),[17] is a strong analytical method for mapping complex disease genes. The TDT is a test for linkage disequilibrium, that is, the simultaneous presence of linkage and association. The test is very simple. Using data from families with at least one affected offspring, it evaluates the transmission of a marker allele (often one previously identified as putatively disease-associated) from heterozygous parents to affected children. Unless both linkage and association are present, the marker allele will be transmitted with a probability of 50 per cent to affected offspring; possible departure from 50 per cent is tested with chi-square or equivalent tests.

Given sufficient numbers of markers and appropriate DNA samples (example parental DNAs) LD analysis can be used for replication and fine mapping studies of susceptibility intervals, identification of aetiological mutations and novel susceptibility loci. Evidence for LD has been reported for several of the *IDDM* loci listed in Table 4.

## *IDDM2* – The insulin gene (INS) region

The immune-mediated process leading to type 1 diabetes is highly specific to pancreatic β-cells. The insulin gene, therefore, is a plausible candidate susceptibility locus since insulin or insulin precursors may act as autoantigens. Alternatively, insulin levels could modulate the interaction between the immune system and the β-cells.

A unique minisatellite (VNTR) which arises from tandem repetition of a 14–15 bp oligonucleotide sequence is located in the 5′ regulatory region of the human insulin gene (*INS*) on chromosome 11p15.5. Repeat number varies from about 26 to over 200, and VNTR alleles occur in three discrete size classes: class I (26–63 repeats), class II (mean of 80 repeats), and class III (141–209 repeats). Class II alleles are virtually absent in Caucasoid populations where the frequencies of class I and class III alleles are 0.71 and 0.29 respectively. The class I/I homozygous genotype is associated with a 2- to 5-fold increase in risk of developing type 1 diabetes, whereas class III alleles seem to provide dominant protection.

**Table 3** Critical polymorphic residues of the HLA-DRB1*04 beta chain associated with predisposition to type 1 diabetes

| DRBI 1*04 allele | Polymorphic residues | | | | | | | Disease predisposition |
| --- | --- | --- | --- | --- | --- | --- | --- | --- |
| | 37 | 57 | 67 | 70 | 71 | 74 | 86 | |
| 0401 | Tyr | Asp | Leu | Gln | Lys | Ala | Gly | + + |
| 0402 | Tyr | Asp | Ile | Asp | Glu | Ala | Val | +/− |
| 0403 | Tyr | Asp | Leu | Gln | Arg | Glu | Val | − − |
| 0404 | Tyr | Asp | Leu | Gln | Arg | Ala | Val | +/− |
| 0405 | Tyr | Ser | Leu | Gln | Arg | Ala | Gly | + + + |
| 0406 | Ser | Asp | Leu | Gln | Arg | Glu | Val | − − − |
| 0407 | Tyr | Asp | Leu | Gln | Arg | Glu | Gly | − − − |

**Table 4** Non-HLA loci, identified by genome scans, predisposing to type 1 diabetes

| IDDM locus | Markers(s) | Chromosomal localization | Maximum lod score | Reference |
| --- | --- | --- | --- | --- |
| IDDM2 | D11S922–INS VNTR | 11p15.5 | 0.6–2.8 | (3,13) |
| IDDM3 | D15S107 | 15q26 | 0.0–2.5 | (7) |
| IDDM4 | FGF3 | 11q13 | 0.4–3.9 | (3,4,20) |
| IDDM5 | ESR | 6q25 | 1.0–4.5 | (3) |
| IDDM6 | D18S487 | 18q21 | 1.6 | (3,24) |
| IDDM7 | D2S152 | 2q31 | 0.4–1.3 | (3,25) |
| IDDM8 | D6S446–D6S281 | 6q27 | 1.1–3.6 | (9,11) |
| IDDM10 | D10S191–D10S220 | 10p11–q11 | 0.2–4.7 | (3,6) |
| IDDM11 | D14S67 | 14q24–q31 | 0.0–4.0 | (10) |
| IDDM12 | CTLA4 | 2q33 | 0.0–0.9 | (27) |
| IDDM13 | D2SI164 | 2q34 | 3.34 | (30) |
| IDDM15 | D6S283 | 6q21 | 6.2 | (12) |
| IDDM17 | D10S592–D10S554 | 10q24–q25 | | (31) |

This susceptibility locus, *IDDM2*, has been mapped and identified as being the *INS* VNTR locus.[13] Data suggest that the VNTR may modulate *INS* transcription in pancreas and thymus.[18,19] Class III alleles, as compared with class I alleles, correlate with low *INS* mRNA levels in pancreas but with higher levels in thymus. Greater *INS* expression in thymus may explain the dominant protective effect of class III VNTR alleles reported in type 1 diabetes by enhancing tolerance to the preproinsulin protein.

## IDDM3–IDDM17

*IDDM1* and *IDDM2*, that is, the HLA and *INS* components, were both originally identified as candidate genes based on case-control studies. The remaining *IDDM* loci, that is, *IDDM3–IDDM17*, have all been found in linkage studies using affected sib-pair families either in whole or partial genome scans. *IDDM3* was originally reported to be located near *D15S107* on chromosome 15q26.[7] For anonymous DNA sequences, example microsatellites, the convention is to use

D (=DNA) followed by 1–22, X or Y to denote chromosomal location, then S for a unique segment, and finally a serial number. Thus, the interpretation of *D15S107* is '*unique DNA segment number 107 found on chromosome 15*'. Interestingly, for marker *D15S107*, families less predisposed to type 1 diabetes through genes in the HLA region provided most of the evidence for linkage. Although support for linkage for the *IDDM3* locus has been published recently, most other studies have failed to replicate this observation. No specific candidate genes have been investigated for this locus.

Evidence for *IDDM4* was reported simultaneously by different groups.[3,4] *IDDM4* is located near the fibroblast growth factor 3, *FGF3*, locus on chromosome 11q13. Most recently, a huge international effort was taken to fine map *IDDM4* by linkage disequilibrium (LD) analysis. In a two-stage approach 2.042 families were typed and a specific haplotype comprising alleles of the two polymorphic markers *D11S1917* and *H0570polyA* showed decreased transmission (46.4 per cent) to affected offspring and increased transmission (56.6 per cent) to unaffected siblings.[20] Several potential candidate genes map to the region near *FGF3* in humans. These include *ZFM1* (zinc finger protein 162 which encodes a putative nuclear protein) and *MDU1* (encodes a cell-surface protein involved in the regulation of intracellular calcium). Gene products of both *ZFM1* and *MDU1* are demonstrable in the pancreas. More interestingly, the gene encoding the Fas-associated death domain protein (*FADD*) has been mapped to this region as well. Transduction of an apoptotic signal depends on association and interaction between the intracellular 'death domain' of Fas with FADD. Recent experimental findings indicate that binding of the Fas ligand (FasL) on cytotoxic T cells to Fas expressed on β-cells may trigger apoptosis in the insulin-producing β-cells. Very recently, a gene encoding a novel transmembrane protein was identified by sequence analysis of the *IDDM4* locus.[21] The gene, termed low-density lipoprotein receptor related protein (*LRP5*), encodes a protein that contains conserved sequences which are characteristic of the low-density lipoprotein receptor family. The gene is in close proximity to the two markers, *D11S1917* and *H0570polyA*. The exon encoding the signal peptide of LRP5 is only 3 kb downstream the *H0570polyA* marker. Neither the precise biological function nor the nature of the LRP-5 ligand have been determined. Hence, continued genetic analysis is necessary to determine whether the *LRP5* gene is indeed a diabetes susceptibility gene.

Three regions on chromosome 6q with varying degree of linkage have been identified in the genome screenings. These are *IDDM5* on 6q25, *IDDM8* on 6q27, and *IDDM15* on 6q21. Initial evidence of linkage for *IDDM5* was found for the *ESR1*, estrogen receptor 1, marker.[3] *IDDM5* is one of only few susceptibility regions that have been replicated in multiple studies. It maps to a region approximately 40 cM centromeric to *IDDM8*. Fine mapping analysis has localized this locus within a 5 cM region between the markers *D6S476* and *D6S473*. The gene encoding Mn superoxide dismutase (*SOD2*) maps close to this region. There is evidence supporting a role of free oxygen radicals (FOR) in the immune-mediated β-cell destruction.[22] A reduced scavenger potential of β-cells would render them more susceptible to FOR-mediated damage. Also, a RFLP of the *SOD2* gene has been associated with type 1 diabetes.[23] Structurally polymorphic variants of MnSOD protein with reduced activity have been reported and such variants might increase predisposition to type 1 diabetes.

Because of previous evidence of linkage of the region of 18q12–q21 containing the Kidd blood group and the marker *D18S64* to type 1 diabetes fine mapping of this region, now designated *IDDM6*, has been performed.[24] Increased transmission of allele 4 of marker *D18S487* to affected children has been observed. Support for this result was extended to a total of 1,067 families from 4 different countries. Heterogeneity in TDT results between data sets was, in part, accounted for by the presence of more than one common disease-associated haplotype (allelic heterogeneity), which confounded the analysis of individual alleles by TDT. No new candidate genes of the *IDDM6* region have been evaluated.

Several loci on chromosome 2q have been suggested as being linked to type 1 diabetes. One of these loci is *IDDM7* on chromosome 2q31 suggested by linkage of *D2S326* in one of the first genome scans.[3] Subsequent linkage and transmission disequilibrium tests have located *IDDM7* to *D2S152* in several populations, although some controversy exists.[25,26] Part of this region is homologous to the region of mouse chromosome 1 that contains the murine type 1 diabetes susceptibility locus *idd5* in the NOD mouse. A number of

genes has been proposed, and investigated, as candidate genes of the *IDDM7* region. These include the genes of the interleukin-1 gene cluster (that is, *IL1R1*, *IL1R2*, *IL1A*, *IL1B*, and *IL1RN*), *HOXD8*, and *GAD1*. However, for none of these candidate genes linkage has been convincingly demonstrated.

*IDDM8* was initially mapped to chromosome 6q27.[9] Significant evidence of linkage was then obtained through multipoint analyses in additional data sets.[11] Supporting evidence for this locus was also reported in other studies using partially overlapping sets of families.[6,12] Combined evidence from these studies (non-overlapping families) suggest that *IDDM8* meets the criteria for confirmed linkage for complex diseases. The only exception was reported in a recent genome scan.[5] However, this study examined only the *D6S264* marker of the region which is several cM away from the peak loci of *IDDM8*, that is, *D6S446–D6S281*.

Although the *IDDM9* symbol has not been approved, *IDDM9* has been used for a region on chromosome 3q21–q25 demonstrating some evidence of linkage of the *D3S1303* marker in one of the initial genome scans.[3] This observation was to some degree replicated in the more recent study, which found strongest evidence for this locus in DR3/4 heterozygous diabetic offspring.[6] However, this locus needs further studies to be confirmed.

Linkage to type 1 diabetes on human chromosome 10p11–q11 has provided suggestive evidence for a susceptibility locus in this region.[3,6] This locus has been designated *IDDM10*. *GAD2*, encoding GAD65, is closely linked to this region. However, several studies have failed to demonstrate evidence of linkage of *GAD2* to type 1 diabetes.

*IDDM11* is the symbol for a possible susceptibility locus on 14q24.3–q31. This locus was identified by demonstration of significant linkage to *D14S67*.[10] The subset of families in which affected children did not show increased sharing of HLA genes provided most of the support for *D14S67* linkage. Significant linkage heterogeneity between HLA-defined subsets of families suggests that *IDDM11* may be an important susceptibility locus in families lacking strong HLA region predisposition. However, no other studies have been able to replicate the original observation.

The *IDDM12* locus maps to chromosome 2q33 and strongest evidence for linkage has been obtained for the *D2S72–CTLA4–D2S116* region which includes a microsatellite in the 3' untranslated region of the *CTLA4* gene.[27] In addition, two single nucleotide polymorphisms (SNPs) within the *CTLA4* sequence have been identified, one in the promoter region and one in exon 1. By means of TDT analysis these polymorphisms – most extensively the exon 1 SNP – have been investigated in several populations, and the combined data support linkage to type 1 diabetes of the *CTLA4* locus.[27–29] Interestingly, some evidence has been produced to suggest that differences between populations exist.

The role of the cytotoxic T-lymphocyte-associated-4 (*CTLA4*) gene has been examined in various autoimmune diseases. CTLA4 is expressed only on activated T-lymphocytes and function to down regulate T-cell function. Blockage of this pathway will lead to maintenance of the activated state of the T-cells which may have implication for the development of type 1 diabetes. In addition, *CTLA4* has been shown to mediate antigen-specific T-cell apoptosis, and biochemical abnormalities related to apoptosis are associated with autoimmune disease in patients and animal models. Even though *CTLA4* is the most likely candidate gene for *IDDM12*, further studies are needed to fully clarify this.

The *IDDM13* locus maps to 2q34, and strongest evidence for linkage has been obtained for the *D2S137–D2S164* region.[30] Thus, *IDDM12* and *IDDM13* is separated by 17–18 cM only, and *IDDM7*, *IDDM12* and *IDDM13* cover a region of approximately 27 cM. Additional evidence for *IDDM13* has been obtain in few other studies.[26,29] A recent study found evidence for linkage to type 1 diabetes of the *D2S1327–D2S1471* region which spans 3.5 cM. Several candidate genes of the *IDDM13* region have been investigated. These include *IA-2, IGFBP2, IGFBP5,* and *NRAMP1*. No evidence for any disease contributing mutation in any of these genes has been found.

*IDDM15* is the symbol for a susceptibility locus that has been linked to 6q21, in the region of *D6S283–D6S1580*.[12] Additional support for this locus came from one of the recent genome scans.[5] Interestingly, it has been suggested that this region on chromosome 6 contains a gene responsible for transient neonatal diabetes mellitus which could be a candidate gene of this region.

*IDDM17* was identified on the basis of a genomic search for linkage in a large Bedouin Arab family to type 1 diabetes.[31] A locus contributing to type 1 diabetes susceptibility was located on chromosome 10q25. The family contained 19 affected relatives, all of whom carried 1 or 2 high risk HLA-DR3 haplotypes that were rarely found in other family members. The susceptibility locus was mapped to an 8 cM interval between *D10S1750* and *D10S1773*. Two adjacent markers, *D10S592* and *D10S554*, showed evidence of linkage disequilibrium with the disease locus. The *FAS* gene maps to this region (10q24.1), but was excluded as the disease contributing mutation of this region. This particular region has not been identified in other genome scans.

In the most recent genome scans,[5,6] a few novel chromosomal regions, with no approved *IDDM* symbols yet, showing some evidence of linkage were identified. These include 1q (*D1S1644-AGT*), 7p (*GCK*), 14q12–q21 (*D14S70–D14S276*), 16q22–q24 (*D16S515–D16S520*), 19p13 (*D19S247–226*), and Xp13-p11 (*DXS1068*).

## Variation in observed evidence for linkage

As evident from the text and Table 4 most of the initially reported chromosomal regions showing some evidence of linkage have not been unambiguously confirmed in new studies. The exceptions are *IDDM4, IDDM5, IDDM8, IDDM12,* and *IDDM15*. Variation between studies may arise from one or more of the following reasons: (i) Small sample sizes in published studies. (ii) Genetic heterogeneity. (iii) Random variation. Variation due to chance is difficult to distinguish from genetic heterogeneity. Weak linkages are expected to occur in genome scans due to random variation, and it cannot at present be excluded that some of the claimed *IDDM* loci are observations due to false-positive findings (type 1 errors). (iv) Stratification or lack of identical stratification of data sets. Heterogeneity in susceptibility factors may exist in relation to example HLA-encoded susceptibility, age-at-onset, autoantibody positivity, and complication profile. Often, information on these variable is not available in all data sets.

It is a tough and enormous challenge to identify polygenes in a multifactorial disorder like type 1 diabetes, because of the combination of locus, allelic, and clinical heterogeneity. Evidence of linkage in affected sib-pair families (the most common pedigree

configuration in studies of common polygenic diseases) should be sought in several different populations. Most information can probably be obtained from family data sets that are drawn from isolated populations, for example Finns and Sardinians. If only one data set shows positive evidence of linkage to a chromosomal region, evidence of replication should be sought by collecting more families from the same country.

## Alternative avenues to identification of new susceptibility loci

Support for the different regions may come from different sources: (i) Identification of candidate genes in such regions, that is positional candidate gene cloning. (ii) Identification of syntenic regions, that is regions demonstrating correspondence in gene order between the chromosomes of different species, conferring susceptibility to diabetes in the spontaneous animal models, that is the NOD mouse and the BB rat. (iii) Overlapping with regions identified through genome scans in other autoimmune or inflammatory diseases.[32] The occurrence of common features of autoimmune diseases and the co-association of multiple autoimmune diseases in the same individual or family support the notion of common genetic factors that predispose to autoimmunity. Indeed, compiling data from existing genome scans in other human autoimmune diseases reveal an overlap with already identified type 1 diabetes susceptibility loci, Table 5. This clustering of autoimmune susceptibility loci suggests that there may be related genetic background contributing to susceptibility of clinically distinct diseases, and that the genes to be identified in these clusters are most likely involved in primary or secondary regulation of the immune system. (iv) The study of sub phenotypes like maturity-onset of diabetes of the young (MODY). MODY is a genetically heterogeneous form of diabetes characterized by an autosomal

**Table 5** *IDDM* loci for which susceptibility loci for other autoimmune diseases have been mapped to the same region

| Locus | Other autoimmune disease |
| --- | --- |
| *IDDM1* | All autoimmune diseases |
| *IDDM2* | MS |
| *IDDM3* | Celiac disease |
| *IDDM6* | RA |
| *IDDM9* | RA |
| *IDDM12* | RA, MS, AITD, AD |
| *IDDM13* | RA |
| 16q22–q24 | Psoriasis, asthma, CD |
| 12p; CD4 | MS |
| GCK | CD/UC, MS |
| DXS998 | MS |

MS: Multiple sclerosis; RA: Rheumatoid arthritis; AITD: Autoimmune thyroid disease; CD: Crohn's disease; UC: Ulcerative colitis.

dominant inheritance, early age of onset (<25 years of age), and a primary defect in β-cell function.[33] Five known MODY subtypes, MODY1, MODY2, MODY3, MODY4 and MODY5, are caused by mutations in genes encoding the hepatocyte nuclear factor-4α (*HNF-4α*), glucokinase, hepatocyte nuclear factor-1α (*HNF-1α*), the insulin promoter factor-1 (IPF-1), and hepatocyte nuclear factor-1β (*HNF-1β*), respectively. Whereas the diabetic phenotype of MODY2 is characterized by mild elevations in fasting and postprandial blood glucose concentrations, the MODY1 and MODY3 subtypes present more severe phenotypes characterized by severe fasting hyperglycaemia, frequent insulin requirement and occurrence of microvascular complications. MODY4 and MODY5 are both very rare. It was recently shown that about 10 per cent of HLA-DR3 and -DR4 negative subjects originally classified as type 1 diabetes patients had mutations in the *HNF-1α* gene and thus were misclassified MODY3 patients.[34] This highlights the difficulties in distinguishing MODY3 patients treated with insulin from patients with type 1 diabetes on the basis of clinical phenotype alone. Although no consensus has yet been reach it has been suggested that patients with a family history of diabetes compatible with an autosomal mode of inheritance (diabetes in 3 consecutive generations), with insulin secretion deficiency, and without autoantibodies should be examined for mutations in the HNF-1α gene. This may have implications for genetic counselling and for ongoing genetic dissection of type 1 diabetes.

## Conclusion and future strategies

Molecular genetics and epidemiological research over the last decade has increased our knowledge of the aetiopathogenesis of type 1 diabetes. A complex picture emerges where not one but several genes provide the necessary polygenetic background to type 1 diabetes. Epidemiological research strategies have identified a number of risk determinants that may be causally related to the development of type 1 diabetes.

Genes located within the HLA region are by far the most important in conferring susceptibility but several other susceptibility regions have been implicated. Fine mapping of all susceptibility regions should facilitate genetic population screening for individuals at high risk and ultimately lead to identification of the pathophysiological relevant mutations of the individual genes.

However, to further unravel the genetics of type 1 diabetes difficult tasks remain. First, combined analyses of data from existing genome scans are needed. Although, close to 1.000 type 1 diabetes affected sib pair families of Caucasian ancestry have been genotyped in various scans, no combined analysis have been performed so far. A combined analysis will be important to assess the role of various susceptibility loci and to understand the variation of linkage evidence between data sets. If new genome scans are to be performed, they should be carried out in very homogenous populations and preferable in isolated populations (few founders). Secondly, confirmation of suggested loci is important. This may be accomplished by linkage disequilibrium studies. Thirdly, fine mapping of confirmed intervals and positional cloning to identify the specific disease genes and mutations within these genes are needed. Finally, there is an urgent demand for functional genomics. The number of identified susceptibility genes may continue to grow, but the elucidation of their function in the pathogenesis will be the most important factor for understanding the molecular pathogenesis of type 1 diabetes. The study approaches will vary accordingly to the function of the genes, but will include expression studies and generation of transgenic and knockout animal models.

## References

1. **Kyvik K, Green A, Beck-Nielsen H**. Concordance rates of insulin dependent diabetes mellitus: a population based study of young Danish twins. *British Medical Journal*, 1995; **311**: 913–17.

2. **Nerup J et al**. HLA antigens and diabetes mellitus. *Lancet,* 1974; **II**: 864–6.

3. **Davies JL et al**. A genome-wide search for human susceptibility genes. *Nature*, 1994; **371**: 130–6.

4. **Hashimoto L et al**. Genetic mapping of a susceptibility locus for insulin-dependent mellitus on chromosome 11q. *Nature*, 1994; **371**: 161–4.

5. **Concannon P et al**. A second-generation screen of the human genome for susceptibility to insulin-dependent diabetes-mellitus. *Nature Genetics*, 1998; **19**: 292–6.

6. **Mein C et al**. A search for type-1 diabetes susceptibility genes in families from the United Kingdom. *Nature Genetics*, 1998; **19**: 297–300.

7. **Field LL, Tobias R, Magnus T**. A locus on chromosome 15q26 (IDDM3) produces susceptibility to insulin-dependent diabetes mellitus. *Nature Genetics*, 1994; **8**: 189–94.

8. **Rowe RE, Wapelhorst B, Bell GI, Risch N, Spielman RS, Concannon P**. Linkage and association between insulin-dependent diabetes mellitus (IDDM) susceptibility and markers near the glucokinase gene on chromosome 7. *Nature Genetics*, 1995; **10**: 240–2.

9. **Luo D-F, Bui MM, Muir A, MacLaren NK, Thomson G, She J-X**. Affected sib-pair mapping of a novel susceptibility gene to insulin-dependent diabetes mellitus (IDDM8) on chromosome 6q25–q27. *American Journal of Human Genetics*, 1995; **57**: 911–19.

10. **Field LL, Tobias R, Thomson G, Plon S**. Susceptibility to insulin-dependent diabetes mellitus maps to a locus *(IDDM11)* on human chromosome 14q24.3–q31. *Genomics*, 1996; **33**: 1–8.

11. **Luo D-F et al**. Confirmation of three susceptibility genes to insulin-dependent diabetes mellitus. *IDDM4, IDDM5* and *IDDM8. Human Molecular Genetics*, 1996; **5**: 693–8.

12. **Delépine M et al**. Evidence of a non-HLA susceptibility locus in type 1 diabetes linked to HLA on chromosome 6. *American Journal of Human Genetics*, 1997; **60**: 174–87.

13. **Bennett ST et al**. Susceptibility to human type 1 diabetes at *IDDM2* is determined by tandem repeat variation at the insulin gene minisatellite locus. *Nature Genetics*, 1995; **9**: 284–91.

14. **Sheehy MJ et al**. A diabetes-susceptible HLA haplotype is best defined by a combination of HLA-DR and DQ alleles. *Journal of Clinical Investigations*, 1989; **83**: 830–5.

15. **She J-X**. Susceptibility to type 1 diabetes: HLA-DQ and DR revisited. *Immunology Today*, 1996; **17**: 323–9.

16. **Cucca F, Todd J**. HLA susceptibility to type 1 diabetes. In: Browning M, McMichaels A, eds. *HLA and MHC: Genes, Molecules and Function*. Oxford: BIOS Scientific Publishers Ltd, 1996: 383–406.

17. **Spielman RS, McGinnis RE, Ewens WJ**. Transmission test for linkage disequilibrium: the insulin gene region and insulin-dependent diabetes mellitus (IDDM). *American Journal of Human Genetics*, 1993; **52**: 506–16.

18. **Pugliese A et al**. The insulin gene is transcribed in the human thymus and transcription levels correlate with allelic variation at the *INS VNTR-IDDM2* susceptibility locus for type-1 diabetes. *Nature Genetics*, 1997; **15**: 293–7.

19. **Vafiadis P et al**. Insulin expression in human thymus is modulated by *INS VNTR. Nature Genetics*, 1997; **15**: 289–92.

20. **Nakagawa Y et al**. Fine mapping of the diabetes susceptibility gene *IDDM4* on chromosome 11q13. *American Journal of Human Genetics*, 1998; **63**: 547–56.

21. **Hey P** *et al.* Cloning of a novel member of the low-density lipoprotein receptor family. *Genetics*, 1998; **216**: 103–11.

22. **Nerup J** *et al.* On the pathogenesis of IDDM. *Diabetologia*, 1994; **37** (suppl. 2): 82–9.

23. **Pociot F** *et al.* Genetic susceptibility markers in Danish patients with type 1 (insulin-dependent) diabetes – evidence for polygenecity in man. *Autoimmunity*, 1994; **19**: 169–78.

24. **Merriman T** *et al.* Evidence by allelic association-dependent methods for a type 1 diabetes polygene (IDDM6) to chromosome 18q12. *Human Molecular Genetics*, 1997; **6**: 1003–10.

25. **Copeman JB** *et al.* Fine localisation of a type 1 diabetes susceptibility gene (IDDM7) to human chromosome 2q by linkage disequilibrium mapping. *Nature Genetics*, 1995; **9**: 80–85.

26. **Esposito L** *et al.* Genetic analysis of chromosome 2 in type 1 diabetes. Analysis of putative loci *IDDM7*, *IDDM12*, and *IDDM13* and candidate genes *NRAMP1* and *IA-2* and the interleukin-1 gene cluster. *Diabetes*, 1998; **47**: 1797–9.

27. **Nisticò L** *et al.* The ctla-4 gene region of chromosome 2q33 is linked to, and associated with, type-1 diabetes. *Human Molecular Genetics*, 1996; **5**: 1075–80.

28. **Marron MP** *et al.* Insulin-dependent diabetes mellitus (IDDM) is associated with *CTLA4* polymorphisms in multiple ethnic groups. *Human Molecular Genetics*, 1997; **6**: 1275–82.

29. **Larsen Z** *et al.* IDDM12 (CTLA4) and *IDDM13* on 2q34 in genetic susceptibility to type 1 diabetes (insulin-dependent). *Autoimmunity*, 1999; **31**: 35–42.

30. **Morahan G, Huang D, Tait BD, Colman PG, Harrison LC.** Markers on distal chromosome 2q linked to insulin-dependent diabetes mellitus. *Science*, 1996; **272**: 1811–13.

31. **Verge CF** *et al.* Evidence for oligogenic inheritance of type 1 diabetes in a large Bedouin Arab family. *Journal of Clinical Investigations*, 1998; **102**: 1569–75.

32. **Becker K** *et al.* Clustering of non-major histocompatibility complex susceptibility candidate loci in human autoimmune diseases. *Proceedings of the National Academy of Sciences of the United States of America*, 1998; **95**: 9979–84.

33. **Froguel P, Vaxillaire M, Velho G.** Genetic and metabolic heterogeneity of maturity-onset diabetes of the young. *Diabetes Reviews*, 1997; **5**: 123–30.

34. **Møller A, Dalgaard L, Pociot F, Nerup J, Hansen T, Pedersen O.** Mutations in the hepatocyte nuclear factor-1a gene in Caucasian families originally classified as IDDM. *Diabetologia*, 1998; **41**: 1528–31.

## 2.2 The natural history of type 1 diabetes

*Edwin Gale*

## Historical background

Long before the discovery of insulin, physicians noticed that patients with diabetes fell into two clinical categories. Young patients, generally thin, presented with acute symptoms, an intolerable thirst and rapid weight loss. Although the onset of diabetic ketoacidosis could be deferred by a rigorous starvation regimen, their existence was unpleasant and life expectancy was short. In contrast, older patients, often overweight, presented with milder symptoms and could survive for many years with careful diet.

In the 1930s Himsworth[1] observed that young thin patients were sensitive to the action of injected insulin, whereas older and fatter patients were not. From this he correctly inferred that one type of diabetes was due to insulin deficiency and the other to insulin insensitivity. The terms type 1 and type 2 diabetes were probably introduced by Lister[2] in 1951, and described as follows:

'…two broad groups of diabetics – the young, thin, non-arteriosclerotic group with normal blood pressure and usually an acute onset to the disease, and the older, obese, arteriosclerotic group with hypertension and usually a gradual onset. These types we have provisionally designated type I and type II, respectively.'

Despite this clear description, the concept of heterogeneity was vigorously resisted by many diabetologists who supported the prevailing view that diabetes was a spectrum. A favoured hypothesis was that older patients possessed one copy of a diabetes susceptibility gene, whereas younger patients were homozygous for the same gene. The rediscovery of type 1 diabetes began many years later when Gepts[3] identified lymphocytic infiltration of the islets in 1965 and tentatively suggested that immune factors might be involved. This was followed by identification of **HLA** (human leucocyte antigens) associations and the discovery of islet cell antibodies in 1973–74. These observations made it possible to distinguish type 1 from other forms of diabetes on the basis of its immune and genetic characteristics. With evidence of humoral and cellular immunity directed against the target organ, lymphocytic infiltration of that organ, HLA-associated disease susceptibility, overlap with other organ-specific autoimmune disorders, and strong suspicion of an environmental trigger, type 1 diabetes was now seen to fit within the paradigm of an autoimmune disorder.

Early attempts at classification were based around the operational criterion of insulin use, but the distinction between 'insulin-dependent' and 'non-insulin dependent' diabetes was never really satisfactory. Patients with autoimmune diabetes may not require insulin, at least initially, while many with type 2 diabetes benefit from insulin therapy. Another problem is the lack of useful markers of type 2 diabetes, which is therefore characterized largely by the absence of features of type 1 diabetes. In an attempt to reach a more satisfactory classification, the American Diabetes Association has proposed total insulin deficiency as the main criterion for type 1 diabetes. The major category of insulin-deficient diabetes due to presumed autoimmunity is currently known as type 1A, whereas insulin deficient diabetes of unknown aetiology is referred to as type 1B. Although patients at opposite ends of the clinical spectrum are easily distinguished, distinction between type 1 and type 2 diabetes remains difficult at the clinical level, particularly in middle age. A useful rule of thumb – in Western countries at least, is that 95 per cent of those under the age of 30 will fit the category of type 1 diabetes, whereas 95 per cent of those over the age of 60 can be considered to have type 2 diabetes.

## Type 1 diabetes and age

Type 1 diabetes is a condition mediated by autoimmune processes that result in insulin deficiency. The rate of beta cell destruction can be highly variable, typically rapid in young children, but slower in adults. The epidemiology of childhood diabetes is relatively simple to study, since children with diabetes have a distinctive phenotype, almost all have the autoimmune form of the disease, and are highly visible within the health-care system. Such children have a characteristic pattern of HLA susceptibility – although this pattern varies between populations. HLA DR3/4 heterozygotes are strongly represented in children, but their prevalence declines rapidly with increasing age, whereas the DR2-associated protective allele DQB1*0602, scarcely represented in early onset cases, becomes more prevalent with increasing age. Differences are also seen in the pattern of circulating islet autoantibodies (**IAA**), such that antibodies to insulin (IAA) and protein tyrosine phosphatase/IA-2 (IA-2-Ab) are inversely related to age, whereas islet cell antibodies (ICA) and antibodies to glutamic acid decarboxylase (GADA) are associated with autoimmune diabetes at any age.

The phenotype of autoimmune diabetes in later life is much less distinctive. Some lean adults present with acute insulin deficiency and resemble children with diabetes in terms of HLA susceptibility and humoral anti-islet immunity.[4] Others are arrayed along a spectrum of insulin deficiency, HLA type and islet autoantibodies (predominantly ICA and GADA) which blurs imperceptibly into the larger mass of middle aged and elderly patients with non-immune diabetes.[5] The term 'latent autoimmune diabetes of adults' (LADA) has been coined for this group of patients, but lack of clear phenotypic characterization remains a major obstacle to epidemiological analysis.

Another insight into understanding of late-onset autoimmune diabetes has come from analysis of long-term risk of diabetes in the relatives of patients with type 1 diabetes. This indicates that the lifetime risk of inheriting type 1 diabetes has been underestimated. A Danish study suggests that long-term sibling risk is around 15 per cent, rather than the 6 per cent frequently quoted for onset prior to age 20, and that the lifetime risk of autoimmune diabetes may be around 1 per cent for the population as a whole.[6] Earlier reports that non-insulin-dependent diabetes is over-represented in families with type 1 diabetes should be reinterpreted; it was not appreciated at the time that an early need for insulin therapy and autoimmune diabetes are not necessarily synonymous.

## Gender and type 1 diabetes

Gender bias is characteristic of autoimmune disease. It has been estimated that 6.7 million women are affected by autoimmune diseases in the USA, as against 1.8 million men. The six most prevalent conditions, accounting for 93 per cent of the total, are Graves'/hyperthyroidism, rheumatoid arthritis, thyroiditis, type 1 diabetes and pernicious anaemia, followed by multiple sclerosis.[7] It is commonly stated that there are no gender differences in type 1 diabetes, but this is incorrect. A review of gender differences in children presenting under the age of 15 has noted a minor male excess in Europe and populations of European origin, while a female excess could be noted in populations of African or Asian origin. Male sex was weakly associated with high frequency of diabetes, but a more striking observation was that all populations with an incidence higher than 23/100 000 had a male excess, whereas all populations with a rate below 4.5/100 000 had a female excess.[8] In contrast to the heterogeneous pattern seen with children, a clear male preponderance

with an approximate 3 : 2 ratio has emerged from all studies of patients with type 1 diabetes diagnosed between 15–40 years.[9,10] Adult type 1 diabetes therefore appears to differ from other common autoimmune diseases, which typically show a strong female predominance, as does the NOD (non obese diabetic) mouse, the main animal model of type 1 diabetes.

## The geography of type 1 diabetes

Type 1 diabetes is most prevalent in populations of European origin, although there is evidence that it is becoming more frequent in other ethnic groups. The patchwork tapestry of childhood onset diabetes in Europe has largely been filled in over the past 15 years. Within Europe, the highest rate of childhood diabetes is found in Finland and countries in Scandinavia and northwest Europe in general have high rates of the disease. There are however important exceptions to this. For example, Estonians, although ethnically related to the Finns, have only one third of the incidence of diabetes. Another important exception is the island of Sardinia, which has the second highest rate of type 1 diabetes in the world. In general, however, northwest Europe has the highest rates, and incidence falls as you move towards southern or eastern Europe. A child in Macedonia is, for example, ten times less likely to develop diabetes than a child in Finland.[11]

Why should these differences exist? It seems on present evidence that the distribution of high risk HLA alleles can provide only part of the explanation. An environmental component seems likely and the quest for potential determinants of the disease will be described later in this chapter.

Elsewhere in the world the incidence of Type 1 diabetes remains relatively low, except in regions occupied by populations of north European origin. Many countries have however reported a rising incidence of the disease, so it cannot be assumed that non-Europeans have some form of genetic protection from the disease. Migrant studies are particularly suggestive. For example, Samoan children moving to New Zealand, or Indians or Pakistanis moving to the UK, are reported to take on the local risk of childhood diabetes. Indicative as they may seem, such studies should be interpreted with caution in the absence of accurate estimates of diabetes incidence in the countries of origin.

## Rising incidence of childhood diabetes

There is unequivocal evidence that the incidence of type 1 diabetes is rising steadily across Europe and in many other parts of the world. A recent report from Finland describes a four-fold increase in the incidence of diabetes in children under 14 since 1953, with a linear increase in incidence stretching back over 40 years, equivalent to an annual increase of 3.4 per cent per annum. By 2010 the projected incidence will be 50/100 000 in Finland.[12] Similar observations have now been made in other countries across Europe, with annual increments ranging from 2 to 4 per cent. Occasional abrupt jumps in incidence have been recorded, and have been reported as local 'epidemics', but the overview suggests an inexorable linear increase in most well-studied populations. There is no reliable report of a population in which the incidence of the disease has fallen. It should however be noted that there are very few accurate estimates of the incidence of type 1 diabetes over the age of 15, so it remains uncertain whether the lifetime risk of autoimmune diabetes has increased, or whether the disease is manifesting earlier in a susceptible subgroup of the population (the 'spring harvest' hypothesis). The public health implications of this trend are considerable.

## Environmental influences

The rapid and progressive increase in incidence of type 1 diabetes within genetically stable populations has inevitably suggested that environmental influences are at work. There are sound reasons to believe that these influences are encountered very early in life, sometimes even before birth. Studies of autoantibody appearance in the offspring or siblings of individuals with type 1 diabetes suggest that autoimmune responses to islet antigens are generally well established by age 2–5 year, even though the disease may not develop until adult life.[13] As in type 2 diabetes, prenatal and early post-natal factors may influence subsequent risk of type 1 diabetes. These include intrauterine exposure to viral infection with rubella or enterovirus, extremes of birth weight and high maternal age at delivery. A recent study has extended these observations by demonstrating that risk of diabetes in the child increases in linear fashion from above a maternal age of 25. The effect is quite powerful, such that the child born to a mother in her 40s is 3–4 times more likely to develop diabetes than the child born to a mother in her early 20s. The trend to later childbirth in the Western world can therefore partly account for the rising incidence of type 1 diabetes in these populations.[14]

The implication of these observations is that the autoimmune process leading to onset of diabetes is triggered very early in life and reflects interaction between the immature immune system and its environment. Coeliac disease presents an interesting analogy, in that it has a number of clinical features in common with type 1 diabetes, including common alleles at some Class II HLA loci, autoantibodies, and a slow smouldering clinical course. Dietary gluten plays the key role in development of coeliac disease but clinical disease may not develop until decades after first exposure to this ubiquitous environmental agent. Many investigators have searched for a similar trigger factor in type 1 diabetes, whether dietary or infective. Important criteria in support of such an agent would include epidemiological evidence of exposure, similarity between antigens presented by the agent and islet autoantigens involved in autoimmune diabetes (molecular mimicry) and evidence of cross-reactivity between cellular immune responses to islet autoantigens and to the putative agent. Harrison[15] has provided a set of criteria which should be satisfied when assessing the role of an environmental agent in causation of an autoimmune disease:

- Immune responses to the antigen are disease specific
- Immune responses to the antigen precede the onset of disease
- Immune responses to the antigen reflect disease pathology; that is, are surrogate markers
- Antigen specific antibodies or T cells mediate disease
- Immunization with antigen reproduces disease
- Antigen peptides co-purify with disease associated MHC molecules
- Manipulation of antigen expression modifies disease expression

- Administration of antigen via tolerizing mode or route prevents disease

At present, no candidate agent fulfils all these criteria; the self-antigens proinsulin and insulin perhaps come closest. Two particular problems which limit progress in this area are the lack of standardization of T-cell proliferation studies and the need for HLA matching in both immunological and epidemiological analyses.

The earliest contacts between the developing immune system of the fetus or neonate and the external environment take the form of antigens derived from infective agents or food. On the assumption that potentially harmful immune responses are keyed into the immune memory early in development, these agents are therefore prime aetiological candidates for autoimmunity.

## Viruses and type 1 diabetes

An association between onset of juvenile diabetes and outbreaks of mumps in the community was first proposed in 1927. Many years later interest in a viral aetiology was stimulated by demonstration that diabetes could be induced in mice by the encephalomyocarditis virus and by coxsackie B4. Serological and epidemiological studies seemed to implicate mumps or coxsackievirus in recently diagnosed patients and it was also recognized that congenital rubella infection predisposed to childhood diabetes, although evidence that this represented typical type 1 diabetes remains scanty.

The difficulty of establishing an infective aetiology for an autoimmune condition is greater than might appear at first sight.[16] For example, the majority of virus infections are asymptomatic or trivial in their consequences and exposure might precede clinical onset of the disease by years or even decades. A further difficulty is that common viruses infect everyone in a community, so the timing or frequency of the exposure or the particular strain of virus involved may be critical. Finally, there are many potential mechanisms by which viral infection might promote autoimmunity, ranging from acute cell rupture with exposure of intracellular antigens which the immune system does not recognize, to persistent or latent infection with subtle effects upon the way in which the affected cell interacts with cells involved in immune surveillance.

In recent years, there has been particular interest in the role of enteroviral infection in type 1 diabetes. More than 40 seroepidemiological studies in recently diagnosed patients have been reported with conflicting results. Even though many of these studies have demonstrated elevated antibody levels in people with recent diabetes, this might represent a stronger response to viral infection in people with diabetes-associated HLA types rather than any aetiological role for the infection. Only one study to date has reported presence of circulating virus at onset of the disease and this has yet to be reproduced. Further, since autoimmune diabetes has a long prodrome, recent infection cannot be the cause of diabetes, although it might precipitate it.

It is therefore of more fundamental interest that case-control studies have shown that mothers whose children subsequently develop type 1 diabetes are more likely to show serological evidence of enteroviral infection in pregnancy.[17] Comparisons should however be adjusted for HLA, since many of the mothers will also carry disease-associated HLA types, and the fraction of cases in which there is a suggestion of maternal infection is in any case small.

The enterovirus that has been most intensively studied in relation to type 1 diabetes is coxsackie.[18] Sequence homology with an identical PEVKEK motif exists between coxsackie B4 and the islet antigen GAD65[20,21] but reports of immune cross-reactivity are conflicting. At present, therefore, and despite some suggestive items of evidence, no firm conclusions can be reached about the role of viral infection in the causation of type 1 diabetes.

## Early nutrition and type 1 diabetes

Coeliac disease has features analogous to those of type 1 diabetes and shares some of the same HLA susceptibility haplotypes. Coeliac disease is triggered by dietary gluten encountered soon after birth but the disease may develop many years or even decades following first exposure. It is therefore tempting to consider that an ubiquitous dietary antigen could be involved in the pathogenesis of type 1 diabetes. The possibility that cow's milk might be the 'gluten' of type 1 diabetes was first suggested by the observation that children from Samoa never seemed to develop type 1 diabetes on their home island, where little milk was consumed, but were susceptible to the disease if they emigrated to New Zealand. Broad correlations between the consumption of cow's milk and its products and the incidence of diabetes were noted in later studies, and it was demonstrated that standard animal diets, containing milk casein, carry a higher risk of diabetes in the NOD mouse and bio-breeding (BB) rat than do synthetic amino acid diets or casein hydrolysate. Later studies in the BB rat suggest that plant products from wheat and soya beans may be more important than milk.[22] The animal data are therefore somewhat confused and complex.

Many human studies have now been performed in an attempt to confirm or refute the link between milk and diabetes. One obvious complication is that there is a direct correlation between short duration of breast feeding and early exposure to cow's milk products, making it difficult to tell which of these factors – if either – is critical to development of diabetes. Case-control comparisons of children with and without diabetes show some bias towards a positive effect of early introduction of cow's milk, but the positive studies generally show weak effects, and many other studies have proved negative. Another approach has been to study patterns of antibody formation to constituents of milk in affected and unaffected children. This is complicated by the fact that milk has many constituents and antibodies to these are almost ubiquitous. Most of the studies show that affected children are more likely to carry one or other type of milk antibody but no consistent pattern has emerged. As with the viral studies, excess antibody formation in affected children might either be a feature of the immune abnormality leading to diabetes, or be associated with HLA susceptibility alleles. As an example of the latter, children with *DQB1*0201* may be more likely to develop antibodies to bovine serum albumin. In such an event, excess formation of milk antibodies would have no pathogenic significance. One study does however suggest that some types of milk antibody are more common in cases than in siblings sharing the same HLA alleles.[23] An alternative approach to study of milk antibodies has been to examine the development of islet autoantibodies in relation to early nutrition in prospective studies of children at high risk of diabetes. No clear association has as yet emerged from these relatively small studies. Yet another way of approaching the issue has been to study cellular immune responses to milk constituents in cases and controls. Many studies have been performed but these are largely vitiated by lack of standardization of methods and failure to match for HLA.[15]

The most interesting recent observation in this area is that cow's milk contains small amounts of bovine insulin, which may be sufficient to stimulate formation of insulin antibodies cross-reactive with human insulin in the infant receiving the feed.[24] This provocative study is however far from conclusive and more studies are needed.

## Other changes in the early environment

All lines of evidence – admittedly sometimes rather circumstantial – appear to converge on early childhood as the window of opportunity for diabetes development. It is therefore particularly frustrating that despite many teasing reports, and despite the work of many investigators over many years, the viral and milk hypotheses remain unconfirmed. It may therefore be worth considering the alternative possibility that global changes affecting fetal development and early infancy could affect the developing immune system in ways that bias it towards autoreactivity.

For example, there has been a constant trend towards earlier maturation of children over the past century, shown by rising heights and weights of children at each year of age, by faster growth for both sexes during adolescence, and by earlier onset of menstruation. Separate studies now suggest that the risk of diabetes is enhanced within a given population by more rapid growth *in utero*,[25] in infancy,[26] or around the time of puberty.[27] The other change in early childhood that has been emphasized is that children grow up in a more sterile environment. According the 'hygiene hypothesis', early stimulation of the immune system by repeated bacterial or viral infection may in some way induce protective early maturation of the immune system.

The importance of these considerations is that they shift the emphasis away from specific environmental agents – several of which might be involved – and towards factors influencing host susceptibility. Experiments in mice suggest that the common factor could be maturation of the mucosal immune system in the gut.[15] Breast milk, for example, contains multiple growth factors and cytokines involved in the maturation of intestinal mucosal tissues. Lack of these factors must influence development of mucosa-mediated tolerance to dietary antigens, whether nutritional or viral. Interactions of a relatively sterile environment with reduced breast feeding and rapid growth could easily be imagined. Better understanding of the early development of gut immunity may in time allow these speculations to be converted into testable hypotheses.

## Summary

Childhood type 1 diabetes has increased steadily in prevalence since the mid-century and shows a continued linear increase across Europe and in many other parts of the world. It is not certain whether the lifetime risk of autoimmune diabetes has increased, or whether the disease is presenting at an earlier age within a genetically susceptible sub-population. The HLA system has a dominant role in modulating age of onset but the condition is polygenic and non-HLA genes may play a more important role in later life. On current evidence, it seems likely that progression to disease is determined by an interaction between the developing immune system and the early environment in genetically predisposed individuals and that this interaction often – if not typically – occurs before 1 year of age. Humoral immune responses to multiple antigenic determinants, established by 3–5 years of age, remain stable over time and predict autoimmune diabetes in later life, although the latent period may be very lengthy.

The inexorable increase in childhood diabetes in genetically stable populations implies a role for an environmental factor or factors. The two candidate risk factors that have attracted most interest are viral infection or early exposure to cow's milk proteins. Evidence has accumulated in support of both points of view but neither provides a satisfactory explanation for the steady increase in incidence over many years. Conventional patterns of viral infection would be expected to produce rapid fluctuations in incidence rather than a sustained increase, and breast feeding was widely promoted in many countries over the period during which the rise has occurred. Rising maternal age at delivery of the first child can provide a partial explanation for the rising incidence but the mechanism for this effect remains obscure.

The history of medicine contains examples of diseases such as infective hepatitis or lung cancer whose aetiology appeared complex until a single causal agent emerged and we should therefore continue to pursue the possibility of a simple explanation. We may also need to confront the possibility that the disease process in this and other autoimmune conditions is intrinsically complex, with multiple genetic, immune and environmental determinants. If the latter view turns out to be correct, disease prevention could prove complicated.

# References

1. Himsworth HP. Diabetes mellitus. Its differentiation into insulin-sensitive and insulin-insensitive types. *Lancet*, 1936; **I**: 127–30.

2. Lister J, Nash J, Ledingham U. Constitution and insulin sensitivity in diabetes mellitus. *British Medical Journal*, 1951; **I**: 376–9.

3. Gepts W. Pathologic anatomy of the pancreas in juvenile diabetes mellitus. *Diabetes*, 1965; **14**: 619–33.

4. Karjalainen J, Salmela P, Ilonen J, Knip M. A comparison of childhood and adult type 1 diabetes mellitus. *New England Journal of Medicine*, 1989; **320**: 881–6.

5. Tuomi T *et al*. Clinical and genetic characteristics of type 2 diabetes with and without GAD antibodies. *Diabetes*, 1999; **48**: 150–7.

6. Lorenzen T, Pociot F, Hougaard P, Nerup J. Long term risk of IDDM in first degree relatives of patients with IDDM. *Diabetologia*, 1994; **37**: 321–7.

7. Jacobson DL, Gange SJ, Rose NR, Graham NM. Epidemiology and estimated population burden of selected autoimmune diseases in the United States. *Clinical Immunology and Immunopathology*, 1997; **84**: 223–43.

8. Karvonen M, Pitkaniemi M, Pitkaniemi J, Kohtamaki K, Tajima N, Toumilehto J. Sex difference in the incidence of insulin-dependent diabetes mellitus: an analysis of the recent epidemiological data. *Diabetes and Metabolism Reviews*, 1997; **13**: 275–91.

9. Blohme G *et al*. Male predominance of type 1 diabetes mellitus in young adults: results from a 5-year prospective nationwide study of the 15–34 year age group in Sweden. *Diabetologia*, 1992; **35**: 56–62.

10. Vandewalle CL *et al.*, the **Belgian Diabetes Registry**. Epidemiology, clinical aspects, and biology of IDDM patients under age 40 years. *Diabetes Care*, 1997; **20**: 1556–61.

11. Green A, Gale EAM, Patterson CC, for the EURODIAB ACE Study Group. Incidence of childhood onset insulin-dependent diabetes mellitus: the EURODIAB ACE Study. *Lancet*, 1992; **339**: 905–9.

12. Tuomilehto J *et al.*, and the **Finnish Childhood Type 1 Registry Group**. Record high incidence of type 1 (insulin-dependent) diabetes mellitus in Finnish children. *Diabetologia*, 1999; **42**: 655–60.

13. Ziegler A-G, Hummel M, Schenker M, Bonifacio E. Autoantibody appearance and risk for development of childhood diabetes in offspring of parents with type 1 diabetes. *Diabetes*, 1999; **48**: 460–8.

14. Bingley PJ, Douek IF, Gale EAM. Risk of childhood diabetes rises with increasing maternal age at delivery. *British Medical Journal*, 2000; **321**: 420–4.

15. Harrison LC, Honeyman MC. Cow's milk and type 1 diabetes. The real debate is about mucosal immune function. *Diabetes*, 1999; **48**: 1501–7.

16. Rose NR. The role of infection in the pathogenesis of autoimmune disease. *Immunology*, 1998; **10**: 5–13.

17. Dahlquist G, Ivarsson S, Lindberg B, Forsgren M. Maternal enteroviral infection during childhood as a risk factor for childhood IDDM: a population-based case-control study. *Diabetes*, 1995; **44**: 408–13.

18. 

19. Graves PM, Norris JM, Pallansch MA, Gerling IC, Rewers M. The role of enteroviral infections in the development of IDDM. Limitations of current approaches. *Diabetes*, 1997; **46**: 161–8.

20. Expert Committee. Report of the expert committee on the diagnosis and classification of diabetes mellitus. *Diabetes Care*, 1997; **20**: 1183–97.

21. Atkinson MA, Maclaren NK. The pathogenesis of insulin-dependent diabetes. *New England Journal of Medicine*, 1994; **331**: 1428–36.

22. Atkinson M *et al*. Cellular immunity to a determinant common to glutamate decarboxylase and coxsackie virus in insulin-dependent diabetes. *Journal of Clinical Investigations*, 1994; **94**: 2125–9.

23. Scott FW. Milk and type 1 diabetes. *Diabetes Care*, 1996; **19**: 379–83.

24. Saukkonen T *et al.*, and the DiMe Study Group. Significance of cow's milk protein antibodies as a risk factor for childhood IDDM: interactions with dietary cow's milk intake and HLA-DQB1 genotype. *Diabetologia*, 1998; **41**: 72–78.

25. Vaarala O *et al.*, cow's milk formula feeding induces primary immunization to insulin in infants at genetic risk for type 1 diabetes. *Diabetes*, 1999; **48**: 1389–94.

26. Dahlquist G, Bennich SS, Kallen B. Intrauterine growth pattern and risk of childhood onset type 1 diabetes: population bases case-control study. *British Medical Journal*, 1996; **313**: 1174–7.

27. Johansson C, Samuelsson U, Ludvigsson J. A high weight gain early in life is associated with an increased risk of type 1 diabetes. *Diabetologia*, 1994; **37**: 91–4.

28. Blom L, Persson LA, Dahlquist G. A high linear growth is associated with an increased risk of childhood diabetes mellitus. *Diabetologia*, 1992; **35**: 528–33.

## 2.3 Type 1 diabetes: immunology

*Mark Atkinson*

## Type 1 diabetes: immune or autoimmune?

### The debate continues

Early evidence ascribing an immunological basis for the development of type 1 diabetes derived from investigations of its association with idiopathic Addison's disease, an organ specific disorder involving lymphocytic infiltration and destruction of the adrenal cortex.[1] Similar patterns of lymphocytic infiltration referred to as insulitis were noted in histological specimens from the pancreases of individuals who died shortly after diagnosis of type 1 diabetes.[2] Further evidence of an *autoimmune* origin came with the discovery that specific alleles of human leucocyte antigens (**HLA**) were associated with type 1 but not with type 2 diabetes,[3] together with identification of autoantibodies directed against the cytoplasm of pancreatic islet cells in persons with polyendocrine autoimmunity including type 1 diabetes.[4] Additional evidence consistent with either an immune or an autoimmune pathogenesis includes the findings of recurrent disease in diabetic patients receiving HLA-matched pancreatic grafts and observations that immunosuppressants (for example, cyclosporin A, azathioprine) preserve $\beta$-cell function in new-onset type 1 diabetes patients.[5]

As the 1990s began, immunologists were hopeful that the debate between an immune versus an autoimmune basis for type 1 diabetes could soon be settled,[6,7] and continued to uncover a number of critical features supporting an autoimmune basis for type 1 diabetes. These included the biochemical identification of a series of molecules (that is, self-antigens) that serve as targets of the humoral and cellular immune response, characterization of multiple immunoregulatory defects associated with the disease, description of cell surface molecules necessary for immune activation and $\beta$-cell destruction, and the definition of peptide binding motifs of the HLA molecules conferring susceptibility or resistance to the disease.[8,9] These findings in humans were greatly facilitated by investigation of two spontaneous animal models for the disease, the BB rat and non-obese diabetic (NOD) mouse.[10,11]

While an abundant body of evidence continues to support an autoimmune pathogenesis for the disorder, we still lack a clear understanding of the interplay between genetic susceptibility and the aberrant immune response of the role for environmental agents in modifying the autoimmune response, and of the process underlying the timing and development of type 1 disease. Each in turn contributes to the debate as to where aberrant 'healthy' immunity ends and autoimmunity begins.

## Pathology

The pancreas of an individual with established type 1 diabetes is often smaller and weighs less (that is, approximately 50 per cent of total organ- and 30 per cent of endocrine-weight) than its healthy counterpart (Fig. 1).[2] This difference is a consequence of the progressive atrophy of exocrine tissue that comprises about 98 per cent of the total pancreatic volume. Islets of recently diagnosed type 1 diabetes patients can also be characterized by a diffuse lymphocytic infiltration (that is, insulitis) with onset of atrophy of the islet cords. Insulitis is an elusive lesion to detect in human pancreas, and is rarely found after one year of overt type 1 diabetes.[12] With prolonged duration of disease, a progressive distortion of islet architecture develops with a tendency for $\alpha$- and $\delta$ cells to leave the islet and spread as single cells into the exocrine parenchyma. Regenerating islets have also been observed in the pancreas of recently diagnosed type 1 diabetes patients (Fig. 2).[13] Newly formed islet cells derive from the epithelium of a duct. However, evidence of such regeneration is rare in type 1 diabetes and usually found only in those dying shortly after disease onset.

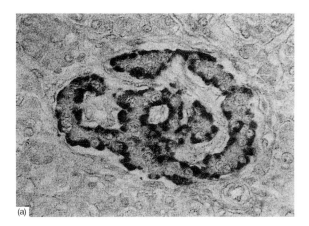

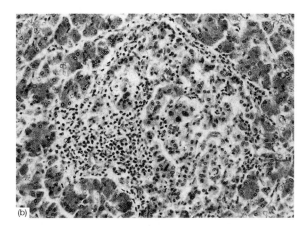

**Fig. 1** The pathology of a pancreatic specimen from a patient with recent onset type 1 diabetes. (a) This panel displays an insulin-deficient islet. The section has been stained for glucagon, somatostatin and pancreatic polypeptide by an immuno-alkaline phosphatase method ($\times$ 1150). All endocrine cells appear to have been stained, confirming the lack of $\beta$ cells. (b) This panel shows insulitis. A chronic inflammatory cell infiltrate is centered on the islet. Haematoxylon and eosin stained ($\times$ 300). (From: Atkinson MA, Maclaren NK. The pathogenesis of insulin dependent diabetes. *New England Journal of Medicine*, 1994; **331**: 1428–36, with permission.)

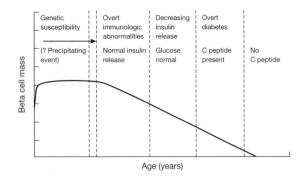

**Fig. 2** The natural history of type 1 diabetes. (Adapted from: Eisenbarth GS. Type I diabetes mellitus: a chronic autoimmune disease. *New England Journal of Medicine*, 1986; **314**: 1360–8, with permission.)

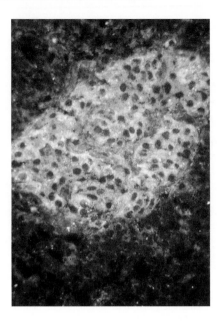

**Fig. 3** Islet cell autoantibodies (ICA) identified by indirect immuno-fluorescence assay using human blood group O pancreas.

## Natural history of disease formation

Based on the collected knowledge of the pathology, immunology (discussed in detail below), and endocrinology of type 1 diabetes, the natural history of the disorder has been modelled by many authors into a disease comprised of five stages (Fig. 2).[5] Stage 1 involves genetic susceptibility (both major histocompatibility complex (MHC) and non-MHC) with intact β-cell mass. Stage 2 is a period in which – following a probable environmental insult in the first months to years of life – insulitis is initiated. Due to a genetic predisposition that does not properly regulate immune responses, the process of β-cell destruction begins. Autoantibodies to islet cell antigens develop marking the autoimmune disease process, yet no measurable β-cell dysfunction in terms of metabolic output occurs at this stage. Stage 3 is characterized by a gradual decline in β-cell mass, with the slope highly variant between individuals (that is, months to years). Incipient β-cell damage is first detectable as an abnormal intravenous glucose tolerance test (IVGTT) with deficient first phase insulin response. Stage 4 is distinguished by an advanced degree of β-cell damage, symptomatic hyperglycaemia with minimal C-peptide production and exogenous insulin dependence. With fulminant β-cell destruction, Stage 5 occurs when C-peptide becomes undetectable and autoantibody markers of disease decline and in most instances, eventually disappear.

## Humoral and cellular immunity

### Autoantibodies

Islet cell cytoplasmic autoantibodies (ICA) are present in the serum of approximately 75 per cent of individuals at the onset of type 1 diabetes versus 0.4 per cent of healthy individuals.[14] ICA are routinely detected by indirect immunofluorescence assay utilizing human blood group O pancreas (Fig. 3). These autoantibodies react with all cells within the islet including those that secrete insulin (β cells), glucagon (α cells), somatostatin (δ cells), and pancreatic polypeptide (PP cells); although ICA specific to β cells have been identified.

Autoantibodies against a variety of islet cell constituents have now been described (Box 1). These include autoantibodies to insulin

(IAA), proinsulin, glutamic acid decarboxylase (GADA), carboxypeptidase H, insulinoma-associated autoantigen-2 (IA-2; also referred to as ICA512), a sialoglycolipid, and several other ill-defined antigens of different molecular weights from 37 to 150 $M_r$.[15] These autoantibodies are reportedly present in 15–85 per cent of patients either at onset or in the period prior to clinical appearance of the disease.[14,15] Of these, four (that is, ICA, IAA, GADA and IA-2 autoantibodies) have gained widespread acceptance by virtue of scientific confirmation, high frequency of expression and superior disease sensitivity and specificity. One of the more promising features of these autoantibodies is that they can be used to predict future cases of type 1 diabetes. Figure 4 represents a life-table analysis indicating the probability of remaining free of type 1 diabetes stratified by the appearance of ICA and IAA in relatives of probands with disease. As can be observed, risk is higher in those with two autoantibodies, and approximately 50 per cent of such individuals develop the disease within four years.[16] The presence of IAA, GADA and IA-2 (that is, three autoantibodies) in addition to ICA greatly increases the risk of subsequent clinical type 1 disease compared to ICA alone.[14,17] Prediction apart, humoral components are important diagnostic markers of type 1 diabetes. Indeed, studies of GADA support their use in identifying type 1 disease in persons with other related disorders (Table 1).

When ICA were first discovered, it was thought that all individuals with ICA would eventually develop overt type 1 disease. This is not the case. Some studies suggest that ICA have a much lower risk of disease in individuals from the general population than in ICA positive relatives of type 1 patients,[17] although others have reported that these markers are equally predictive of subsequent disease in both groups.[18] ICA appear to be less predictive of diabetes when detected in non-diabetic individuals with other autoimmune disorders, and in those with protective Euro-Caucasian HLA haplotypes (for example, DQ*0602).[19] In addition, several subsets of ICA have been identified with varying risks of type 1 disease. One subset termed 'restrictive' due to a staining pattern limited to β cells and

## Box 1 Autoantibody markers of islet immunity in human type 1 diabetes

- ◆ Described in the 1970s
  - ▪ Islet cell cytoplasmic autoantibodies (ICA)
  - ▪ Islet cell surface autoantibodies (ICSA)
- ◆ Described in the 1980s
  - ▪ 64 kDa autoantibodies
  - ▪ Carboxypeptidase-H autoantibodies
  - ▪ Heat shock protein (HSP) autoantibodies
  - ▪ Insulin autoantibodies (IAA)
  - ▪ Insulin receptor autoantibodies
  - ▪ Proinsulin autoantibodies
- ◆ Described in the 1990s
  - ▪ 37 kDa/40 kDa tryptic fragment autoantibodies
  - ▪ 52 kDa rat insulinoma (RIN) autoantibodies
  - ▪ 51 kDa aromatic-L-amino-acid decarboxylase autoantibodies
  - ▪ 128 kDa autoantibodies
  - ▪ 152 kDa autoantibodies
  - ▪ Chymotrypsinogen-related 30 kDa pancreatic autoantibodies
  - ▪ DNA topoisomerase II autoantibodies
  - ▪ Glucose transporter 2 autoantibodies
  - ▪ GAD 65 autoantibodies
  - ▪ GAD 67 autoantibodies
  - ▪ Glima 38 autoantibodies
  - ▪ Glycolipid autoantibodies
  - ▪ GM2-1 islet ganglioside autoantibodies
  - ▪ ICA512/IA-2 autoantibodies
  - ▪ IA-2$\beta$ autoantibodies
  - ▪ Phogrin autoantibodies

displaceable with glutamate decarboxylase (GAD), is less predictive than ICA which reacts with all islet endocrine cells. Autoantigens thus far implicated in the ICA reaction include sialoglycolipids (for example, GM1 gangliosides), the neuroendocrine enzyme GAD, and the tyrosine phosphatase molecule IA-2.

In summary, autoantibodies to islet constituents have proved valuable as predictive markers for type 1 diabetes. The functional and pathogenic relationship between these autoantibodies, $\beta$-cell autoimmunity, and the development of overt type 1 diabetes is very complex and still not fully understood.

## Cellular immunity

An abundant body of evidence suggests that type 1 diabetes results from a cellular immune mediated destruction of islet $\beta$-cells.[20]

This includes:

- demonstration of $\beta$-cell antigen-specific T-cell responses in type 1 diabetes and in those at increased-risk for the disease,
- mononuclear cell infiltrate of the pancreatic islets,
- observations of animal models which suggest that T cells are required for and actively involved in $\beta$-cell destruction (for example, adoptive transfer, lymphocyte depletion, etc.),
- beneficial responses in humans with type 1 diabetes to immunospecific therapy aimed at cellular immune activity.[5–9]

Markers of cellular immunity would therefore be expected to serve as excellent markers with which to delineate the natural history of type 1 diabetes. In practice, this role has been filled by humoral autoantibodies combined with metabolic testing.[14] This is partly because these markers are easier to measure, and partly because the literature is marked with considerable controversy regarding the functional characteristics of T cells or peripheral blood mononuclear cells (PBMC) obtained from individuals with – or at increased risk of – type 1 diabetes.[21,22] Many promising observations have not been reproducible, or were not reported in a standardized format, thereby rendering comparison between laboratories difficult.

Phenotypic markers identified by cytometric analysis may provide a more practical means of disease prediction and pathogenesis. Multiple abnormalities of lymphocyte populations have been reported in association with type 1 diabetes including a reduced percentage of CD4 (helper) and CD8 (cytotoxic) lymphocytes, a decreased CD4/CD8 ratio, and enrichment of lymphocytes possessing HLA class II molecules and interleukin-2 receptors (that is, markers of cellular activation).[23] These investigations have not always proved reproducible and many of these issues remain controversial.

The availability of islet cells and rodent cell lines (for example, RIN, HIT, NIT, etc.) has also led to assays of cellular proliferation (that is, blastogenesis) and generation of T-cell lines to monitor the role of cellular immunity in type 1 diabetes.[21] One theoretical advantage of using islet cells/lines is that they provide all potential sources of $\beta$-cell autoantigen and can be useful for biochemical identification of target molecules. T-cell lines from type 1 diabetic patients generated against an insulinoma (that is, is rat RINm5F cell) membranes eventually resulted in the biochemical identification of a 38 kDa autoantigen.[22] Other studies have demonstrated enhanced PMBC proliferation from cells of type 1 diabetes patients in the presence of adult human islets and fetal pig proislets. However, the scarcity of islet cells and concerns over specificity, and assay variability have made the performance of such assays difficult.

The biochemical identification and recombinant production of putative $\beta$-cell autoantigens targeted by autoantibodies has allowed for investigations measuring the T-cell activity against these compounds. These studies may be able to distinguish antigens involved in the pathogenesis of type 1 diabetes. Insulin is an obvious candidate antigen, yet surprisingly few reports have analysed cellular immunity against insulin in non-insulin treated subjects and the results of these are somewhat conflicting. Enhanced PBMC responses to insulin have been reported in autoantibody positive relatives of patients with type 1 diabetes, as compared with healthy controls, but a greater body of evidence suggests GAD as a target of cellular immunity in type 1 diabetes, and suggest an inverse relationship between GAD antibody

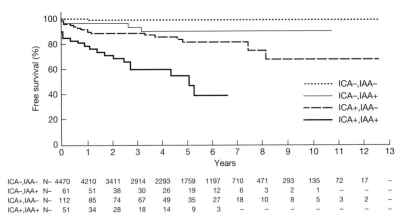

**Fig. 4** A life-table analysis indicating the probability of remaining free of type 1 diabetes stratified by the appearance of islet cell cytoplasmic autoantibodies (ICA) and insulin autoantibodies (IAA) in relatives of probands with disease. The number of relatives followed from the time since the autoantibody was identified is displayed at the bottom for each group. (From: Krischer JP et al. Insulin and islet cell autoantibodies as time-dependent covariates in the development of insulin-dependent diabetes: a prospective study in relatives. *Journal of Clinical Endocrinology and Metabolism*, 1993; **77**: 743–9, with permission.)

**Table 1** Prevalence of GAD autoantibodies and their potential utility in identification of autoimmune activity.

| Subject group | Autoantibody frequency (%) |
| --- | --- |
| Healthy controls | 0.3–0.6 |
| Relatives (first degree) of type 1 diabetes patients | 3–4 |
| Other autoimmune endocrine disorders | 1–2 |
| Newly diagnosed type 1 diabetes | 55–85 |
| Type 2 diabetes | 10–15 |
| Gestational diabetes | 10 |

Investigations (summarized in representative form here) indicate that GAD autoantibodies, in addition to serving as a marker for predicting future cases of – and diagnosing new cases of – type 1 diabetes, may also be useful in identifying autoimmunity in persons diagnosed with other forms of diabetes. Such identifications may be useful in terms of imparting appropriate diabetes management and clinical care.

titer and PBMC reactivity to GAD. Newly diagnosed type 1 patients also have been reported to have enhanced cellular immune activities to various components of cow's milk including bovine serum albumin, β-lactoglobulin, β-casein and α-casein.[23] It has been hypothesized that ingestion of cow's milk in early life can initiate β-cell destruction through molecular mimicry between an amino acid sequence common to cow's milk antigen and a β-cell protein (for example, bovine and human insulin). Unfortunately, most studies of T-cell responses to these antigens suffer a number of deficiencies including a disappointingly low degree of confirmation by other investigators and a low definition for a positive response (that is, a stimulation index of greater than 1.5). The latter is very important as it influences both the sensitivity and specificity of the assay for discriminating between individuals at risk of developing type 1 diabetes and those not so predisposed. Attempts to standardize such tests have thus

far been disappointing, and hence the value of cellular immune makers for the prediction of type 1 diabetes is currently limited and their contribution to β-cell destruction remains unclear.

# Mechanisms of β-cell destruction: perspectives from spontaneous animal models

## Strengths and weaknesses of animal models

For both ethical and practical reasons, limited direct information is available on the mechanisms of β-cell destruction in humans. Therefore much of our understanding of these processes derive from studies of animal models of spontaneous diabetes. The endocrine disorder in both the NOD mouse (Table 2) and BB rat (Table 3) appears remarkably similar to human type 1 diabetes.[10,11] From a research perspective, the NOD mouse has eclipsed the BB rat as the favoured model, and hence will be discussed in far more detail. Reasons for this include a better-defined genome, more monoclonal reagents for analysis of immune system components and considerably lower maintenance costs

Although an understanding of the pathogenic mechanisms underlying type 1 diabetes development in NOD mice has been developed,[11,24] unavoidable genus-specific differences limit their interpretation as a surrogate for human diabetes. In addition to certain NOD strain-specific characteristics that distinguish these mice from humans at risk for type 1 diabetes (for example, deafness, absence of C5 complement), important genus-specific features distinguish the murine from human diabetes. These include resistance to ketoacidosis, and absence of the murine homologue of HLA-DR molecules on antigen presenting cells (APC). Investigators have not always considered that these mice are so highly inbred that they must be viewed as a single case study in humans. Indeed, the combination of NOD strain-specific features as well as inherent differences between genera may explain why identification of non-MHC

**Table 2** The NOD mouse model of type 1 diabetes

| Characteristic | NOD mice |
|---|---|
| Disease onset | Spontaneous, 13–30+ weeks of age |
| Gender bias | Female predominance |
| Disease frequency | Strong inter-colony variation; 50–80% female, 20–50% male typical rates at 26 weeks of age |
| Clinical presentation | Hyperglycaemia, mild ketosis, polydipsia, polyuria, weight loss, insulin dependency |
| Additional disease model | Thyroiditis, sialoadenitis (Sjögrens syndrome), deafness |
| Insulitis | Appears in non-destructive (5–12 weeks) and destructive (13+ weeks) phases; macrophages, dendritic cells, T- and B-lymphocytes, NK cells |
| Genetic susceptibility | MHC plus >15 non-MHC loci |
| Immune markers | Autoantibodies, autoreactive T cells |

**Table 3** The BB rat model of type 1 diabetes

| Characteristic | BB rats |
|---|---|
| Disease onset | Spontaneous, 8–14 weeks of age |
| Gender bias | None |
| Disease frequency | Minor inter-colony variation; 40–70% at 12 weeks of age |
| Clinical presentation | Hyperglycaemia, mild ketosis, polydipsia, polyuria, weight loss, insulin dependency |
| Additional disease model | Thyroiditis, T-cell lymphopenia |
| Insulitis | Rapidly progressive; appears near time of disease onset; macrophages, dendritic cells, T- and B-lymphocytes, NK cells |
| Genetic susceptibility | MHC plus *Lyp* (T-lymphopenia ) locus (chromosome 4) |
| Immune markers | Autoantibodies, autoreactive T cells |

diabetogenic loci in mice have not generally been direct guideposts to identification of homologous loci in outbred humans at risk for type 1 diabetes. Nevertheless, certain immunogenetic and immunopathogenic aspects of type 1 diabetes in this mouse 'case study', particularly the major pathogenic contributions made by MHC genes, clearly justify intensive investigation into why MHC-associated deficiencies in immune function allow development of an autoreactive T-cell repertoire.

## Disease pathology and pathogenesis in NOD mice

The aetiology of type 1 diabetes in this model is both complex and multifactorial.[11,24] By way of summary, both CD4 and CD8 T cells comprise the effector arm, while underlying functional defects in bone marrow-derived APC including macrophages, dendritic cells, and B lymphocytes have been shown to be essential components in selection/activation of the autoimmune repertoire.[20] Multiple CD4 and CD8 T-cell lines and clones with diabetogenic potencies against a variety of identified and unidentified antigens have been established from both islets and spleen.[21] If there is a single T-cell receptor clonotype distinguishing the 'primordial' diabetogenic T-cell, its primacy has not yet been demonstrated.[21] Destruction of β cells apparently entails both necrotic and apoptotic events in response to

invasion of the islets by leucocytes (that is, insulitis). The number of leucocytes in the insulitic infiltrates of NOD mice are striking, almost suggesting lymph node formation around islets. One of the strain-specific peculiarities of NOD mice is accumulation of high percentages of T cells in peripheral lymphoid organs, pancreas and submandibular salivary glands.[24] This T-lymphoaccumulation possibly reflects low interleukin-2 (IL-2) levels and resistance of thymocytes and peripheral T cells to the induction of apoptosis.

## Insulitis: the NOD mouse perspective

The natural history of pancreatic inflammation suggests that the disease process begins with an inflammatory response adjacent to the pancreatic islet ('peri-insulitis' focused in the region adjacent to the islet that carries small pancreatic ducts and blood vessels. As the process progresses, the inflammatory lesion spreads to the islet itself. The insulitis lesion is comprised of a number of inflammatory cells (that is, T cells, B cells, macrophages), but the resulting destructive process appears very specific (that is, β cells are destroyed while α cells remain intact). In the latest stages, the islet collapses into an α-cell like islet, and the integrity of other cellular components of the pancreatic islet is maintained. It has recently been proposed that the period of actual β-cell killing occurs immediately prior to symptomatic onset (Fig. 5).

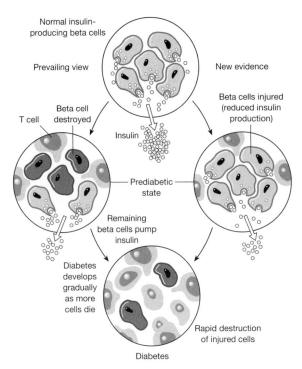

**Fig. 5** A new model portending a rapid destruction of $\beta$ cells in the pathogenesis of type 1 diabetes is shown. Until recently, most models assessing the rate of $\beta$-cell destruction in type 1 diabetes have presumed a gradual (that is, modified linear, see Fig. 2) endocrine cell loss characterized by small periods of 'waxing and waning' in the immune response. However, recent investigations of NOD mice have suggested a different scenario wherein the period of actual $\beta$-cell destruction occurs in a very limited time period immediately prior to symptomatic onset. The composition of the insulitic lesion and/or destructive activity prior to this event would be of non- or limited-destructive capacity. Evidence for this model in terms of human type 1 diabetes is limited but the subject of ongoing investigation.

## Lymphocyte subsets in NOD diabetes

The development of diabetes in the NOD mouse is clearly a thymus-dependent process.[24] Studies of cell transfer, treatment with monoclonal reagents and investigations of disease that develops following cyclophosphamide treatment of disease-prone male animals suggest that both CD4 and CD8 T-lymphocytes are required for the initiation of disease process.[20,24] CD4 T cells are thought to be involved in the inflammatory reaction through provision of helper function for both CD8 T-cells and B-lymphocytes. CD8 T cells are most often considered to play a role in direct cellular killing. Thus, the requirement for both CD4 and CD8 T cells has been interpreted by some as indicating that the initiation of disease requires an interaction between CD4 and CD8 T cells and that the CD8 cytotoxic T-cell is the effector cell causing islet damage. This cytotoxic model implies that diabetes results from a direct attack of CD8 cytotoxic T cells on islet $\beta$ cells, and provides an explanation for the specificity of the disease process. Other studies support the notion that both CD4 and CD8 T cells are required for the initiation of disease, but do

not support the concept that the effector phase is a CD8 T-cell dependent process.

## Cytokines in immune regulation and destruction

The cytokines have been the most commonly implicated inflammatory mediators to date.[25–27] Cytokines are produced by lymphoid cells to regulate immune responses, haemopoiesis and inflammation. More than two dozen cytokines have thus far been identified, most having several actions that produce local or general immunomodulatory effects. Cytokines are primarily produced by lymphoid cells, but other cells (for example, fibroblasts, endothelial cells) can also produce these compounds. Among the cytokines thought most important as inflammatory mediators are IL-1, interferon gamma (IFN-$\gamma$) and tumour necrosis factor-$\alpha$ (TNF-$\alpha$).

IFN-$\gamma$ is a product of T cells containing antiviral and anti-proliferative activities. IL-1 and TNF-$\alpha$ are predominantly produced by macrophages and monocytes.[27] These promote local pro-inflammatory actions (for example, increased vascular permeability, phagocyte stimulation, free radical production and chemotaxis). IL-1 and TNF-$\alpha$ are also responsible for induction of fever and cortico-steroid release. Positive and negative feedback loops between cytokines regulate the magnitude of the inflammatory response.[25] IFN-$\gamma$ increases MHC class I antigen expression on cells, facilitating cytotoxic T-cell killing of target cells. It also induces expression of MHC class II antigens on macrophages and adhesion molecules on endothelial cells and APC.

In one widely recognized model (Fig. 6), CD4 T cells are divided into two T-helper (Th) subsets, termed Th1 and Th2, based on cytokine secretion patterns and presumed function.[8,20,25] Th1 cells produce IL-2, IFN-$\gamma$ and TNF-$\beta$. Th2 cells secrete IL-4, IL-5, IL-6 and IL-10. These two types of CD4 T cells mediate different immunological responses. The Th1 subset is predominantly involved in delayed-type hypersensitivity (DTH) reactions, whereas Th2 cells are responsible for B-lymphocyte helper function and antibody production. As discussed later in this chapter, the balance between the two responses appears to regulate the pathogenesis and expression of diabetes in NOD mice.[25]

## *In vitro* effects of cytokines on $\beta$ cells

A large body of evidence exists to suggest that cytokines can either stimulate or inhibit insulin secretion of islet cells as well as promote their death.[27] These effects are largely dose dependent, and IL-1 has often been considered largely responsible for these effects. However, TNF ($\alpha$ or $\beta$) and IFN-$\gamma$ are also capable of reversibly impairing $\beta$-cell function *in vitro*. When present in combination, these agents can exert a synergistic cytotoxic effect. *In vitro* toxicity of monolayer cultured islet has also been observed. The *in vitro* cytotoxic effects of IL-1$\beta$, TNF and IFN-$\gamma$ are not observed in all situations and concentrations specific for $\beta$ cells. Indeed, other islet cell lineages (for example, $\alpha$ cells) can also be damaged under similar conditions of testing. However, selective inhibition of $\beta$-cell function and preservation of glucagon production have been demonstrated using purified preparations of $\beta$- and $\alpha$ cells, respectively.

The ability of IFN-$\gamma$ to increase the density of cellular MHC antigen expression has already been indicated. *In vitro* treatment of islet

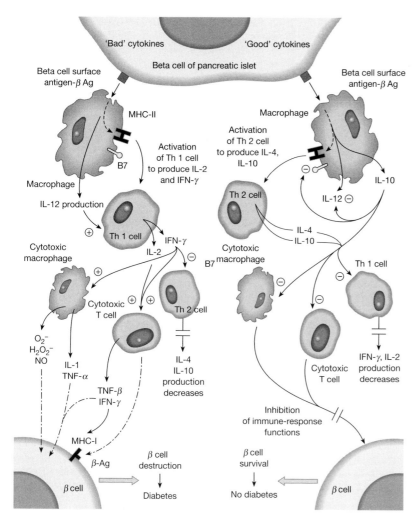

**Fig. 6** The Th1/Th2 model for immune regulation is shown. Studies both *in vivo* and *in vitro* have supported the notion that activities of CD4 + 'helper-T' cells may directly and/or indirectly relate to the production of specific cytokines. Evolutionary immunologists indicate the compartmentalization of such responses provides for a more efficient distinction in the development of an immune response against pathogens of divergent origins and modes of evasion. While somewhat of an overgeneralization, Th1 cytokines are viewed as enhancing cellular immune activities whereas Th2 cytokines support those of humoral immunity. Specifically, Th1 activity appears enhanced by production of the lymphokines IFN-γ, IL-2 and IL-12. Conversely, Th2 augmentation of humoral immunity occurs through the release of IL-4 and IL-10. IL-4 appears to be a strong inhibitor of Th1 immunity. The production of specific cytokines, both systemic and at the site of pancreatic inflammation, may have important implications on the pathogenesis of diabetes as well as the potential for developing methods aimed at disease prevention (see Table 4).

cells with IFN-γ and TNF can induce *de novo* synthesis of MHC class II molecules on β cells. 'Aberrant' MHC class II antigen expression on β cells has been reported to occur in NOD mice as well as in patients with new-onset type 1 diabetes. Hence, a pathogenic role for aberrant presentation of islet autoantigens in spontaneous diabetes has been suggested. However, this hypothesis has not been supported by studies of transgenic mice expressing MHC class II molecules on their β cells, since these animals do not develop spontaneous diabetes. In addition, other studies of aberrant MHC class II antigen expression on β cells obtained from patients with recent onset of diabetes have not supported the early findings.

## Cytokine transgenic mice

The introduction of gene sequences coding for cytokines combined with regulatory (that is, promoter) elements of the insulin gene into fertilized mouse eggs allows for the production of highly artificial but informative transgenic animals. These mice have provided interesting clues as to the role of cytokines in the development of insulitis and diabetes in otherwise non-diabetes-prone mouse strains.[24] For example, mice transgenic for IFN-γ develop severe insulitis leading to islet destruction and overt diabetes. As neither insulitis nor diabetes develops when the transgene is expressed in severe combined immunodeficiency mice, this cytokine would appear to induce lymphoid cells capable of mediating β-cell destruction.

IFN-α may also be involved in the pathogenic process leading to diabetes, since animals transgenic for this cytokine develop pancreatic pathology characterized by progressive islet infiltration, β-cell destruction, persistence of α- and δ cells and islet atrophy. Insulin deficiency and clinical diabetes develop in approximately one-half of these animals. IFN-α activates macrophages, natural killer cells, and induces IL-2 production by activated T cells. Local production of IFN-α may promote an inflammatory reaction involving several cell lineages that impart β-cell destruction.[27]

Not all cytokine transgenic animals develop type 1 diabetes, as shown by animals expressing TNF-α and TNF-β. The phenotype of these animals is one of progressive insulitis in the absence of diabetes, demonstrating that insulitis can occur in the absence of diabetes.

In somewhat similar fashion, IL-10 production in pancreatic islets from mice transgenic for this cytokine is marked by diffuse pancreatic extravasation of leucocytes (that is, not islet focused) without overt diabetes. Hyper-expression of MHC class II antigens and of adhesion molecules on endothelial cells is also observed in these animals. Thus, it appears that IL-10 may provide a recruitment signal for leucocyte migration, yet this effect alone is not in and of itself sufficient to initiate β-cell destruction.[20,26]

Taken together, studies of transgenic animals indicate that several cytokines may be involved in the pathogenic process leading to type 1 diabetes. Some of these (for example, IFN-γ) have previously been associated in both *in vivo* and *in vitro* analyses as promoting the development of diabetes. By way of contrast, the role of other inflammatory molecules (for example, IL-1, TNF) in the pathogenesis of this disease remain in doubt, since their effect *in vivo* was not consistent with that observed *in vitro*.

## Cytokine immunoregulation in diabetes

As IFN-γ is predominantly produced by the Th1 subset of T cells and IL-4 and IL-10 are products of the Th2 subset, one widely recognized but controversial model (Fig. 7) suggests that type 1 diabetes develops in genetically prone individuals when Th1 and Th2 T-cell-dependent effects are unbalanced.[8,25] Evidence supportive of this model in NOD mice includes the observations of decreased IL-4 production, the protective effects of *in vivo* IL-4 administration, and numerous therapeutic studies suggesting that immunomodulation to a high IL-4/low (decreased) IFN-γ ratio promotes disease prevention. In addition, as IFN-γ appears to be important in the initiation and expression of β-cell damage and both IL-4 and IL-10 suppress IFN-γ production *in vivo*/ *in vitro*, a large body of evidence would indicate that cytokine regulation is of central importance in the pathogenesis of autoimmune diabetes. However, this model has also been challenged since IL-4 secreting T-cell

clones have been reported which promote diabetes, and therapies capable of diabetes prevention work with equivalent effectiveness in standard NOD mice as well as in NOD mice lacking IL-4 (that is, IL-4 knockout).

Even in the absence of a strict Th1/Th2 model, cytokines may play an important role in the activation and development of clinical disease. Indeed, the balance of the counteracting cytokine-dependent effects may be influenced by environmental stimuli.[7] Specifically, while all animals of the disease-prone genotype develop insulitis, only those that develop destructive insulitis develop diabetes. Hence the proportion developing the destructive autoimmune response may be inversely related to exposure to environmental antigenic challenge.

## Free radicals and type 1 diabetes

Cytokines (for example, IL-1, TNF-α) may also influence the pathogenesis of diabetes through the production and activation of free radicals. Free radicals are metabolites that display an unpaired electron within their outer molecular orbital (for example, $O_2^-$, $OH^-$). This unique electronic configuration lead to a highly reactive and unstable molecule capable of damaging or disrupting cellular membranes, enzymatic pathways and DNA. Under normal conditions cells continuously neutralize the deleterious activities of free radicals through antioxidants (for example, catalase, glutathione peroxidase and superoxide dismutase) or quenchers of radical damage (for example, vitamin E). Both IL-1 and TNF-α have been shown to induce free radical formation in a variety of cell types including pancreatic β cells. One model of islet damage proposes that the production of free radicals may represent the final common pathway responsible for β-cell dysfunction and damage (Fig. 8).

In terms of oxidative damage, the superoxide ($O_2^-$) free radical can be converted to the reactive hydroxyl radical within a cell and promote oxidation of molecules and DNA breakage. DNA damage activates the repair enzyme poly-(ADP-ribose)-synthetase, a process dependent on adenosine diphosphate (ADP). This repair process depletes nicotine adenine dinucleotide (NAD) from cellular stores thereby decreasing protein synthesis. As NAD is also required in

CD4T Cells: Peptide + MHC class II

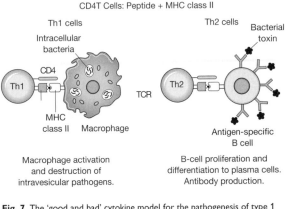

**Fig. 7** The 'good and bad' cytokine model for the pathogenesis of type 1 diabetes is shown. Production of Th2 cytokines would be viewed as providing a pathway of avoidance of β-cell destruction (hence the label of a 'good' cytokine). Specifically, production of IL-4 and IL-10 would block the destructive actions of the cellular immune response. By contrast, immune responses characterized by 'bad' Th1 cytokines would be considered as promoting β-cell destruction through enhancement of actions ascribed to cytotoxic T cells or macrophages (through radical mediator damage).

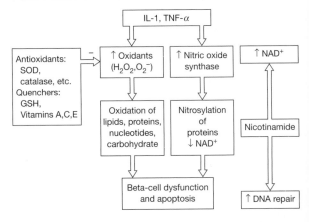

**Fig. 8** The lymphokine model for β-cell destruction in type 1 diabetes.

radical scavenging, a damaged cell becomes more susceptible to further radical attack. This process is especially important for $\beta$ cells in that they are highly sensitive to oxygen free radical injury due to their high rate of metabolism and relatively low activity of scavenging enzymatic systems (for example, superoxide dismutase).

Another interesting and highly multi-functional molecule, nitric oxide (NO), has been shown to inhibit platelet aggregation, serve in neurotransmission and vasodilatation. NO is the primary means by which cells of the immune system (for example, macrophages) destroy intracellular bacteria and parasites. NO is produced from L-arginine; a pathway regulated by either of the two isoforms of the enzyme nitric oxide synthase (NOS). The constitutive form of nitric oxide synthase (cNOS) produces only limited quantities of NO and is associated with the physiological functions of the molecule. The inducible isoform (iNOS), is responsive to both cytokines (for example, IL-1, IFN-$\gamma$, TNF-$\alpha$) as well as to bacterial endotoxin. Contrary to cNOS, the iNOS enzyme is capable of stimulating the production of large quantities of NO. High quantities of intracellular NO can lead to the depletion of NAD stores, activation of iron and thiol groups of enzymes leading to inefficient oxidative phosphorylation, impaired glycolosis, protein nitrosylation and strand breakage in DNA. NO may be responsible for the inhibition of insulin secretion by IL-1. In addition, iNOS activation in response to nonspecific inflammatory tissue damage may result in specific $\beta$-cell destruction. Selective $\beta$-cell destruction observed in type 1 diabetes may thus be the result of the unusual sensitivity of these cells to inflammatory mediators including NO. Free radicals thus appear to be implicated in $\beta$-cell destruction but their specific role in type 1 diabetes awaits clarification.

## NOD mice as a model for disease prevention

While important for understanding the cause(s) and pathogenesis of type 1 diabetes, this model can also be used to test therapies for its prevention. Over 125 interventions which induce the prevention or delay of diabetes in NOD mice have been identified.[11] The ease by which immunomodulation diverts the immune system in these mice is best understood by considering the effect of their exposure to extrinsic microbial pathogens. The inbreeding of NOD mice has genetically fixed a number of immunodeficiencies that, in aggregate, impair communication between APC and T cells. NOD macrophages exhibit impaired ability to activate regulatory T cells in an autologous mixed lymphocyte reaction. Comparable impairment in dendritic cell function has been observed in recent onset type 1 diabetes patients. The NOD immunodeficiencies are partially correctable in a natural environment where a full range of microbial and viral antigens would be encountered. It is only when NOD mice are maintained under stringent specific pathogen-free conditions that full disease penetrance is observed in both sexes. Hence immunostimulation by a variety of treatments ameliorates the weak communication between the innate and adaptive immune system components and restores more normal control over autoreactive T cells. Unfortunately, in a genetically heterogeneous human population containing individuals at high risk for type 1 diabetes development, there is little evidence of a comparable set of immune deficiencies that would prove as malleable. At the same time, the observation that cleaning up the extrinsic environment of the NOD mouse sets the stage for activation of autoimmune T cells raises the question of whether a hypersanitized rearing environment for human infants might predispose children with autoimmune-permissive HLA haplotypes to higher risk for eventual penetrance of autoimmune diseases.

In NOD mice, type 1 diabetes development is well choreographed when all the relevant environmental factors are held constant (pathogen status, diet, etc.). Specific time windows can be defined in which an immunomodulator can be either protective or destructive. By contrast, the natural history of type 1 diabetes in humans is such that the age of disease onset is extremely broad; with symptoms occurring at any time from the first years of life to well beyond 50 years of age. Intervention studies in NOD mice can however be designed in which therapeutic regimens are initiated at birth, at a presymptomatic stage prior to the occurrence of insulitis (that is, less than three weeks post-partum); before the onset of symptomatic disease (that is, four to eight weeks post-partum) at a time when considerable numbers of $\beta$ cells are still intact; or at the diagnosis of type 1 diabetes when the $\beta$-cell damage has appreciated to the extent of overt hyperglycaemia. However, studies of in NOD mice must be viewed for their functional as well as their practical applicability to therapeutic intervention in human disease. For example, agents effective in NOD mice from birth may not be useful in treatment of humans identified immediately prior to the onset of type 1 diabetes when significant $\beta$-cell destruction has occurred.

At a minimum, investigations of NOD mice have enhanced our appreciation of the aetiological complexity of type 1 diabetes in humans and provide an illustration of how promising results obtained in an animal model can be translated into human clinical trials (Table 4). Thus, although the mouse and rat models can never be complete surrogates for humans, they will provide essential insights as to the interactions between genes and environment that together trigger a complex disease.

**Table 4** Treatments aimed at inducing clinical remissions or preventing human type 1 diabetes

| Group studied | Agent or treatment |
|---|---|
| New onset type 1 patients | Cyclosporine |
| | Azathioprine |
| | Anti-CD5 antibodies (CD5+) |
| | Intensive insulin therapy |
| | High-dose insulin therapy |
| | Antibody against IL-2 receptor |
| | Nicotinamide |
| | Intravenous immune globulin |
| | Plasmapheresis |
| | Anti-lymphocyte globulin |
| | Prednisone |
| | Bacille Calmette–Guerin |
| Subjects at high risk for type 1 disease | Intensive therapy with intravenous insulin |
| | Prophylactic insulin therapy |
| | Nicotinamide |
| | Oral insulin |
| | Avoidance of cow-milk based infant formulas |

# Hypothetical models for the pathogenesis of type 1 diabetes

## Environmental agents: key to understanding pathogenesis

Type 1 diabetes appears to either result from or be strongly influenced by the action of an environmental agent(s) in persons genetically susceptible to the disease. A plethora of potential environmental agents have been proposed, most being of dietary or infectious origin, but no single all-encompassing agent has been identified. In addition, identification of the pathogenic mechanisms underlying the disease is complicated by its heterogeneous natural history (that is, months to decades), complex patterns of genetic susceptibility and resistance, limited understanding of a primary autoantigen (if such even exists), and the finding that not all persons displaying signs of autoimmunity progresses to overt disease. While not specific in their early pathogenic features, the following models have been the most cited examples of potential models that may underlie the disease.

## The lymphokine model for β-cell destruction in type 1 diabetes

In this scenario, lymphokines produced in response to a nonspecific inflammatory event (for example, trauma) produce a limited degree of initial β-cell destruction due to a usual susceptibility of β cells to such agents (Fig. 8). The predominant lymphokines in this model are produced by macrophages and include TNF-α and IL-1. Anti-β-cell immunity would persist in those genetically susceptible to the disease, with continuing β-cell destruction produced by various cytotoxic agents (for example, superoxides, NO) as well as a lack in activity of numerous compounds associated with cellular and/or DNA repair mechanisms (for example, superoxide dismutase). Nicotinamide, an agent that reportedly prevents type 1 diabetes in persons at high-risk for the disease and NOD mice, may provide a beneficial role in averting β-cell destruction by increasing intracellular NAD and DNA repair mechanisms.

## Role for viruses in the pathogenesis of type 1 diabetes; molecular mimicry model

In this model (Fig. 9), the autoimmune process is triggered by a 'normal' immune response to a cell infected with a virus whose proteins share similar sequence to that of a β-cell protein. The infected cells display processed viral antigens (via class I molecules) to CD8+ T cells. Macrophages, having phagocytosed and processed virus, present the viral peptides to CD4+ T cells through class II molecules. The CD4+ T cells amplify the actions of the CD8+ T cells to become cytotoxic effector cells that can kill β cells expressing a peptide common to the viral protein. Despite exhaustive research efforts to demonstrate molecular mimicry as an underlying cause of type 1 diabetes, it remains an unproven hypothetical model. Contemporary support predominantly derives from studies demonstrating amino acid sequence similarity between β-cell proteins (for example, GAD, IA-2) with those of viruses (for example, Coxsackie, Rota virus), and the ability of HLA molecules with susceptibility/resistance for type 1

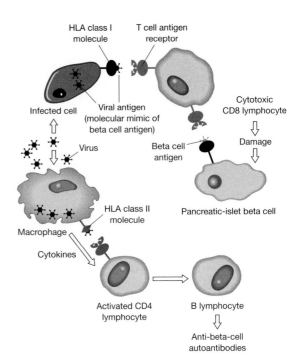

**Fig. 9** Role for viruses in the pathogenesis of type 1 diabetes; molecular mimicry model.

disease to bind these regions of mimicry. However, studies (particularly those of cellular immunity) of the natural history of diabetes in humans and NOD mice have failed to elevate this model beyond the hypothetical stage.

## Role for viruses in the pathogenesis of type 1 diabetes; β tropic virus/viral superantigen models

In this model (Fig. 10), the autoimmune process is initiated following the direct viral infection of β cells or the expression in β cells of a virus acting as a superantigen. In either situation, leucocytes are recruited to pancreatic islets. Recruitment increases the release of cytokines (for example, interferon α) and the adhesion of leucocytes within the pancreatic islets. In the β-cell tropic model, the infected β-cell is susceptible to direct attack by anti-viral cytotoxic lymphocytes. Under both models, cytokines and free radicals produced by macrophages activated within the islet may augment the cytotoxic response to the β cells; the cytokines also recruit CD4+ T cells to the lesion. Macrophages present autoantigens derived from virus damaged β cells, thus leading to the development of lymphocytes and autoantibodies that react with β cell proteins. Support for both of these models exists, yet they remain hypothetical. Whereas viruses capable of β-cell destruction have been isolated from an extremely limited number of human pancreata, examination of an extensive number of these tissues from type 1 diabetes patients have failed to reveal the presence of such viruses. Support for the superantigen model exists through the identification of T cells characteristic of

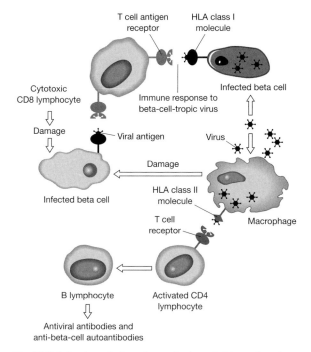

**T cell antigen receptor**

**HLA class I molecule**

**Cytotoxic CD8 lymphocyte**

**Infected beta cell**

**Immune response to beta-cell-tropic virus**

**Damage**

**Viral antigen**

**Virus**

**Infected beta cell**

**Damage**

**HLA class II molecule**

**T cell receptor**

**Macrophage**

**B lymphocyte**

**Activated CD4 lymphocyte**

**Antiviral antibodies and anti-beta-cell autoantibodies**

**Fig. 10** Role for viruses in the pathogenesis of type 1 diabetes; $\beta$ tropic virus/viral superantigen models.

superantigen activation in the pancreas of a limited number of new onset type 1 diabetes patients. However, to date, no such viral superantigen has been unequivocally identified.

# References

1. **Nerup J**. The clinical and immunological association of diabetes mellitus and Addison's disease. In: Bastenie PA, Gepts W, Addison AM, eds. *Immunity and Autoimmunity in Diabetes Mellitus*. Amsterdam: Excerpta Medica, 1974: 149–83.

2. **Gepts W**. Pathologic anatomy of the pancreas in juvenile diabetes mellitus. *Diabetes*, 1965; **14**: 619–33.

3. **Nerup J, Platz P, Anderssen OO**. HLA-antigens and diabetes mellitus. *Lancet*, 1974; **2**: 864–6.

4. **Bottazzo GF, Florin-Christiansen A, Doniach D**. Islet cell antibodies in diabetes mellitus and autoimmune polyendocrine deficiencies. *Lancet*, 1974; **2**: 1279–83.

5. **Eisenbarth GS**. Type I diabetes mellitus: a chronic autoimmune disease. *New England Journal of Medicine*, 1986; **314**: 1360–8.

6. **Castano L, Eisenbarth GS**. Type 1 diabetes: a chronic autoimmune disease of human, mouse and rat. *Annual Reviews of Immunology*, 1990; **8**: 647–79.

7. **Atkinson MA, Maclaren NK**. The pathogenesis of insulin dependent diabetes. *New England Journal of Medicine*, 1994; **331**: 1428–36.

8. **Tisch R, McDevitt H**. Insulin-dependent diabetes mellitus. *Cell*, 1996; **85**: 291–7.

9. **Bach JF, Chatenoud L, Herbelin A, Gombert JM, Carnaud C**. Autoimmune diabetes: how many steps for one disease? *Research in Immunology*, 1997; **148**: 332–8.

10. **Rossini AA, Mordes JP, Like AA**. Immunology of insulin dependent diabetes mellitus. *Annual Reviews of Immunology*, 1985; **3**: 289–320.

11. **Atkinson MA, Leiter EH**. The NOD mouse model of type 1 diabetes: as good as it gets? *Nature Medicine*, 1999; **5**: 601–4.

12. **Foulis AK** *et al.* The histopathology of the pancreas in type I (insulin-dependent) diabetes mellitus: a 25-year review of deaths in patients under 20 years of age in the United Kingdom. *Diabetologia*, 1986; **29**: 267–74.

13. **Gepts W, LaCompte PM**. The pancreatic islets in diabetes. *American Journal of Medicine*, 1981; **70**: 105–15.

14. **Palmer JP**. Predicting IDDM. The use of humoral immune markers. *Diabetes Reviews*, 1993; **1**: 104–15.

15. **Atkinson MA, Maclaren NK**. Islet cell autoantigens in insulin-dependent diabetes. *Journal of Clinical Investigation*, 1993; **92**: 1608–16.

16. **Krischer JP** *et al.* Insulin and islet cell autoantibodies as time-dependent covariates in the development of insulin-dependent diabetes: a prospective study in relatives. *Journal of Clinical Endocrinology and Metabolism*, 1993; **77**: 743–9.

17. **Bingley PJ, Bonifacio E, Gale EAM**. Can we really predict IDDM? *Diabetes*, 1993; **42**: 213–20.

18. **Schatz D** *et al.* Islet cell antibodies predict insulin-dependent diabetes in United States school age children as powerfully as in unaffected relatives. *Journal of Clinical Investigation*, 1994; **93**: 2403–7.

19. **Gianani R** *et al.* Prognostically significant heterogeneity of cytoplasmic islet cell antibodies in relatives of patients with type I diabetes. *Diabetes*, 1992; **41**: 347–53.

20. **Janeway C**. Immunology relevant to diabetes. In: Porte D, Sherwin RS, eds. *Ellenberg and Rifkin's Diabetes Mellitus*, 5th edn., 1997: 287–301.

21. **Haskins K, Wegmann D**. Diabetogenic T-cell clones. *Diabetes*, 1996; **45**: 1299–305.

22. **Roep BO**. T-cell responses to autoantigens in IDDM. The search for the Holy Grail. *Diabetes*, 1996; **45**: 147–56.

23. **Harrison LC, Honeyman LC**. Cow's milk and type 1 diabetes: the real debate is about mucosal immune function. *Diabetes*, 1999; **48**: 1501–7.

24. **Leiter EH, Serreze D, Prochazaka M**. The genetics and epidemiology of diabetes in NOD mice. *Immunology Today*, 1990; **11**: 147–9.

25. **Rabinovitch A**. Immunoregulatory and cytokine imbalances in the pathogenesis of IDDM. Therapeutic intervention by immunostimulation? *Diabetes*, 1994; **43**: 613–21.

26. **Rabinovitch A**. An update on cytokines in the pathogenesis of insulin-dependent diabetes mellitus. *Diabetes/Metabolism Reviews*, 1998; **14**: 129–151.

27. **Burkart V, Kolb H**. Macrophages in islet destruction in autoimmune diabetes mellitus. *Immunobiology*, 1996; **195**: 601–13.

## 3.1 Genetic subtypes of diabetes

*Katharine Owen and Andrew Hattersley*

## Genetic influences and genetic subgroups in diabetes

Diabetes is a collection of discrete disorders characterized by chronic hyperglycaemia. The different aetiologies are reflected in different clinical patterns, which require different management. This heterogeneity of aetiology and management is most clearly seen in type 1 and type 2 diabetes. Recently a large number of discrete subtypes have been identified on the basis of genetic mutations in single genes. These genetic subtypes can be characterized, may have a very different clinical course, and require a different approach to treatment than type 1 or type 2 diabetes. This chapter outlines the molecular genetic definition, clinical characteristics and management of these genetic subgroups.

### Genes in type 1 and type 2 diabetes

Genetic influences play an important role in the aetiology of type 1 and type 2 diabetes (Chapters 2.2 and 3.2) but they are not important in determining clinical management. Type 1 diabetes is a homogeneous disorder but it is likely that the group of disorders at present called type 2 diabetes will in the future be broken down into other aetiological sub-groups. This further subclassification may well be on the basis of molecular genetics, especially if a single gene mutation causes some subtypes of type 2 diabetes. Such a classification will not be possible if there are multiple gene mutations predisposing to diabetes in a single patient. The advances in the molecular genetics of type 2 diabetes to date (outlined in Chapter 3.3) have been inconsistent and could not form the basis of a clinically robust classification.

### Evidence for genetic influence in type 2 diabetes

There is considerable evidence for genetic influences in the aetiology of type 2 diabetes from observations in families. Twin studies showed a concordance of 80–90 per cent in monozygotic twins compared with 30–40 per cent in dizygotic twins.[1,2] There is an increased familial risk and the prevalence in siblings of a patient with type 2 diabetes is 3–4 fold the general population. If both parents have type 2 diabetes the life time risk of developing the disease increases to 70–80 per cent. Although type 2 diabetes is clustered in families, its inheritance rarely follows a simple Mendelian pattern.[3] The variation in prevalence between ethnic groups also provides evidence for the role of genes. There are populations with high prevalence (for example, native Americans and Polynesians), medium prevalence (Indian subcontinent and Afro-Caribbean) and low prevalence (European caucasian). Although some of the differences in diabetes risk between ethnic groups reflect obesity and other environmental influences, migration studies suggest that genetic predisposition varies markedly between races in the same environment.

### Genetics of type 2 diabetes

Despite clear evidence for a genetic aetiology the genes involved have not been identified in the majority of patients with type 2 diabetes. Most of the major advances in understanding genetic disease have been in rare conditions that are caused by mutations in a single gene (monogenic) rather than the common diseases where there are multiple genetic (polygenic) and environmental influences. Diabetes is a good example of this; causative gene mutations have been identified in the majority of patients with the rare, monogenic subgroup maturity onset diabetes of the young (**MODY**), but little progress has been made in defining the genes in the common, polygenic, type 2 diabetes.

The main problem is that in the common form of type 2 diabetes the genes involved predispose to developing diabetes rather than causing it; an important distinction. An individual develops type 2 diabetes because of the interaction between the genes he inherits and the environment he lives in (Fig. 1). The multiple predisposing genetic factors, and the major role of environmental influences present considerable methodological difficulties in attempting to define the genes.

As the primary pathophysiology is not known in type 2 diabetes it has been difficult to focus the search for predisposing genes. A mutation in a gene for a key protein in any of the pathways involved in the secretion or the action of insulin could result in a predisposition to diabetes. This has led to two main approaches in the investigation of putative type 2 diabetes genes. The first is to investigate specific candidate genes based on the role of the protein they encode (for example, the glucose transporter GLUT-2). The genes need to be identified and studied in detail for mutations or polymorphisms that

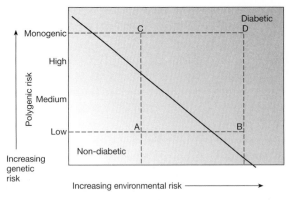

**Fig. 1** Genetic and environmental interaction in type 2 diabetes. A and B – Subjects with a mild genetic predisposition to type 2 diabetes and differing obesity for example, offspring of a caucasian subject with type 2 diabetes. C and D – Subjects with a major genetic predisposition to diabetes and differing obesity for example, patients with *HNF1α* mutations. As genetic risk increases environmental influences have less effect on phenotype. So an individual with low polygenic risk for diabetes for example, A and B only develop diabetes if there are adverse environmental influences such as obesity. Subject A is thin so is not diabetic whereas B is obese and thus diabetic. However in a monogenic condition with high penetrance (for example, *HNF1α* MODY mutations) environmental influences have little or no effect on the diagnosis of diabetes. Therefore both sibs C and D are diabetic even though C is thin.

are increased in patients with diabetes. The second approach, positional cloning, involves searching the whole genome for a region (for example, a portion of the long arm of chromosome 12) that is inherited more frequently in family members with diabetes. The region is then further investigated to determine which of the genes in this region is important.

## Candidate genes and regions in type 2 diabetes

Over 250 candidate genes have been investigated in type 2 diabetes but none have been shown to be major predisposing genes. Several polymorphisms have been reported to have an increased prevalence in diabetes in preliminary reports but these have not been reproduced in other study populations and reduced function of the polymorphism has rarely been shown in *in vitro* studies. The best evidence is probably for the insulin gene where the count of variable number of tandem repeats (VTNR) in the promoter alters susceptibility to type 2 diabetes as well as type 1 diabetes and polycystic ovarian disease.[4]

In many different populations total genome searches have been performed in families with at least two affected siblings. These have not shown evidence for a single major predisposing gene of similar magnitude to HLA in type 1 diabetes in any population. The different genome searches have identified many different regions of genetic susceptibility. The most important finding to date has been the localization of an area of linkage on the short arm of chromosome 2 in Mexican Americans.[5] The critical gene in this region is thought to be Calpain 10, a cysteine protease, but the mechanism of action is not yet known.[6]

# Genetic subtypes of diabetes

An important minority of type 2 diabetic patients (2–5 per cent) have diabetes that results from a mutation in a single predisposing gene that may result in either *β*-cell dysfunction or, less frequently, insulin resistance. The commonest genetic subtypes are the dominantly inherited MODY and maternally inherited diabetes and deafness (MIDD).

## Genetic defects of *β*-cell function

### Maturity onset diabetes of the young

The heterogeneous clinical entity MODY was initially recognized in the pre-insulin era when it was noted that some patients with familial diabetes could survive in the absence of insulin.[7] This was recognized as an autosomal dominant form of non-insulin dependent diabetes in 1974.[8] MODY is characterized by:[9]

*Early onset, non-insulin dependent diabetes*: at least one and ideally two family members diagnosed before age 25. Other family members may be diagnosed later. Subjects are considered non-insulin dependent if five years after diagnosis they are not on insulin or, for those on insulin, have evidence of circulating C-peptide indicating endogenous insulin secretion.

*Autosomal dominant inheritance*: at least two generations with diabetes and ideally three generations and cousins showing a similar phenotype. Subjects where both parents have type 2 diabetes are normally excluded as this would be unlikely to be monogenic and early onset of the disease might be due to a 'double gene dose'[10] (Fig. 1).

### MODY genes and phenotypes

The definition of the genes causing MODY was relatively simple because its early onset made it easy to collect large multi-generation families (Fig. 2) and a single gene was responsible for diabetes within a family. Five different genes, the glycolytic enzyme – glucokinase and the transcription factors hepatocyte nuclear factors (*HNF*) *1α, 4α* and *1β* and insulin promoter factor (*IPF*)-*1*, cause MODY.[9,11] The clinical and molecular characteristics are summarized in Table 1.

### Glucokinase mutations (MODY 2)

Glucokinase mutations result in a distinct phenotype with stable mild hyperglycaemia throughout life.[9] Glucokinase is a hexokinase enzyme, catalysing the first step in glucose metabolism; phosphorylation of glucose to glucose-6-phosphate. In pancreatic *β*-cells glucokinase acts as the glucose sensor for pancreatic *β*-cells, ensuring insulin secretion is appropriate for the ambient glucose concentration. Over 60 mutations in the glucokinase gene have been identified.[9,12] The phenotype of those affected is almost identical, with the exception of one mutation that leads to hyperinsulinaemia.[13] Patients with glucokinase mutations have lifelong mild fasting hyperglycaemia – usually between 5.5–9 mmol/l. This results from resetting of the fasting glucose level by altered glucose sensing at the *β*-cell andhepatocyte. There is characteristically a small increment (below 3 mmol/l) in the two hour glucose above the fasting value during an oral glucose tolerance test so many patients will not have diabetes as classified by the two hour value. In keeping with the mild stable hyperglycaemia, symptoms are unusual, and most causes are detected

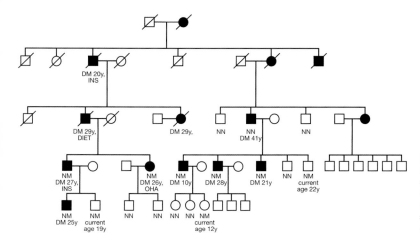

**Fig. 2** Typical pedigree of a family with MODY due to *HNF1α* mutation. The family shows autosomal dominant inheritance with affected cousins and several affected members diagnosed under the age of 25. Predictive testing is now able to find mutation carriers who are not yet diabetic.

**Table 1** Sub-types of maturity onset diabetes of the young (MODY)

|  | HNF-4α (MODY 1) | Glucokinase (MODY 2) | HNF-1α (MODY 3) | IPF-1 (MODY 4) | HNF-1β (MODY 5) | MODY x |
|---|---|---|---|---|---|---|
| Chromosomal location | 20q | 7p | 12q | 13q | 17q | Unknown |
| Frequency in a large UK series | 5% | 15% | 65% | <1% | 1% | 13% |
| Penetrance of mutations at age 40 years | >80% | >95% fasting hyperglycaemia, 45% diabetic | >90% | Limited data | ?>90% | Not known |
| Onset of hyperglycaemia | Adolescence early adulthood | Early childhood (from birth) | Adolescence early adulthood | Early adulthood | Similar to HNF-1α | Uncertain |
| Severity of hyperglycaemia | Progressive may be severe | Mild with minor deterioration with age | Progressive may be severe | Limited data | Progressive may be severe | Variable |
| Micro-vascular complications | Frequent | Rare | Frequent | Not known | Not known | Variable |
| Pathophysiology | β-cell dysfunction | β-cell dysfunction | β-cell dysfunction | β-cell dysfuction | β-cell dysfunction | β-cell dysfunction |
| Abnormality of glucose sensing? | No | Yes | No | No | No | Not known |
| Non-diabetes related features | Low plasma triglycerides | Reduced birth weight | Low renal threshold and sensitivity to sulphonylureas | Pancreatic agenesis in homozygotes | Renal cysts, proteinuria, renal failure |  |

by routine screening. Pharmacological treatment is rarely needed and microvascular complications are very rare. Intensive medical follow up is therefore not required.

These asymptomatic patients are frequently detected in pregnancy, and in European caucasian populations account for approximately 3–6 per cent of patients with gestational diabetes. If subjects are selected for specific clinical characteristics of glucokinase mutations up to 75 per cent will be affected.[12] As these patients have mild hyperglycaemia their children would be at risk of macrosomia, but it has been shown that this is only the case if the fetus does not carry a glucokinase mutation. The presence of a fetal glucokinase mutation

reduces birthweight by decreasing fetal insulin secretion as a result of reduced fetal β-cell glucose sensing.[14] If affected mothers have an affected fetus, growth is normal because maternal hyperglycaemia causes a normal level of insulin secretion. This can be judged by normal fetal growth on ultrasound and treatment with insulin in pregnancy is probably not necessary.

The frequency of glucokinase mutations appears to vary between populations (France over 50 per cent, UK 24 per cent and Japan below 1 per cent). Some of this variability is artefactual due to differing research approaches in recruiting families, however it is likely that there is a genuine variation in genetic frequency between racial groups.

### Hepatic nuclear factor 1α (MODY 3)

HNF1α is the commonest cause of MODY, accounting for 70 per cent of UK MODY families and 1–2 per cent of caucasian diabetic patients.[9] This DNA-binding transcription factor, found in many tissues, was not an obvious MODY gene and was identified using a positional cloning approach. Over 70 mutations have been described in this gene.[9] About 20 per cent of families have a common frameshift mutation (a C insertion at position 291) which is a hotspot for mutations.

Patients with *HNF1α* mutations are born normoglycaemic but develop a progressive β-cell defect which is detectable in adolescence and early adulthood.[15] It is likely that this results from disruption of fetal pancreatic development or β-cell metabolism by altering the regulation of other critical genes.

*HNF1α* mutations have a life-time penetrance of over 95 per cent. Figure 3 illustrates how the prevalence of diabetes varies with age in *HNF1α* mutation carriers. In a large UK series 63 per cent were diagnosed by age 25 and 79 per cent by age 35.[16] Most patients present with osmotic symptoms and may be incorrectly diagnosed as type 1 diabetes if the significance of the family history is not appreciated. Glucose tolerance continues to decline as β-cell function deteriorates further in middle age and thus treatment requirements increase. Approximately equal proportions of patients are treated with diet, oral agents and insulin. Obesity is not typical although poorer glycaemic control is seen in obese patients due to increasing insulin resistance. HNF1α patients develop diabetic microvascular and macrovascular complications, and retinopathy and nephropathy are common. The pattern of complications is similar to type 1 diabetes, so in contrast to patients with glucokinase mutations long term monitoring and follow up is necessary.

### Hepatic nuclear factor 4α (MODY 1)

*HNF4α* mutations are an unusual cause of MODY. A mutation in *HNF4α* was found to cause diabetes in the largest and most studied MODY family, the North American RW family.[17] *HNF4α* regulates the expression of *HNF1α*, so β-cell dysfunction probably results from alterations in *HNF1α*. Patients with *HNF4α* mutations have a similar phenotype to those with *HNF1α* mutations except the average age of onset is slightly later and the penetrance lower,[9] with 10–20 per cent

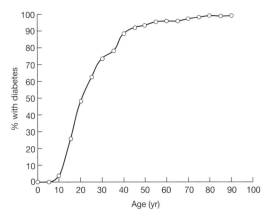

**Fig. 3** The prevalence of diabetes with age in HNF1α mutation carriers.

of those with mutations having normal glucose tolerance. As with *HNF1α* progressive β-cell dysfunction is seen requiring treatment with insulin and severe microvascular complications may occur. Altered transcription of lipoprotein lipase may explain why some families have reduced triglyceride levels in marked contrast to the elevated levels seen in type 2 diabetes.[18]

### Insulin promoter factor-1 (MODY 4)

IPF-1 is a transcription factor that plays a critical role both in the development of the pancreas and in the regulation of gene transcription (especially the insulin gene) in the β-cell.[19] Transgenic mice in whom both *IPF-1* genes were 'knocked out' had agenesis of the pancreas while those with a single gene 'knocked out' had glucose intolerance and diabetes. IPF-1 is also the principle regulator of insulin gene transcription in response to hyperglycaemia.

The phenotype associated with mutations in *IPF-1* in man depends on the type and dose of mutation. In a single family a severe *IPF-1* mutation has been shown to cause pancreatic agenesis in a child who was homozygous for the mutation and MODY in the child's relatives who were heterozygous.[20,21] One per cent of a European caucasian population are heterozygote carriers of milder missense mutations in this gene and these are predisposed to type 2 diabetes.[22]

### Hepatic nuclear factor 1β (MODY 5) – renal cysts and diabetes (RCAD)

The transcription factor HNF1β is closely related to HNF1α, with which it forms a heterodimer. Mutations in *HNF1β* result in autosomal dominant renal cysts and diabetes.[23,24] While *HNF1β* mutations are a rare cause of MODY it may be a relatively common cause of familial cystic kidney disease in children. As the diabetes is similar to HNF1α diabetes it rarely presents before early adult life. This means that these patients may present to paediatric nephrology clinics rather than diabetic clinics. Renal manifestations are varied: all subjects appear to have cysts, but this ranges from a few isolated cysts in an adult to severe cystic disease resulting in renal failure *in utero*. Most have reduced renal function and chronic renal failure has been described in approximately 40 per cent of middle aged mutation carriers. Histology is variable and includes cystic dysplasia, hypoplastic glomerulocystic disease and oligomeganephronia. HNF1β is expressed in the developing kidney and the clinical manifestations of mutations confirm that it plays a critical role in human renal development.

### 'MODY X'

The MODY gene remains elusive in up to a fifth of UK and French families and over 70 per cent of Japanese families. Phenotypes are variable within these families, suggesting that more than one additional gene remains to be identified.

### Do MODY genes cause type 2 diabetes?

Do MODY gene mutations cause type 2 diabetes as well as MODY? A mild mutation in a MODY gene might predispose to late onset diabetes fitting the criteria for type 2 diabetes. The insulin promoter factor 1 mutations (MODY 4) are a good example of this, with severe mutations causing MODY and milder mutations predisposing to type 2 diabetes in caucasians (see above). However the *HNF1α* and *HNF4α* genes are not commonly implicated in type 2 diabetes in European or

Japanese patients. The few cases that were discovered can be classified as 'missed MODY' or a true late onset due to unexplained low penetrance. Patients with glucokinase mutations are often diagnosed in later life, but their mild hyperglycaemia is lifelong and so this represents a late diagnosis rather than a late onset of diabetes.

Susceptibility genes to type 2 diabetes have been localized close to the HNF1α gene on the long arm of chromosomes 12 (NIDDM 2) and close to the HNF4α gene on the long arm of chromosome 20 in some, but not all, genome scans of large numbers of European caucasian families.[25] No mutations have been found in the coding regions of the MODY genes but it is possible that an unidentified regulatory polymorphism altering expression could explain these results.

### Mitochondrial gene lesions – maternally inherited diabetes and deafness

Mitochondria have their own small circular genome coding some of the genes needed for mitochondrial components. Mitochondrial DNA is inherited maternally as the paternal mitochondria in the sperm tail are discarded when the nuclear genetic material enters the ovum. Each mitochondrion has several copies of its genome and there are many mitochondria in each cell. As each mitochondrion in the ovum can have a discrete genome, it follows that there is a great deal of heterogeneity in the mitochondrial genetic material in our cells. Diseases due to mitochondrial mutations are recognized by a maternal dominant inheritance and a variable penetrance due to different proportions of the abnormal gene in each tissue. This is termed heteroplasmy and accounts for some of the unusual features of mitochondrally inherited diseases.

The first mitochondrial diseases to be recognized affected tissues with a high energy demand; such as the brain and muscle. Pancreatic β-cells have a shared ontogeny with neurones and they too rely on oxidative phosphorylation for their energy requirements. It became apparent that diabetes was a common accompaniment to neurological manifestations.[26] A family was then observed where the nine children of a mother with type 2 diabetes also had diabetes accompanied by hearing loss. In the third generation only the children of affected females inherited the condition.[27] This pedigree was strongly suggestive of a mitochondrial disease and subsequent investigation confirmed a mutation at position 3243 in the mitochondrial genome.[27] This gene codes for a leucine transfer RNA (tRNA(Leu,UUR)). This form of diabetes is characterized by sensorineural deafness in young adult life and is designated MIDD. A typical pedigree is illustrated in Figs 4 and 5.

### The mitochondrial 3243 mutation

The 3243 tRNA(leu) mutation is by far the best characterized and commonest mutation in the mitochondrial genome. Interestingly its effect is not confined to causing diabetes and deafness. It is also responsible for the mitochondrial syndrome MELAS (myopathy, encephalopathy, lactic acidosis, and stroke-like episodes).[28] The two syndromes appear to be distinct, although overlap is observed in large families. It seems likely that the degree of heteroplasmy in different tissues affects the phenotype.

The prevalence of this mutation among diabetics varies between racial groups being highest in Japan and probably accounts for about 0.5–3 per cent of diabetics with a family history.[26]

The tRNA(leu) gene has been noted to have a variety of other mutations, some of which have been linked to diabetes. Large deletions and duplications in the mitochondrial genome may also result in diabetes and deafness.

### Mitochondrial diabetic phenotype

Patients with mitochondrial diabetes have early onset type 2 diabetes that frequently progresses to insulin requirement due to progressive β-cell loss.[29] They tend to be non-obese and may have evidence of neurological and optic features seen in mitochondrial disorders. Diagnosis may be complicated by low levels of heteroplasmy in cells such as blood cells that are accessible for sampling. If initial tests are negative oral mucosa cells or muscle biopsy can be used.[29]

### Abnormal insulins

A few individuals have hyperglycaemia and hyperinsulinaemia with a normal response to exogenous insulin.[30] Investigations have shown them to have point mutations in the insulin gene giving rise to a structurally abnormal insulin, typically a single amino acid substitution in the insulin B chain. In some patients, alterations in the structure of proinsulin may prevent normal cleavage leading to a similar phenotype except with hyperproinsulinaemia rather than

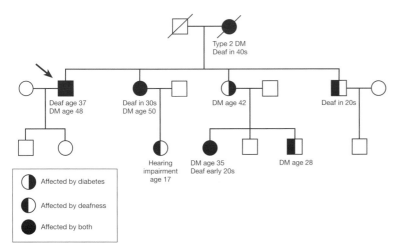

Fig. 4 Typical pedigree of family with MIDD. The proband developed sensorineural deafness and then diabetes in young adult life. His mother had a similar phenotype and other family members show diabetes, deafness and neurological features associated with the mitochondrial 3423 mutation. In the third generation only children of affected mothers have inherited the mutation.

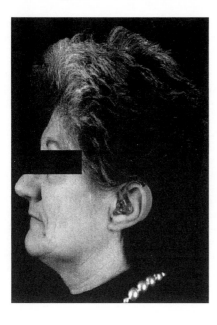

**Fig. 5** Diabetic patient with hearing aid (MIDD). Clinical clues should prompt appropriate history taking and investigations.

hyperinsulinaemia. Diabetes is not always a feature of mutation carriers. These mutant insulins or proinsulins are a very rare cause of diabetes with less than 20 families described to date.

## Genetic defects in insulin action

### Genetic causes of insulin resistance

Insulin resistance is of primary importance in the development of type 2 diabetes. It is influenced by many factors. Here we will concentrate on the established syndromes of inherited severe insulin resistance. These syndromes do not contribute greatly to the prevalence of type 2 diabetes; in fact many patients remain normoglycaemic, compensating for their insulin resistance with hyperinsulinaemia. However, as with MODY and β-cell function, it is hoped that by studying monogenic causes of insulin resistance lessons will be learnt about the commoner, polygenic causes.

### Clinical features of genetic severe insulin resistance

Insulin resistance is characterized by hyperinsulinaemia due to compensatory β-cell hypersecretion and loss of the normal receptor-mediated clearance of insulin. Some of the manifestations of insulin resistance listed below are due to normal sensitivity of certain tissues to these raised circulating insulin levels. A characteristic of genetic causes of severe insulin resistance is that the following stigmata of insulin resistance occur in the absence of obesity:

*Acanthosis nigricans* is the cutaneous manifestation of severe insulin resistance. The pathophysiology is not yet completely defined, but it may be due to the action of insulin on insulin-like growth factor-I receptors within the skin.

*Ovarian hyperandrogenism* is caused by stimulation of insulin and insulin-like growth factor-I receptors on ovarian thecal cells. This results in excess production of ovarian androgens leading to menstrual disturbance, acne, hirsutism and other features of polycystic ovarian disease as well as virilization in children.

*Impaired glucose tolerance* occurs when β-cell compensation is inadequate to overcome insulin resistance in liver and muscle.

*Precocious growth* is seen in children with inherited insulin resistance syndromes probably due to the crossover stimulation of insulin-like growth factor-I receptors, but early fusing of epiphyseal plates means that final height is reduced.

*Lipodystrophy* may be a feature as a result of impaired fat storage.

### Mechanisms of insulin resistance

Stimulation of the insulin receptor activates a complex signalling mechanism. This is still not fully characterized and thus defects in signalling responsible for many cases of severe insulin resistance remain elusive. The insulin receptor itself is the most obvious and best studied target and a variety of insulin receptor gene mutations have been described.[31] Where the insulin receptor structure is demonstrated to be normal the defect is assumed to be either on the post-receptor signalling pathway or in the processing and regulation of the insulin receptor.

### Type A insulin resistance syndrome

This condition is characterized by insulin resistance, acanthosis nigricans and hyperandrogenism in women usually presenting in the second decade of life.[32] Contrary to some initial reports, men are also affected, but are less readily diagnosed because they do not present with hyperandrogenism. Obesity is unusual and lipodystrophy is absent. Diabetes is not always present.

A type A variant has also been described which has features of acromegaly in the absence of excess growth hormone, possibly mediated via the anabolic actions of insulin on sensitive tissues.

The inheritance of type A syndrome is variable, suggesting more than one aetiology. Several mutations of the insulin receptor have been described in association with type A syndrome. However, more than half the cases do not possess insulin receptor mutations and therefore must be accounted for by other signalling defects.[33]

### Rare syndromes caused by insulin receptor mutations

*Leprechaunism* is a syndrome of severe insulin resistance with onset *in utero* and death in early infancy. Features include intra-uterine growth retardation, acanthosis nigricans, lipoatrophy, virilization, dystrophic facies and failure to thrive. The syndrome is caused by homozygous or compound heterozygous insulin receptor mutations.

*Rabson–Mendenhall syndrome* is a rare condition characterized by moderately severe insulin resistance with onset in infancy as a result of insulin receptor mutations. The defect appears to affect synthesis and insertion of the insulin receptor into the plasma membrane.[33] Other features include dental dysplasia, pineal hyperplasia and dysmorphic features. The children develop insulin resistant diabetes with poor control, ketoacidosis and early onset of complications.

### Lipodystrophies

Insulin resistance is a feature of this heterogeneous group of disorders of lipid storage characterized by lipodystrophy.

#### Congenital generalized lipoatrophy (Berardinelli–Seip syndrome)

An autosomal recessive condition with almost complete absence of adipose tissue. Hepatomegaly and muscular hypertrophy occur due to increased fat and glycogen stores. Hyperlipidaemia, reduced final height, features of insulin resistance, diabetes and liver cirrhosis also occur. Premature death has been noted due to hypertrophic cardiomyopathy.[34] The primary pathology appears to be deficient lipid storage. The insulin receptor has not been shown to be abnormal, so the defect may lie in the post receptor pathways. Recently linkage has been shown in several pedigrees to chromosome 9, but a gene product has not yet been identified.[35]

*Familial partial lipodystrophy (Dunnigan syndrome)*

This dominant condition is characterized by an onset of degeneration of adipose tissue in young adult life, confined to the limbs or trunk accompanied by hyperlipidaemia and insulin resistant diabetes. Mutations in the *LMNA* gene coding for nuclear lamin A/C have been demonstrated in patients with familial partial lipodystrophy.[36]

### PPARγ mutations and the metabolic syndrome

The peroxisome proliferator-activated receptor γ is a nuclear receptor found in adipose tissue. *PPARγ* is the target for the thiazolidinedione drugs. Two families with severe insulin resistance, early onset type 2 diabetes and hypertension have been found to have dominant negative mutations in the *PPARγ* gene co-segregating with disease.[37]

## Monogenic multi-system diseases that include diabetes

Diabetes is a feature of a wide variety of inherited conditions. Some of these are relatively common, others extremely rare. Although these syndromes represent a small percentage of the diabetes it is important to recognize them as it will explain the associated clinical features and alter management. An additional reason is that knowledge of the genetic lesion may provide clues about the function of genes predisposing to diabetes and offer new insights into the pathophysiology of hyperglycaemia. The wide variation in the genes and their function and chromosomal location reminds us of the complexity of the genetic influences on diabetes. The commoner and more clinically relevant monogenic conditions that include diabetes are discussed below. Table 2 summarizes the remainder where the association with diabetes is well established, grouped according to their aetiology. The contents are mainly limited to those cited in the Online Mendelian Inheritance in Man which is an excellent source of further information (http://www.ncbi.nlm.nih.gov/omim/) as well as published reviews.[38,39]

## Diabetes as a feature of systemic disease

### Cystic fibrosis

Cystic fibrosis occurs in approximately one in 2500 live births in European populations. Pancreatic exocrine dysfunction is an early feature of cystic fibrosis, but later in the disease process the islets become disrupted as a consequence of the degeneration of the exocrine tissue. In centres where routine screening occurs, the prevalence of diabetes in cystic fibrosis is 40–50 per cent by age 30.[40] Routine screening is recommended as diabetes can have an insidious onset with clinical decline seen before diabetes is diagnosed. In general those patients with diabetes have a higher mortality than

those without, but it is uncertain whether this is due to the adverse effect of diabetes on the other disease processes or if diabetes is a manifestation of severe disease.

Diabetes generally presents in the second or third decade of life and is initially characterized by a delayed first phase response of insulin secretion. Although diabetes in cystic fibrosis requires insulin treatment, the insulin deficiency is not absolute and ketogenesis does not usually occur.

Management of diabetes in cystic fibrosis differs in some important respects from standard management of type 1 diabetes. The coexistent malabsorption generally leads to a poor nutritional state and low body mass index (BMI). Patients with diabetes must be encouraged to take adequate nutrition accompanied by pancreatic enzyme supplementation and must be prescribed adequate insulin doses to metabolize their calories. A multiple injection regimen is the most logical treatment so long as it is acceptable to an individual who is already on numerous other therapies. Overnight enteral feeding will require adjustments in insulin therapy.

Glycaemic control will deteriorate sharply during infective episodes, particularly if corticosteroids are required. The increasing use of outpatient antibiotic treatment means that intensive educational input on self-management of these episodes must be in place. Poor glycaemic control prolongs recovery time from pulmonary infections. As patients with cystic fibrosis increasingly survive into middle age, diabetic complications become more prevalent and there is no evidence that microvascular disease is encountered any less frequently than in the general diabetic population.[40]

### Haemochromatosis

Genetic haemochromatosis is one of the commonest monogenic conditions affecting European populations (1 in 500 of the population are homozygotes although far fewer present with diagnosed disease). Excess absorbed iron is sequestered in many tissues including the pancreatic islets, the liver and the gonadotroph cells of the anterior pituitary. Although fibrosis is observed on pancreas histology, there is evidence of β-cell dysfunction at a much earlier stage of the disease.[41] The mechanism of direct iron toxicity on β-cells is not completely clear. Insulin resistance is also evident in the early stages of haemochromatosis, presumably due to the hepatic involvement. Early diagnosis and initiation of venesection to remove excess iron prevents further deterioration and can restore normal life expectancy in those without tissue damage. Now that the gene is known, family members can be screened. The combination of diabetes with abnormal liver function tests, unexplained arthropathy or cardiac impairment (in the absence of known ischaemic heart disease) should warrant investigation with a transferrin saturation or serum ferritin. However, ferritin has the disadvantage of sometimes being raised in those diabetics with poor control or fatty liver as well as in acute phase reactions.[41] There is insufficient evidence at present to screen diabetic populations for haemochromatosis, as it is not clear that it occurs more commonly than in the normal population.

The management of diabetes in haemochromatosis is conventional, with most requiring insulin treatment. Ketoacidosis is unusual. Hypoglycaemia may be troublesome, particularly in those with liver disease.

**Table 2** Genetic syndromes featuring diabetes

| Syndrome | Inheritence/OMIM | Locus | Clinical features | Diabetic mechanism |
|---|---|---|---|---|
| **Pancreatic disorders** | | | | Insulin deficiency |
| Pancreatic agenesis | AR 600089 | 6 | | |
| | AR 260370 | 13q12 | Permanent neonatal diabetes | |
| Pancreatic hypoplasia | Various | | | |
| Absence of islets | AR/XR | | | |
| Hereditary relapsing pancreatitis | AD 167800 | 7q33 | Abdominal pain | |
| Cystic fibrosis | AR 219700 | 7q31 | Respiratory disease, malabsorption, diabetes | |
| Haemochromatosis | AR 235200 | 6p21 | Hepatic disease, cardiac failure, hypogonadism | |
| α-1 Antitrypsin deficiency | AR 107400 | 14q32 | Emphysema | |
| Pearson Marrow-pancreas syndrome | Mt 557000 | Mitochondrial | Sideroblastic anaemia, exocrine pancreas dysfunction | |
| Renal-hepatic-pancreatic dysplasia | AR 263600 | 6p21–12 | Variant of infantile polycystic kidney disease | |
| **Metabolic conditions** | | | | |
| Hyperlipidaemia (Types I, III–VI) | Various | | Type 2 DM, vascular disease | Type 2 DM |
| Thiamine-responsive megaloblastic anaemia | AR 249270 | 1q23 | Megaloblastic anaemia, deafness, situs inversus, aminoaciduria | IGT |
| **Endocrine** | | | | |
| **Polyglandular endocrine syndromes** | | | | |
| Type 1 | 240300 | 21q22.3 | Addison's disease, hypoparathyroidism, mucocutaneous candidiasis | Type 1 DM |
| Type 2 – Schmidt syndrome | 269200 inheritance may not be strictly Mendelian | | Addison's disease, thyroid disease | Type 1 DM |
| Hereditary phaeochromocytoma (MEN 2A and B, von Hippel Lindau, neurofibromatosis) | AD 171400, AD 162300, AD 193300, AD 162200 | 10q11, 10q11, 3p26–25, 17q11 | Labile hypertension, sweating, tremor | IGT due to catecholamine excess |
| **Neuromuscular** | | | | |
| Bardet–Biedl syndrome | AR 209900 | | Obesity, visual loss, polydactyly, hypogonadism, learning difficulties | |
| DIDMOAD | AR 222300 | 4p16 | Visual loss, deafness, diabetes insipidus | Insulin requiring |
| Fredriech's ataxia | AR 229300 | 9q13 | Cerebellar signs, cardiomyopathy, pes cavus | Ketosis prone |
| Herrmann's syndrome | AD 186500 | 17q22 | Skeletal abnormalities, deafness | |
| Machado–Joseph syndrome | AD 109150 | 14q24–32 | Spinocerebellar ataxia, muscle atrophy, nystagmus | |
| Myotonic dystrophy | AD 160900 | 19q13 | Myotonia, muscle wasting, frontal balding, hypogonadism, cardiac conduction defects, cataract | IGT |
| **Obesity related** | | | | Insulin resistance |
| Alstrom syndrome | AR 203800 | 2p13 | Obesity/visual loss/nystagmus/deafness | |

**Table 2** Continued

| Syndrome | Inheritence/OMIM | Locus | Clinical features | Diabetic mechanism |
|---|---|---|---|---|
| Prader–Willi | AD 176270 | 15q11 | Hyperphagia, obesity, hypogonadism, learning difficulties | |
| Achondroplasia | AD 100800 | 4p16 | Characteristic skeletal abnormality | Secondary to obesity |
| Chromosomal abnormalities | | | | |
| Down's syndrome | | Trisomy 21 | Characteristic facies, learning difficulties, cardiac abnormalities, premature ageing | IGT |
| Klinefelter's syndrome | | XXY | Hypogonadism, gynaecomastia | IGT |
| Turner's syndrome | | X0 | Ovarian dysgenesis, short stature | IGT |
| Defects in DNA stability/repair | | | | |
| Ataxia telangiectasia | AR 208900 | 11q22 | Telangiectasia, ataxia, immunodeficiency, malignancy | |
| Bloom syndrome | AR 210900 | 15q26 | Telangiectasia, skin pigmentation, immunodeficiency, malignancy | IGT |
| Cockayne syndrome | AR 216400 | 5 | Short stature, retinopathy | IGT |
| Werner's syndrome | AR 277700 | 8p11–12 | Features of premature ageing, malignancies | Insulin resistance |
| Miscellaneous | | | | |
| Walcott-Rallison syndrome | AR 226980 | +2p12 | Multiple epiphyseal dysplasia, organomegaly | Permanent neonatal diabetes |
| Hereditary Stiff Man syndrome | AD 184850 | | Episodic stiffness (most cases not inherited) | Autoimmune type 1 DM |

## Monogenic causes of hyperlipidaemia

Hyperlipidaemia is a further example of a heterogeneous condition that can be a result of polygenic and monogenic influences as well as acquired causes. Derangements in plasma lipids are very frequently seen in type 2 diabetes as part of the metabolic syndrome, but diabetes can also be a consequence of certain of the monogenic causes of abnormal lipids. These are characterized by marked hypertriglyceridaemia (usually above 30 mmol/l) which causes severe insulin resistance and $\beta$-cell dysfunction and may even result in ketoacidosis. In acute exacerbations, patients may present with pancreatitis, eruptive xanthoma, lipaemia retinalis and organomegaly. The serum shows characteristic lipaemia. Treatment of triglyceridaemia with fibrates and correction of precipitating causes such as hyperglycaemia (which may initially require high dose insulin), hypothyroidism, and excess alcohol can result in a dramatic improvement in both glucose and lipid levels.

Monogenic causes predisposing to massive hypertriglyceridaemia can be separated on the basis of their inheritance, molecular genetics, biochemistry and clinical features. These include:

*Lipoprotein lipase deficiency (WHO phenotype 1a)*: lipoprotein lipase is required to metabolize the chylomicron and very-low-density lipoprotein (VLDL) lipid fractions. This autosomal recessive condition is characterized by hypertriglyceridaemia (10–30 mmol/l) without raised cholesterol and fasting chylomicronaemia, other features include pancreatitis, eruptive xanthomas and diabetes.

*Apolipoprotein C-II deficiency (WHO phenotype Ib)*: this is an activator of lipoprotein lipase and so this autosomal recessive condition leads to a similar phenotype as the above.

*Remnant particle disease (WHO phenotype III)*: this is due to apolipoprotein E (ApoE) defects. Apo E binds to hepatic chylomicron remnant and low-density lipoprotein (LDL) receptors, facilitating hepatic clearance of chylomicron remnants and VLDL. There are three main isoforms of ApoE: E2, E3 and E4. Homozygotes for E2 have been found to have impaired binding to the hepatic receptors. Clinically this is associated with tuberous and palmar xanthomas, premature vascular disease and abnormal glucose tolerance. Cholesterol and triglycerides are raised (cholesterol 8–14 mmol/l, triglycerides 10–15 mmol/l). Possession of this variant alone does not lead to the phenotype, but requires additional metabolic or environmental input such as a further abnormality in lipid metabolism, the development of hypothyroidism, obesity or diabetes or excessive alcohol consumption.

*Familial hypertriglyceridaemia (WHO phenotypes IV and V)*: an autosomal dominant condition caused by raised VLDL levels and characterized by premature atherosclerosis, eruptive xanthomas, pancreatitis and abnormal glucose tolerance. The primary pathophysiology is not known. Cholesterol and triglycerides are raised (cholesterol 6–12 mmol/l, triglycerides 10–30 mmol/l). Alcohol consumption, the oestrogen-containing contraceptive pill, hypothyroidism and poor control of diabetes can exert an environmental influence on the phenotype.

## Genetic obesity syndromes

Type 2 diabetes is increasing in prevalence in childhood and adolescence and this is particularly associated with obesity. It will therefore become increasingly important to differentiate simple obesity from that associated with syndromes such as Prader–Willi, which may have escaped diagnosis in early childhood.

### Prader–Willi syndrome

The Prader–Willi syndrome (PWS) is characterized by obesity, muscular hypotonia, learning disabilities, short stature and hypogonadotrophic hypogonadism. The obesity is due to hyperphagia secondary to an unknown hypothalamic disease process. Diabetes is a consequence of obesity.

PWS is caused by deletion or disruption of a gene or several genes on the proximal long arm of the paternal chromosome 15 or because of the presence of two copies of the maternal chromosome 15 (maternal uniparental disomy 15). The genes on the maternal chromosome(s) 15 are virtually inactive as a result of imprinting in this region.

### Alstrom syndrome

This is an uncommon syndrome characterized by retinal degeneration, childhood obesity, infantile cardiomyopathy, sensorineural deafness and diabetes developing in the second decade. Diabetes is probably secondary to obesity.

Alstrom syndrome is an autosomal recessive condition, with the gene now localized to 2p13 although not yet identified.

## DIDMOAD (Wolfram syndrome)

This autosomal recessive disorder causes a neurodegenerative disorder characterized by diabetes mellitus, diabetes insipidus, optic atrophy, and sensorineural deafness. The gene on chromosome 4 has now been identified, coding for a transmembrane protein.[42] A variety of mutations give rise to a similar phenotype.

Insulin requiring diabetes is usually the first manifestation, and develops in childhood. Visual loss from optic atrophy, renal tract abnormalities and ultimately fatal brainstem/cerebellar degeneration are the other main features.[43]

# Diagnostic approach to defining specific genetic subgroups

This chapter illustrates the advances that have been made in defining sub-groups of non-insulin dependant diabetes caused by genetic mutations. Single gene mutations are known to cause β-cell dysfunction, abnormal insulins and defects in insulin action and diabetes is a feature of several multi-system genetic disorders. Making a precise diagnosis has implications for management of the individual patient as well as predicting genetic risk to other family members. Molecular genetic testing now offers the possibility of confirming clinical diagnoses. Diagnostic testing is now available in most European countries for the commoner forms of MODY as well as more conventional genetic disorders such as Prader–Willi, haemochromatosis and cystic fibrosis.

When considering whether a patient has a discrete genetic cause of their diabetes, a full medical history, family history and examination are very important. Non-diabetic features in the patient or their family may be critical when making a diagnosis for example, cystic renal disease (*HNF1β* mutations) or neural deafness (MIDD). In subjects with diabetes alone the family history is the most important clue to suggest a monogenic cause. If a glucokinase mutation is suspected this should include testing the fasting glucose in both parents as this form of mild hyperglycaemia is often not diagnosed.

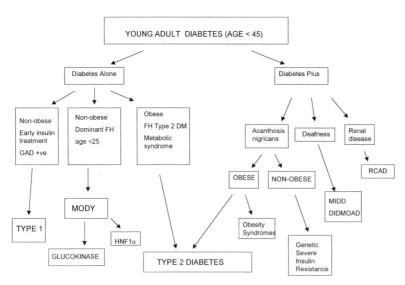

**Fig. 6** Approach to the diagnosis of young adult onset diabetes. Simple guidelines for categorizing diabetics according to aetiology may assist management.

Knowledge of specific genetic subtypes is likely to have most implications in the diagnosis of young adult onset diabetes. Diabetics presenting in their third to fifth decade may have one of a variety of pathologies that can be resolved by a combination of clinical criteria, family studies and laboratory investigations. A scheme is summarized in Fig. 6.

## Summary

Our increasing knowledge about the pathophysiology of diabetes has led to a classification based on aetiology.[44] This classification recognizes specific subgroups according to their underlying mechanism. The well established observation of a strong genetic predisposition in non-insulin dependant diabetes is now being slowly unravelled. In some cases of clear Mendelian inheritance, such as MODY, the precise genetic lesion is now known and can be used to guide clinical management. In the more common type 2 diabetes, despite considerable research, there is no definitive evidence for any gene playing a major role in the genetic predisposition.

## References

1. **Barnett AH, Eff C, Leslie RDG, Pyke DA**. Diabetes in identical twins: a study of 200 pairs. *Diabetologia*, 1981; **20**: 87–93.

2. **Newman B, Selby JV, King MC, Slemenda C, Fabsitz R, Friedman GD**. Concordance for type 2 (non-insulin-dependent) diabetes mellitus in male twins. *Diabetologia*, 1987; **30**: 763–8.

3. **Turner RC, Hattersley AT, Shaw JT, Levy JC**. Type II diabetes: clinical aspects of molecular biological studies. (Review). *Diabetes*, 1995; **44**: 1–10.

4. **Bennett ST, Todd JA**. Human type 1 diabetes and the insulin gene: principles of mapping polygenes. *Annual Review of Genetics*, 1996; **30**: 343–70.

5. **Hanis CL** *et al*. A genome-wide search for human non-insulin-dependent (type 2) diabetes genes reveals a major susceptibility locus on chromosome 2. *Nature Genetics*, 1996; **13**: 161–6.

6. **Horikawa Y** *et al*. Genetic variation in the gene encoding calpain-10 is associated with type 2 diabetes mellitus. *Nature Genetics*, 2000; **26**: 163–75.

7. **Cammidge PJ**. Diabetes mellitus and heredity. *British Medical Journal*, 1928; **2**: 738–41.

8. **Tattersall RB**. Mild familial diabetes with dominant inheritance. *Quarterly Journal of Medicine*, 1974; **43**: 339–57.

9. **Hattersley A**. Maturity-onset diabetes of the young: clinical heterogeneity explained by genetic heterogeneity. *Diabetic Medicine*, 1998; **15**: 15–24.

10. **O'Rahilly S, Turner RC**. Early onset type 2 diabetes versus maturity onset diabetes of youth: evidence for the existence of two discrete diabetic syndromes. *Diabetic Medicine*, 1988; **5**: 224–9.

11. **Frayling T, Beards F, Hattersley AT**. Maturity-onset diabetes of the young: a monogenic model of diabetes. In: Hitman GA, ed. *Type 2 Diabetes: Prediction and Prevention*. Chichester: John Wiley, 1999: 107–26.

12. **Ellard S** *et al*. A high prevalence of glucokinase mutations in gestational diabetic subjects selected by clinical criteria. *Diabetologia*, 2000; **43**: 250–3.

13. **Glaser B** *et al*. Familial hyperinsulinism caused by an activating glucokinase mutation. *New England Journal of Medicine*, 1998; **338**: 226–30.

14. **Hattersley AT, Beards F, Ballantyne E, Appleton M, Harvey R, Ellard S**. Mutations in the glucokinase gene of the fetus result in reduced birth weight. *Nature Genetics*, 1998; **19**: 268–70.

15. **Byrne MM** *et al*. Altered insulin secretory responses to glucose in diabetic and nondiabetic subjects with mutations in the diabetes susceptibility gene *MODY3* on chromosome 12. *Diabetes*, 1996; **45**: 1503–10.

16. **Shepherd M, Hattersley A, Sparkes A**. Genetic testing in maturity onset diabetes of the young (MODY): a new challenge for the diabetic clinic. *Practical Diabetes*, 2001; **18**: 16–21.

17. **Yamagata K** *et al*. Mutations in the hepatocyte nuclear factor 4 alpha gene in maturity-onset diabetes of the young (MODY1). *Nature*, 1996; **384**: 458–60.

18. **Lehto M** *et al*. Mutation in the HNF-4 alpha gene affects insulin secretion and triglyceride metabolism. *Diabetes*, 1999; **48**: 423–5.

19. **Edlund H**. Transcribing pancreas. *Diabetes*, 1998; **47**: 1817–23.

20. **Stoffers DA, Zinkin NT, Stanojevic V, Clarke WL, Habener JF**. Pancreatic agenesis attributable to a single nucleotide deletion in the human *IPF1* gene coding sequence. *Nature Genetics*, 1997; **15**: 106–10.

21. **Stoffers DA, Ferrer J, Clarke WL, Habener JF**. Early-onset type-II diabetes mellitus (MODY4) linked to IPF1. *Nature Genetics*, 1997; **17**: 138–9.

22. **Macfarlane W** *et al*. Missense mutations in the insulin promoter factor 1 (IPF-1) gene predispose to type 2 diabetes. *Journal of Clinical Investigation*, 1999; **104**: R33–9.

23. **Bingham C** *et al*. Abnormal nephron development associated with a frameshift mutation in the transcription factor hepatocyte nuclear factor-1 beta. *Kidney International*, 2000; **57**: 898–907.

24. **Lindner TH, Njolstad PR, Horikawa Y, Bostad L, Bell GI, Vik O**. A novel syndrome of diabetes mellitus, renal dysfunction and genital malformation associated with a partial deletion of the pseudo-POU domain of hepatocyte nuclear factor-1 beta. *Human Molecular Genetics*, 1999; **8**: 2001–8.

25. **Frayling TM** *et al*. No evidence for linkage at candidate type 2 diabetes susceptibility loci on chromosomes 12 and 20 in United Kingdom Caucasians. *Journal of Clinical Endocrinology and Metabolism*, 2000; **85**: 853–7.

26. **Gerbitz K, van den Ouweland J, Maassen J, Jaksch M**. Mitochondrial diabetes mellitus: a review. *Biochimica et Biophysica Acta*, 1995; **1271**: 253–60.

27. **van den Ouweland JM** *et al*. Mutation in mitochondrial tRNA(Leu)(UUR) gene in a large pedigree with maternally transmitted type II diabetes mellitus and deafness. *Nature Genetics*, 1992; **1**: 368–71.

28. **Goto Y, Nonaka I, Horai S**. A mutation in the tRNA(leu,UUR) gene associated with the Melas subgroup of mitochondrial encephalomyopathies. *Nature*, 1990; **348**: 651–3.

29. **Maassen JA, Kadowaki T**. Maternally inherited diabetes and deafness: a new diabetes subtype. *Diabetologia*, 1996; **39**: 375–82.

30. **Shoelson S** *et al*. Three mutant insulins in man. *Nature*, 1983; **302**: 540–3.

31. **Moller DE, Flier JS**. Insulin resistance – mechanisms, syndromes, and implications (see comments). (Review). *New England Journal of Medicine*, 1991; **325**: 938–48.

32. **Kahn CR** *et al*. (Abstract) The syndromes of insulin resistance and acanthosis nigricans. Insulin-receptor disorders in man. *New England Journal of Medicine*, 1976; **294**: 739–45.

33. **Tritos NMC**. Syndromes of severe insulin resistance. *Journal of Clinical Endocrinology and Metabolism*, 1998; **83**: 3025–30.

34. **Seip M, Trygstad O**. Generalized lipodystrophy, congenital and acquired (lipoatrophy). *Acta Paediatrica Supplement*, 1996; **413**: 2–28.

35. **Garg A** *et al*. A gene for congenital generalized lipodystrophy maps to human chromosome 9q34. *Journal of Clinical Endocrinology and Metabolism*, 1999; **84**: 3390–4.

36. **Cao H, Hegele RA**. Nuclear lamin A/C R482Q mutation in Canadian kindreds with Dunnigan-type familial partial lipodystrophy. *Human Molecular Genetics*, 2000; **9**: 109–12.

37. **Barroso I** *et al.* Dominant negative mutations in human PPAR gamma are associated with severe insulin resistance, diabetes mellitus and hypertension. *Nature*, 1999; **402**: 880–3.

38. **Robinson S, Kessling A.** Diabetes secondary to genetic disorders. *Bailliére's Clinical Endocrinology and Metabolism*, 1992; **6**: 867–98.

39. **McKusick-Nathans Institute for Genetic Medicine, John Hopkins University (Baltimore, MD) and National Center for Biotechnology Information.** *Online Mendelian Inheritance in Man. OMIM (TM).* Bethesda, MD: National Library of Medicine 2000.

40. **Hardin D, Moran A.** Diabetes mellitus in cystic fibrosis. *Endocrinology and Metabolism Clinics of North America*, 1999; **28**: 787–800.

41. **Yaouanq J.** Diabetes and haemochromatosis: current concepts, management and prevention. *Diabetes and Metabolism*, 1995; **21**: 319–29.

42. **Strom TM** *et al.* Diabetes insipidus, diabetes mellitus, optic atrophy and deafness (DIDMOAD) caused by mutations in a novel gene (wolframin) coding for a predicted transmembrane protein. *Human Molecular Genetics*, 1998; **7**: 2021–8.

43. **Barrett TG, Bundey SE, Macleod AF.** Neurodegeneration and diabetes: UK nationwide study of Wolfram (DIDMOAD) syndrome. *Lancet*, 1995; **346**: 1458–63.

44. **Alberti K, Zimmet P.** Definition, diagnosis and classification of diabetes mellitus and its complications part 1: provisional report of a WHO consultation. *Diabetic Medicine*, 1998; **15**: 539–53.

## 3.2 The aetiology of type 2 diabetes

*C. Nicholas Hales and Stephen O'Rahilly*

## Introduction

There are many pathological, physiological and biochemical mechanisms which lead to the clinical features of type 2 diabetes. They interact in a complex manner which is far from fully understood. Lack of understanding is due in part to the remaining gaps in our knowledge of the basic science relevant to the condition. We also

suffer from a lack of large, detailed and long-term studies of the natural history of type 2 diabetes in the general population.

It is likely that genetic factors play a part in the production of type 2 diabetes. It remains unclear whether they play a major role or act more subtly in a polygenic fashion to modulate the impact of possibly more important environmental influences. The genetic aspects of type 2 diabetes have been considered in the previous chapter. In this chapter we focus on the pathophysiology of the condition and on the major environmental influences which impact on its development. We present a summary of the evidence which leads to these conclusions and consider what is currently understood of the mechanisms by which they may predispose to type 2 diabetes.

## Pathophysiology of established type 2 diabetes

In established type 2 diabetes both insulin deficiency and insulin resistance are usually apparent (Fig. 1). Indices of insulin resistance as well as poor acute insulin responses to glucose are also predictors of future diabetes in middle aged men.[1]

### Insulin secretory defects in diabetes

Insulin deficiency is usually demonstrable in terms of a poor early response to orally or intravenously administered glucose. It is not entirely clear whether the defective secretory response is specific for glucose or reflects a more general loss of response to a wide range of secretagogues. One difficulty in resolving this question is that glucose potentiates the effects of most other secretagogues. Therefore the fasting hyperglycaemia of type 2 diabetics potentiates the response to another stimulus – an effect which is lacking if a comparison is made with the response in a normoglycaemic control subject. In studies in which normoglycaemic individuals have first been made hyperglycaemic by the administration of glucose or when diabetics have been rendered normoglycaemic by treatment it is usually observed that the insulin secretory response to a non-glucose stimulus is defective. Another problem in relation to answering this question is that

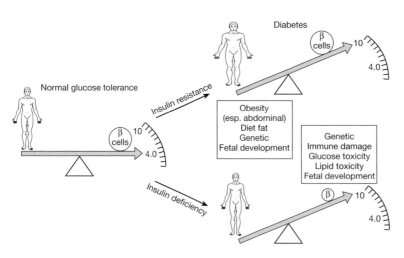

**Fig. 1** The role of beta cell function and insulin resistance in glucose homeostasis. Changes in either or both of these factors may be involved in the production of type 2 diabetes which is a heterogeneous condition. Scale indicates glucose concentration (mM).

chronic hyperglycaemia in itself is damaging to the insulin secretory process – so-called 'glucose toxicity'.[2] This effect may have a degree of specificity for the glucose response by decreasing the expression of glucose transporters in the β-cell. Therefore even if it is found that the glucose response is more defective than the response to other secretogogue this in turn may be the result of chronic hyperglycaemia rather than to any specificity of the pathological process for the effect of glucose. In our opinion the available data which relate to this question support the view that there is a fairly general defect of the insulin secretory response in established type 2 diabetes.

Type 2 diabetes is also characterized by an abnormal control of lipid metabolism. Non-esterified fatty acid (NEFA) concentrations are elevated in the fasting state and are suppressed poorly after oral glucose. There is evidence that chronic elevation of NEFA is also detrimental to insulin secretion.[3]

## Defects of insulin action

Insulin resistance may be demonstrated by a variety of investigations.[4] It is beyond the scope of this chapter to consider the validity and interrelationships of the results of these different methods. However most studies of insulin resistance carried out relate to the effect of insulin to regulate the plasma glucose concentration or the rate of glucose disposal. There are many other known effects of insulin, for example, on lipid and protein metabolism. In remains unclear to what extent resistance to the effects of insulin on glucose metabolism are paralleled by or distinct from its effects on other aspects of metabolism. It is also not entirely clear whether there are equally important defects of insulin action on its three main targets for glucose homeostasis namely muscle, liver, and adipose tissue.

### Muscle

One of the most important actions of insulin in maintaining postprandial glucose homeostasis is its effect to increase glucose uptake by skeletal muscle. In type 2 diabetes the greatest defect in insulin's action on skeletal muscle is in its stimulation of glycogen synthesis. The underlying basis of this defect is less clear. Recent studies using nuclear magnetic resonance spectroscopy to measure intracellular glucose, glucose-6-phosphate and glycogen in muscle non invasively, point to a defect of glucose transport whilst not excluding alterations in glucose phosphorylation or the control of glycogen synthesis itself.[5]

A possible indirect mechanism by which muscle may become resistant to the effects of insulin on its glucose metabolism relates to lipid metabolism. The supply of NEFA to muscle as an alternative fuel to glucose has major effects to reduce glucose metabolism. A large body of work *in vivo* and *in vitro* both in human and animal studies suggests that these effects are of pathophysiological significance and may well play a role in obesity and type 2 diabetes. More recently it has been observed that intramyocellular lipid deposition is related to insulin sensitivity in non-diabetic, non-obese humans.[6] It remains to be established by what mechanism this relationship occurs but it did not appear to be simply a consequence of the fasting NEFA or triglyceride concentration.[7]

### Liver

Insulin potentially reduces hepatic glucose output but there is a debate as to what extent this is a direct or an indirect effect. Insulin

inhibits glucose production by the perfused liver so that it clearly can have a direct effect. However NEFA are capable of increasing hepatic glucose production and therefore some part of insulin's effect on this could be indirect due to its action to reduce NEFA release by adipose tissue. There are also conflicting data in the literature as to whether insulin action on the liver is normal or defective in type 2 diabetes.

Insulin suppresses and NEFA augments hepatic secretion of very-low-density lipoproteins. Hepatic resistance to this action of insulin or adipose tissues resistance to the effect of insulin to suppress NEFA release or both does not explain the raised plasma triglyceride concentration which is a frequent feature of type 2 diabetes and the insulin resistance syndrome.[8]

### Adipose tissue

As adipose tissue is responsible for the uptake of only a small fraction of an oral glucose load, it has been traditionally thought unlikely that insulin resistance at the level of the adipocyte would have much impact on overall glucose homeostasis. On the other hand, an increased adipose mass, particularly if distributed centrally, is a major risk factor for the development of type 2 diabetes.[9] Recently a great deal of scientific attention has focused on the possible mechanisms whereby obesity may lead to diabetes. Plasma levels of NEFA tend to be higher in subjects with diabetes than in controls, and are often poorly suppressed by insulin in the postprandial state. As discussed above, these disturbances of lipid metabolism may have profound secondary consequences on the efficiency of glucose uptake in skeletal muscle. The adipocyte is also a site of synthesis of a number of secreted hormones and cytokines, for example, leptin, tumour necrosis factor-α and interleukin-6 (IL-6) all of which may have an impact on skeletal muscle insulin sensitivity in a paracrine or endocrine fashion. Subjects with body fat largely localized to intra-abdominal sites have a much higher risk of type 2 diabetes than those with a similar total fat mass distributed subcutaneously. This may relate both to the venous drainage of visceral adipose tissue directly into the liver and/or to the fact that visceral adipocytes tend to be more lipolytically active and less responsive to insulin than subcutaneous fat cells. There is little doubt that our increasing appreciation of the complex biology of adipocytes will have profound implications on our understanding of type 2 diabetes.

### Vascular effects of insulin

Hypertension and type 2 diabetes frequently occur together. Insulin resistance is a prominent feature of both. There is a great deal of interest as to whether raised concentrations of insulin might contribute to the production of hypertension or conversely whether defects in the action of insulin on blood vessels might contribute to insulin resistance in terms of glucose homeostasis.[10]

Patients with insulin secreting tumours are not generally hypertensive. However, it is difficult to exclude the possibility that the chronic, possibly life long, hyperinsulinaemia which accompanies insulin resistance could contribute to hypertension through effects on salt retention or other mechanisms.

Insulin increases forearm blood flow and appears to do so via an endothelium-derived nitric oxide (NO)-dependent mechanism. Thus it is possible that this effect of insulin could mediate at least in part its effect on glucose utilization by muscle and indeed even on its own access to muscle insulin receptors. Thus resistance to this effect of insulin could have down stream effects on insulin stimulated glucose utilization by muscle. There is also evidence that elevated NEFA concentrations cause endothelial dysfunction in relation to blood flow providing yet another site at which insulin and NEFA interact in an antagonistic fashion. Type 2 diabetics have been found to have a reduced blood flow response to methacholine chloride but not sodium nitroprusside thereby implicating a blunted endothelium-dependent response. Hyperinsulinaemia failed to augment this response. Again it is not clear whether these changes in diabetes are mediated via changes in NEFA concentration.

## Interaction between β-cell dysfunction and insulin resistance

There is great debate as to the primary pathological process leading to type 2 diabetes whether it is insulin deficiency, insulin resistance or a relatively equal contribution of the two. Part of the reason for this uncertainty is the fact that either change may be capable with the passage of time of leading to the other. Thus in the established chronically abnormal metabolism of type 2 diabetes the fact that both insulin deficiency and insulin resistance exist tells us nothing of the time scale over which they came to be established.

Examples of the way in which insulin deficiency may lead to insulin resistance may be cited. Firstly a major role of insulin in the regulation of metabolism is to suppress the release of NEFA by adipose tissue. Poor insulin secretion leads to increased fatty acid release. Fatty acids provide an alternative source of energy to glucose and in doing so inhibit glucose utilization thereby causing insulin resistance. Fatty acids also increase glucose output by the liver – an effect which may also reduce the ability of insulin to lower plasma glucose concentration. A second potential mechanism by which a primary abnormality of insulin secretion may lead to an apparent defect in insulin action is thorough loss of the normal oscillatory secretion pattern seen in the fasting state. Exogenous insulin administered in a similar oscillatory fashion has been shown to be more effective than insulin infused continuously at a steady rate. One of the earliest changes in insulin secretion observed during the loss of glucose tolerance leading to type 2 diabetes, is a loss of the normal oscillatory pattern of secretion. A consequence of this may be that the insulin secreted is less effective and this in turn may be incorrectly interpreted as insulin resistance. Chronic hyperglycaemia itself may result in the excess glucose being metabolized through the hexosamine pathway. This in turn may result in reduced sensitivity and defective glucose uptake.[11]

Conversely insulin resistance may lead to insulin deficiency. One way in which this could happen is through a rather ill-defined process of 'exhaustion' of the β-cell. In this sequence it is considered that hyper-glycaemia resulting from a primary process of resistance to the effect of insulin to reduce the plasma glucose concentration would damage or even destroy the β-cells as a consequence of the excessive demands placed upon it. Islet amyloid polypeptide (IAPP) is co-secreted with insulin. The physiological function of this apparently endocrine peptide remains unclear but it is increasingly evident that it plays a pathological role in the processes leading to type 2 diabetes (Fig. 2). As a consequence of its amino acid sequence in the human, the polypeptide is highly prone to aggregate into fibrils. These fibrils are the main basis of the amyloid deposits seen commonly in the islets of subjects with type 2 diabetes. Studies of transgenic mice expressing the human polypeptide have

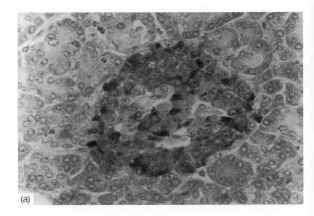
(a)

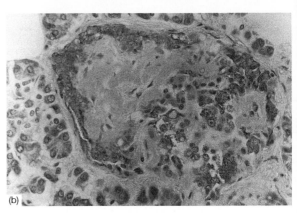
(b)

**Fig. 2** Post-mortem human pancreatic islet (a) from a non-diabetic subject labelled for insulin (brown). Insulin secreting cells occupy approximately 80 per cent of the islet volume; (b) from a type 2 diabetic subject labelled for insulin (brown) and amyloid (pink with Congo red). Amyloid has replaced central parts of the islet which would normally contain insulin secreting cells. (We are grateful to Dr A Clark, Radcliffe Infirmary, Oxford, for these illustrations.)

shown that in conditions of insulin resistance compensatory increased secretion of insulin is accompanied by increased secretion of IAPP. This in turn leads to deposition of amyloid fibrils in the islets. These deposits – either by a direct toxic effect on β cells or due to deleterious structural changes in the islets themselves – appear to cause β-cell damage and death. In this way secondary insulin deficiency would result. Intensive treatment of type 2 diabetics with insulin to produce a normal plasma glucose concentration considerably improves their insulin secretory response. Treatment does not however normalize the response. Also the production of chronic hyperglycaemia by the infusion of glucose is damaging to the insulin secretory response. This is the effect referred to as glucose toxicity to which we have alluded earlier.

One way of trying to resolve the issue of the relative importance of insulin deficiency compared with insulin resistance in the pathogenesis of type 2 diabetes is to study a population either cross sectionally or prospectively. In a cross sectional study of a large population one observes people with glucose tolerances ranging from the very best to the worst. If one makes the assumption that an individual deteriorating

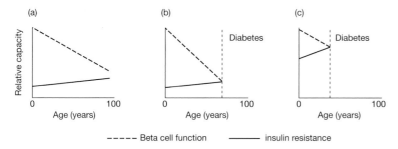

**Fig. 3** The age dependent changes in decreasing β-cell function and increasing insulin resistance. As long as β-cell function exceeds the demands posed by insulin resistance there is normal glucose tolerance. In many people this is true throughout their lifespan (a). In populations which are relatively insulin sensitive (for example, Japanese) the decline in β-cell function must be enhanced before glucose intolerance develops (b). In highly insulin resistant populations (for example, Pima Indians) diabetes occurs without a large reduction in β-cell function (c).

from the best to the worst tolerance follows the apparent sequence of changes which the whole population displays at one time, one can trace the apparent pathogenic time course. In this way one can determine whether signs of insulin deficiency or resistance appear 'first'. In our own studies of a predominantly Caucasian population in the UK (in Ely, Cambridgeshire), it was not possible to separate the apparent evolution of indices of insulin deficiency from those of resistance.

## Heterogeneity of type 2 diabetes

These findings of course relate to the whole population. It is of great importance to establish the degree of heterogeneity which exists at the level of the individual. Are there individuals whose type 2 diabetes appears to be the consequence of insulin deficiency or resistance entirely (Fig. 3) and still others who exhibit a roughly equal mixture of the two? It seems highly probable that all three types of individuals exist. There are undoubtedly thin individuals who appear to have type 2 diabetes and are insulin deficient but insulin sensitive. In our studies these were more frequently female. However the question arises as to whether such people are misclassified and really represent those with late onset type 1 diabetes. Depending on the populations studied it is possible that as many as 15–20 per cent of 'type 2' diabetics may fall into this category. Further research and better criteria for the separation of the two entities are required before this question can be resolved definitively. An increasing number of single gene disorders resulting in type 2 diabetes are being recognized. Although individually rare, together they may account for a small but significant percentage of type 2 diabetes. As the natural history and response to therapy of these disorders may dictate specific management strategies, it is important that steps are taken to recognize these individuals within the general population of diabetics.

## Aetiological factors

### Genetic influences

This topic has been discussed in the previous chapter and therefore is only briefly considered here. However any discussion of the aetiology of type 2 diabetes must include genetic factors. Indeed the 'thrifty

genotype' hypothesis of Neel put forward nearly 40 years ago continues to dominate thinking in this area. When the hypothesis was proposed no clear distinction was made between type 1 and type 2 diabetes. Thus it was reasonable to consider that a genotype leading to diabetes would potentially have had a negative effect on survival occurring as it (type 1) did during the reproductive phase of life. Thus it was also reasonable to propose that positive effects of the genotype must exist to neutralize consequences which might otherwise have been expected to eliminate the gene(s) by natural selection. Now that it is clear that type 2 diabetes is a disease predominantly affecting those in the post reproductive period of life, this argument is much less persuasive. However the concepts put forward in the thrifty phenotype hypothesis (see below) provide an alternative mechanistic framework for the role of thrifty genotypes. Thus genes which aid the process of metabolic adaptation to a poor fetal environment could well be selected under conditions of poor nutrition. The thrifty phenotype hypothesis proposed that this outcome would only be detrimental if they were manifest during reproductive life and this would only occur if nutrition suddenly improved. Thus the concepts embodied in the thrifty phenotype hypothesis greatly widen the candidate genes for thrifty genotypes.

Recently, evidence that such searches may prove fruitful have begun to emerge. Mutations in the 'glucose sensor' gene glucokinase have suggested that insensitivity to glucose stimulated insulin secretion results in a reduced birth weight.[12] Such an effect was predictable from the well established role of insulin as a fetal growth factor. However it remains an interesting possibility that this very rare genotype might confer a survival advantage under lifelong conditions of poor nutrition. Another interesting linkage between early growth and genetic polymorphisms has emerged from studies of the insulin gene.[13]

### Postnatal environment

The most compelling evidence that the postnatal environment is a major determinant of type 2 diabetes comes from populations migrating from areas of low to areas of high diabetes prevalence. In general, these populations rapidly acquire the high prevalence rates characteristic of the society into which they have migrated. The most likely environmental factors contributing to this phenomenon are alterations in diet and physical activity. As mentioned above, obesity is one of the most potent predictors of type 2 diabetes and therefore any alteration in macronutrient balance that promotes obesity is likely to lead to an increased prevalence of diabetes. Such adverse changes in energy balance could come from an increase in total energy intake, a decrease in energy expenditure, or both. Both of these changes are typical of the move from rural to urban societies. There is evidence, however, that the effects of diet and exercise may be more complex than can be accounted for simply by their effects on body fat mass. Thus, even among individuals with a similar fat mass, regular physical exercise is associated with a reduced prevalence of diabetes. With respect to food intake, there is growing evidence that a diet rich in fat results in greater insulin resistance than a eucaloric high carbohydrate diet. Even within dietary fat, there is increasing interest in the notion that particular types of mono-unsaturated and polyunsaturated fatty acids may have a protective role with respect to the development of diabetes and insulin resistance. While many studies have examined the roles of vitamins, minerals and other micronutrients there is no consistent body of data supporting a major aetiological role for these nutrients in type 2 diabetes.

## Low birthweight and the thrifty phenotype

In recent years poor fetal, and possibly, infant growth have been linked to an increased risk of loss of glucose tolerance[14] and to developing the metabolic syndrome[15] in adult life. Poor early growth has been defined by a variety of indices such as birthweight or weight at one year, thinness or shortness at birth and the ratio of head circumference to length at birth. Historical records of such measurements have been discovered in different centres in the UK and around the world. The associations are reproducible in a wide variety of populations including Pima Indians, Mexican Americans, and Australian aboriginals. The size of the relationship may also be very large. In Hertfordshire, UK there was an 18 fold increased risk of the lightest compared with the heaviest males at birth developing the metabolic syndrome when aged 64. In men and women in Preston, UK, a similar strong trend was observed (Table 1). Identical twins which were discordant for type 2 diabetes had significantly different birthweights such that the non-diabetic twins

were heavier. Whilst this finding does not exclude some role for genetic factors in explaining these associations it does show that the relationship between birthweight and risk of type 2 diabetes can exist independently of genetic differences.

The determination of fetal growth is generally accepted as being predominantly due to maternal factors. Genetic factors play only a small role in contrast to their importance in determining growth in childhood. The thrifty phenotype hypothesis[16] (Fig. 4) attempted to provide a conceptual and mechanistic framework to explain the statistical relationships between parameters of early growth and risk of

(a)

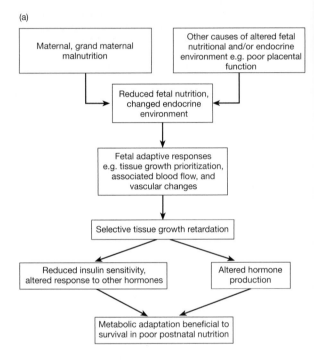

(b)

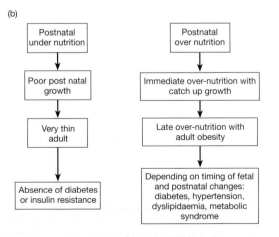

**Fig. 4** Some of the current concepts and questions relating to the proposals put forward as the 'thrifty phenotype' hypothesis (a) prenatal, (b) postnatal.

**Table 1** Odds ratio for the metabolic syndrome in men in Hertfordshire, UK and men and women in Preston, UK according to birthweight

| Hertfordshire birthweight (kg) | Odds ratio[a] | Preston birthweight (kg) | Odds ratio[b] |
|---|---|---|---|
| ≤2.5 | 18 | ≤2.5 | 13.5 |
| −2.95 | 8.4 | −2.95 | 9.0 |
| −3.41 | 8.5 | −3.41 | 5.2 |
| −3.86 | 4.9 | >3.41 | 1.0 |
| −4.31 | 2.2 | | |
| >4.31 | 1.0 | | |

Data with permission from Barker DJP, Hales CN, Fall CHD, Osmond C, Phipps K, Clark PMS. Type 2 diabetes mellitus, hypertension and hyperlipidaemia (syndrome X): relation to reduced fetal growth. *Diabetologia*, 1993; **36**: 62–7.

[a] Adjusted for body mass index (BMI) (p<0.001 for trend).

[b] Adjusted for BMI and sex (p=0.006 for trend).

type 2 diabetes in adult life. It proposed that the underlying factor is the fetal nutritional and endocrine environment. Poor fetal nutrition may be due to a variety of factors. Most commonly poor maternal growth and nutrition are involved. However uterine blood flow, placentation and placental function could also be involved in some circumstances. The fetus subjected to poor nutrition adopts at least two strategies which may be considered as thrifty. In the first, nutrients are distributed selectively in such a way that brain growth is relatively protected in relation to the growth of other organs such as the liver and kidney. A second consequence proposed, is that organ function is adapted in such a way that it aids postnatal survival in an environment in which nutrition is poor (the thrifty phenotype). These adaptations, whilst being beneficial under these circumstances, have detrimental consequences when nutrition is excessive, leading to obesity.

In order to test these ideas, experiments have been carried out in animals which were the offspring of pregnancies in which nutritionally deficient diets have been fed. It has been known for many years that both in humans and a variety of animals, protein deficiency may result in loss of glucose tolerance and poor insulin secretion. These changes may be irreversible on return to a normal diet. The growth of, and insulin secretion by, fetal $\beta$-cells is dependent on the availability of amino acids. Therefore the main manipulation of diet during pregnancy that has been studied, is a reduction in the protein, but with maintenance of the calorie content. However it is by no means certain that protein restriction is the only or even the most important dietary reduction which can lead to adverse consequences for glucose homeostasis in the adult. There is a need for a systematic evaluation of a number of dietary constituents which are recognized to be deficient in different populations world-wide so that these issues may be resolved.

Despite these uncertainties it is clear that protein restriction alone in early life followed by weaning onto a normal or obesity-inducing diet can reproduce a remarkable number of the features associated with type 2 diabetes.[17] It is clear that even such short-term early dietary changes can lead to permanent changes in the structure and function of key tissues involved in glucose homeostasis such as the islets of Langerhans, liver, muscle, and adipose tissue. Some of these changes have a specific molecular basis.[18] Therefore there is the real prospect that specific markers of the metabolic adaptations occurring during fetal growth retardation will be defined. It will then be possible to test whether some or many type 2 diabetics share these characteristics.

The quantity and quality of the post weaning diets interact strongly with the effects of poor early growth and consequent programming of metabolism. Excess nutrition leading to obesity on top of early growth restriction can reproduce the components of the metabolic syndrome in the rat: glucose intolerance, insulin resistance, hypertriglyceridaemia, and hypertension.[19] Insulin resistance consequent upon the consumption of a high fat diet also exacerbates the consequences of poor early growth.

Another issue which has emerged from tests of the thrifty phenotype hypothesis in animal models is the importance of postnatal growth to the outcome of fetal growth restriction. Studies of longevity have shown that in male rats, the life span may be influenced positively or negatively by the interactive effects of fetal and early postnatal growth restriction. Male rats from a normal pregnancy which were postnatally growth restricted by suckling a protein-restricted dam and weaned onto a normal diet exhibited increased longevity. The opposite outcome was observed when fetally growth restricted male pups were able to rapidly catch up in growth postnatally by suckling a normally fed dam.[17] Epidemiological studies of human populations are consistent with rapid postnatal growth and weight gain, as against early growth restriction having detrimental consequences in adult life in relation to hypertension and ischaemic heart disease.

Understanding the role and relative importance of environmentally determined poor early growth in the aetiology of type 2 diabetes is clearly of great importance for at least two reasons. In the first place, it represents a readily available means for the prevention of the condition. Secondly, the precise definition of the resulting phenotype opens up the prospect of rational intervention during adult life aimed at delaying or even preventing the evolution of diabetes. It might, for example, transpire that there are key components of the diet such as fat content which could be altered early in life in those identified on the basis of specific markers as being at greatest risk of subsequent disease. In addition, or as an alternative, the definition of endocrine and metabolic changes which have been programmed could lead to relevant and targeted therapy designed to specifically counteract the effects of the changes.

## Conclusions

There remain many unanswered questions concerning the aetiology of type 2 diabetes. It is undoubtedly a heterogeneous disorder. In recent years, considerable progress has been made in identifying a monogenic basis for some individuals. At present it seems unlikely that such mechanisms will account for anything but a small proportion of the condition. However the identification of specific mutations is important since the treatments used should be as appropriate as possible to the resulting abnormalities. Careful study of such individuals will also continue to teach us a great deal about the role of specific molecules in glucose homeostasis. The majority of type 2 diabetes are due to a mixture of genetic and environmental factors and their interactions. It is important to establish what are the dominant factors so that attention can be directed to better treatment and ultimately to prevention. It is not clear whether the main predisposing factor is the interaction of a variety of polygenic changes or is it the environment. Poor early growth and adult obesity are major factors predisposing to type 2 diabetes. Again it is not yet clear what are the relative roles of genes and environment underlying these associations. An emerging environmental factor is the composition of the diet particularly the quantity of fruit and vegetables consumed and the amount and composition of dietary fat.

Despite the many unanswered questions we remain optimistic that considerable progress will be made in the next few years to increase our understanding of the aetiology of type 2 diabetes.

## References

1. **Skafors ET, Selinus I, Lithell HO**. Risk factors for developing non-insulin dependent diabetes: a 10 year follow up of men in Uppsala. *British Medical Journal*, 1991; **303**: 755–60.

2. **Ling Z, Pipeleers DG**. Prolonged exposure of human $\beta$ cells to elevated glucose levels results in sustained cellular activation leading to a loss of glucose regulation. *Journal of Clinical Investigation*, 1996; **98**: 2805–12.

3. **Shimabukuro M, Zhou Y-T, Levi M, Unger RH**. Fatty acid induced β cell apoptosis: a link between obesity and diabetes. *Proceedings of the National Academy of Sciences of the United States of America*, 1998; **95**: 2498–502.

4. **Whitelaw DC, Gilbey SG**. Insulin resistance. *Annals of Clinical Biochemistry*, 1998; **35**: 567–83.

5. **Cline GW** *et al.* Impaired glucose transport as a cause of decreased insulin-stimulated muscle glycogen synthesis in type 2 diabetes. *New England Journal of Medicine*, 1999; **341**: 240–6.

6. **Krssak M** *et al.* Intra myocellular lipid concentrations are correlated with insulin sensitivity in humans: a $^1$H NMR spectroscopy sudy. *Diabetologia*, 1999; **42**: 113–6.

7. **Paolisso G, Howard BV**. Role of non-esterified fatty acids in the pathogenesis of type 2 diabetes mellitus. *Diabetic Medicine*, 1998; **15**: 360–6.

8. **Malmström R** *et al.* Defective regulation of triglyceride metabolism by insulin in the liver in NIDDM. *Diabetologia*, 1997; **40**: 454–62.

9. **Gautier J-F** *et al.* Evaluation of abdominal fat distribution in non insulin-dependent diabetes mellitus: relationship to insulin resistance. *Journal of Clinical Endocrinology and Metabolism*, 1998; **83**: 1306–11.

10. **Wiernsperger N**. Vascular defects in the aetiology of peripheral insulin resistance in diabetes. A critical review of hypotheses and facts. *Diabetes/Metabolism Reviews*, 1994; **10**: 287–307.

11. **Cooksey RC, Herbert LF, Zhu J-H, Wolford P, Garvey WT, McClain DA**. Mechanism of hexosamine-induced insulin resistance in transgenic mice overexpressing glutamine: fructose-6-phosphate amidotransferase: decreased glucose transporter GLUT 4 translocation and reversal by treatment with thiazolidinedione. *Endocrinology*, 1999; **140**: 1151–7.

12. **Hattersley AT, Beards F, Ballantyne E, Appleton M, Harvey R, Ellard S**. Mutations in the glucokinase gene of the fetus result in reduced birth weight. *Nature Genetics*, 1998; **19**: 268–70.

13. **Ong KKL** *et al.* The insulin gene *VNTR*, type 2 diabetes and birth weight. *Nature Genetics*, 1999; **21**: 262–3.

14. **Hales CN** *et al.* Fetal and infant growth and impaired glucose tolerance at age 64 years. *British Medical Journal*, 1991; **303**: 1019–22.

15. **Barker DJP, Hales CN, Fall CHD, Osmond C, Phipps K, Clark PMS**. Type 2 diabetes mellitus, hypertension and hyperlipidaemia (syndrome X): relation to reduced fetal growth. *Diabetologia*, 1993; **36**: 62–7.

16. **Hales CN, Barker DJP**. Type 2 diabetes mellitus: the thrifty phenotype hypothesis. *Diabetologia*, 1992; **35**: 595–601.

17. **Hales CN, Desai M, Ozanne SE, Crowther NJ**. Fishing in the stream of diabetes: from measuring insulin to the control of fetal organogenesis. *Biochemical Society Transactions*, 1996; **24**: 341–50.

18. **Ozanne SE, Nave BT, Wang CL, Shepherd PR, Prins J, Smith GD**. Poor fetal nutrition causes long-term changes in expression of insulin signalling components in adipocytes. *American Journal of Physiology*, 1997; **273**: E46–51.

19. **Petry CJ, Ozanne SE, Wang CL, Hales CN**. Early protein restriction and obesity independently induce hypertension in year old rats. *Clinical Science*, 1997; **93**: 147–52.

## Further reading

Baron AD, Clark MG. Role of blood flow in the regulation of muscle glucose uptake. *Annual Review of Nutrition*, 1997; **17**: 487–99.

Kahn SE, Andrikopoulos S, Verchere CB. Islet amyloid. A long recognised but underappreciated pathological feature of type 2 diabetes. *Diabetes*, 1999; **48**: 241–53.

McGarry JD. Glucose fatty acid interactions in health and disease. *American Journal of Clinical Nutrition*, 1998; **67**: 5500–4.

Roden M, Shulman GI. Applications of NMR spectroscopy to study muscle glycogen in man. *Annual Review of Medicine*, 1999; **50**: 277–90.

Shepherd PR, Kahn BB. Glucose transporters and insulin action. Implications for insulin resistance and diabetes mellitus. *New England Journal of Medicine*, 1999; **341**: 248–57.

Shulman GI. Cellular mechanisms of insulin resistance in humans. *American Journal of Cardiology*, 1999; **84**: J3–10.

## 3.3 Epidemiology and clinical heterogeneity of adult-onset diabetes

*Leif Groop*

## Definition of diabetes

Diabetes mellitus represents a group of metabolic disorders characterized by chronic hyperglycaemia with or without typical symptoms. The chronic hyperglycaemia of diabetes results from defects in insulin secretion, insulin action or both, and is associated with long-term organ damage, particularly in the eyes, kidneys, nerves, heart and blood vessels. More specifically, these long-term complications of diabetes include retinopathy which can lead to loss of vision, nephropathy leading to renal failure, nephropathy with an increased risk of foot ulcers, amputations and foot deformations, autonomic neuropathy causing cardiovascular, gastrointestinal, genitourinary and sexual dysfunction. Patients with diabetes also have an increased risk of atherosclerotic cardiovascular, peripheral vascular and cerebrovascular disease in addition to an increased incidence of obesity, particularly abdominal obesity, hypertension and lipid disorders. The clustering of abdominal obesity, hypertension, lipid disorders with diabetes (especially type 2 diabetes) and cardiovascular disease is often called a 'metabolic syndrome' or insulin resistance syndrome, to indicate that insulin resistance could be a common denominator for the syndrome. The burden of life-threatening chronic disease may have serious emotional and social impact on the patients and their families and the disease continues to impose a high toll on the society.

## Diagnosis of diabetes mellitus

As diabetes is defined as a condition of chronic hyperglycaemia, the diagnosis requires the establishment of the presence of chronic hyperglycaemia. Therefore, under most circumstances one elevated blood glucose or plasma glucose measurement is not enough, it has to be confirmed by another measurement on another day. The definition of chronic hyperglycaemia has varied over the years. The current WHO definition of chronic hyperglycaemia is based upon a fasting plasma glucose concentration of 7 mmol/l or above and/or a 2 h venous plasma glucose value during an oral glucose tolerance test (**OGTT**) of 11.1 mmol/l or above (equivalent to a venous blood glucose value of 10.0 mmol/l). The rationale for choosing this cutoff level is that it indicates an increased risk of diabetic retinopathy. But the OGTT is cumbersome for diagnostic purposes, therefore the majority of diagnoses are based upon the fasting value, which shows less variation than the 2-h value during the OGTT (6.4 per cent compared with 16.7 per cent). An important argument for the recent lowering of the cutoff level for fasting plasma glucose is that the risk for cardiovascular disease increases already at fasting blood glucose concentrations in this range.[1]

The use of the lower fasting plasma glucose value for diagnosis of diabetes would increase the prevalence of diabetes by about 25 per cent if based upon screening of the entire population with an OGTT. In practice, it does not increase the prevalence of diabetes by more than 8–10 per cent. These new diagnostic criteria for diabetes have been endorsed both by the ADA and WHO.

## Prevalence of diabetes

Ageing and westernization of developing countries have led to a dramatic increase in the worldwide prevalence of diabetes from 100 million in 1994 to an estimated 165 million in 2000 and 230 million in 2010. This increase is primarily due to an increase in type 2 diabetes, particularly in developing countries. There are marked differences in the prevalence of type 1 and type 2 diabetes across different populations.[2] In Europe, about 10–15 per cent of all patients with diabetes have type 1 diabetes. In the age group 0–15 years, the highest incidence of type 1 diabetes is seen in Finland (40/100 000/year) and Sweden (30/100 000/year), while the lowest is seen in Japan (1/100 000/year) (Fig. 1). Although there are no definite explanations for these gross differences, a reciprocal relationship is seen with type 2 diabetes, which is common in countries where type 1 diabetes is rare, for example, Japan. A combination of environmental factors and genetic susceptibility is thought to explain most of these differences. In developing countries, the epidemic of type 2 diabetes is ascribed to accumulation of so called thrifty genes. Genes predisposing to abdominal fat accumulation, energy preservation and insulin resistance might have been beneficial during periods of famine. These so called thrifty genes would have increased the

probability of survival in a harsh environment. With the increase in energy intake and decrease in energy expenditure (exercise), they are no longer survival genes, instead in the wrong environment they are associated with a shorter survival. In general, mortality is increased more than two-fold in patients with type 2 diabetes, cardiovascular mortality is usually increased even more.

At present, the total prevalence of diabetes varies between 0.8 per cent in Africa to 3.6 per cent in Europe and 5.3 per cent in northern America. There are, however, populations with a very high prevalence of diabetes. In India, the prevalence is about 13 per cent in the age group 30–64 years, in Micronesians on the Island of Nauru it is about 40 per cent in the same age-group while it approaches 50 per cent in the Pima Indians from Arizona (Fig. 2). The prevalence of impaired glucose tolerance (IGT) follows a somewhat different geographical pattern, it is about 7 per cent in Europe, 15 per cent in Native Americans and Pima Indians and highest, about 20 per cent in Micronesians.

## Classification of diabetes

The proposed new WHO classification of diabetes encompasses both clinical stages and aetiologic types of diabetes and other categories of hyperglycaemia. The clinical staging considers the fact that many diabetic subgroups progress through several clinical stages during its natural history. All subjects with diabetes mellitus can be categorized according to clinical stage from normoglycaemia to manifest hyperglycaemia; this should be achievable everywhere and worldwide regardless of the availability of sophisticated diagnostic tools. The aetiologic classification is based upon the identification of the underlying disease process.

The clinical staging goes from normoglycaemia (fasting venous plasma glucose below 6.1 mmol/l) to gross hyperglycaemia or diabetes. Diabetes mellitus, regardless of the underlying cause, is subdivided into *non-insulin requiring*, that is, those patients who may be satisfactorily controlled with diet and/or oral antidiabetic agents (formerly non-insulin-dependent diabetes mellitus, NIDDM), *insulin-requiring for control* (a new form corresponding to type 2 diabetic patients requiring insulin therapy for metabolic control rather than for survival) and *insulin requiring for survival* (corresponding to the former class of insulin-requiring diabetes, IDDM).

This staging procedure seems to identify clinically distinct subgroups, the non-insulin requiring patients represent the common form of type 2 diabetes characterized by obesity, insulin resistance, preserved β-cell function, absence of glutamate decarboxylase (GAD) antibodies and moderate risk of chronic diabetic complications. The insulin requiring for survival overlaps with the classical early-onset type 1 diabetes with absolute insulin deficiency, high prevalence of islet cell cytoplasmic autoantibodies (ICA) and GAD antibodies and high risk of microangiopathic complications. The new group, insulin-requiring for control seems to represent an admixture, patients are in general older, they have an increased prevalence of GAD antibodies and may thus represent the so called latent autoimmune diabetes in adults (LADA) type of diabetes (see below) and they are at increased risk of developing both micro and macroangiopathy.[3–5]

The aetiologic types designate disease processes which result in diabetes mellitus. The aetiologic classification may be possible only if appropriate measurements of autoimmune or genetic markers is available.

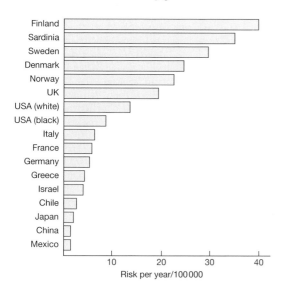

**Fig. 1** Prevalence of type 1 diabetes worldwide.

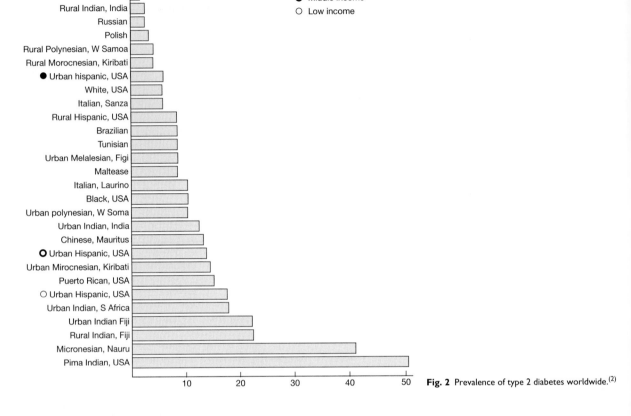

**Fig. 2** Prevalence of type 2 diabetes worldwide.[2]

**Type 1 diabetes** indicates processes of β-cell destruction that may ultimately lead to diabetes mellitus requiring insulin for survival or prevention of ketoacidosis, coma and death. Genetic predisposition determined by the human leucocyte antigen (HLA) locus together with immunological and environmental factors are key players in the pathogenesis of the disease. Autoimmune diabetes is further subdivided into a rapidly progressive form which is commonly observed in children below the age of 15 years, but may also occur in adults and a slowly progressive form which mostly occurs in adults. The latter is also referred to as LADA and defined as GADA positive diabetes with onset after the age of 35. These patients are usually misclassified as type 2 diabetic patients, in fact, about 10 per cent of type 2 diabetic patients have LADA.[6] LADA is genetically different from classical early-onset type 1 diabetes with a much lower prevalence of high risk HLA genotypes like DQβ*0201/0302 and no increase in other susceptibility alleles like the class I alleles of the insulin gene VNTR.[6]

In northern Europe, it is not uncommon that type 1 and type 2 diabetes occur in the same families, about 10–15 per cent of multiplex families are of mixed origin. This may have consequences for the clinical picture, the type 2 diabetic patients from such families often present with an earlier onset of the disease, less obesity and more severe impairment in β-cell function as generally seen in type 2 diabetes.

**Type 2 diabetes** encompasses the group of patients previously called NIDDM. People with type 2 diabetes usually have two metabolic defects, impaired insulin action and insufficient insulin secretion to compensate for the degree of insulin resistance. At least initially, these patients usually do not need insulin to survive. The disease often remains undiagnosed for many years. The patients are at increased risk of both macrovascular and microvascular disease. The aetiology is not known, but there are most likely several different causes of type 2 diabetes. A majority of the patients display features of the metabolic syndrome (insulin resistance syndrome or syndrome X), and these patients are at particular risk of developing macrovascular disease. Evidence is accumulating that insulin resistance may be the common aetiologic factor for the individual components of the metabolic syndrome.

In accordance to the WHO proposal, a person with type 2 diabetes or impaired glucose has the metabolic syndrome if two of the criteria listed below are fulfilled. A person with normal glucose tolerance has the metabolic syndrome if he/she fulfils two of the criteria in addition to being insulin resistant. Insulin resistance is defined as the lowest quartile of measures of insulin sensitivity (for example, insulin stimulated glucose uptake during euglycaemic clamp) or highest quartile of fasting insulin or Homoeostasis Model Assessment

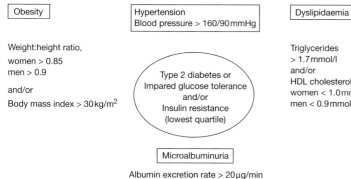

**Fig. 3** Definition of the metabolic syndrome.

(HOMA) insulin resistance index.[1] It should be kept in mind that fasting insulin concentrations or the HOMA index only represent surrogate measures of insulin sensitivity and that changes in insulin sensitivity only explain about 30 per cent of the variance in fasting insulin concentrations. The components of the metabolic syndrome are: (1) hypertension defined as antihypertensive treatment and/or blood pressure above 160/90 mm Hg, (2) dyslipidaemia defined as elevated plasma triglyceride (at or above 1.7 mmol/l) and/or low high density lipoprotein (HDL) cholesterol (below 0.9 mmol/l in men, below 1.0 mmol/l in women) concentrations, (3) obesity defined as high body mass index (BMI) (30 or above) and/or high waist hip ratio (WHR more than 0.90 in men, over 0.85 in women) and (4) micro-albuminuria (overnight urinary albumin excretion rate 20 µg/min or above) (Fig. 3). The cutoff for WHR would make 80–90 per cent of the population obese, it may therefore be wise to increase the cutoff levels for WHR to over 1.00 in men and over 0.90 in women.

## Prevalence and risk associated with the metabolic syndrome

Applying this definition to a population from Scandinavia[7] about 10 per cent of persons with normal glucose tolerance, 40 per cent of persons with impaired glucose tolerance (IGT) and 70 per cent of patients with type 2 diabetes would have the metabolic syndrome. Importantly, the presence of the metabolic syndrome was associated with a three-fold increased risk of coronary heart disease, myocardial infarction and stroke and a three–five-fold increased risk of cardio-vascular death.

Insulin resistance clusters in families and 45 per cent of first-degree relatives of patients with type 2 diabetes are insulin resistant compared with 20 per cent of people without a family history of diabetes.[8,9] Despite this, the heritability for insulin resistance is lower than the heritability for insulin secretion in twin studies. This may simply reflect the fact that insulin resistance is also strongly influenced by environmental factors.

About 40 per cent of the variation in body fat is being attributed to genetic factors.[10] The genetic factor is even more impressing for abdominal obesity; they are considered to explain 60 per cent of the variance in abdominal fat postmenopausal women. First-degree relatives of patients with type 2 diabetes have an increased waist–hip ratio compared with their spouses without a family history of

NIDDM,[8] and this increase in abdominal fat is seen without a significant increase in total body fat. Importantly, the redistribution of fat to the abdominal region is seen at completely normal glucose tolerance. The inheritance of type 2 diabetes thus seems to favour fat accumulation in the intra-abdominal region. Intra-abdominal fat is metabolically very active with a high rate of free fatty acid turnover. Intra-abdominal free fatty acids metabolism is relatively resistant to the effect of insulin in persons with abdominal obesity. Instead, the β-3-adrenergic receptor of visceral fat is sensitive to stimulation by catecholamines. This, in turn, will ensure a large supply of free fatty acids to the portal vein for further transport to liver and other tissues like muscle. In contrast, lipolysis in subcutaneous fat is more sensitive to the inhibitory effect of insulin, which will favour reesterification of free fatty acids to triglycerides.

## Thrifty genotype

Why does the metabolic syndrome develop in individuals switching from a rural to an urban lifestyle? The thrifty gene hypothesis was put forward in 1962 by Neel,[11] who proposed that individuals living in a harsh environment with unstable food supply would maximize their probability of survival if they could maximize storage of surplus energy. Genetic selection would thus favour energy conserving genotypes in such environments. Storage of energy as fat rather than as glycogen would ensure energy during periods of starvation. When this energy storing genotype is exposed to the abundance of food typical of Western society, it becomes detrimental causing glucose intolerance. It can therefore be assumed that thrifty genes predispose to the metabolic syndrome. Such putative genes could be expected to influence lipolysis, fuel oxidation and skeletal muscle glucose metabolism.

## Thrifty phenotype

An alternative explanation has also been proposed by which most of the metabolic syndrome is programmed *in utero*, the so-called thrifty phenotype hypothesis.[12] According to this, intrauterine malnutrition would lead to a low birthweight and increased risk of the metabolic syndrome later in life. Although these findings have been replicated in several studies, it has also been shown that the risk of a small birthweight for the metabolic syndrome is increased particularly in families with the metabolic syndrome, suggesting that a small birthweight could be a phenotype for a thrifty gene. In support of this, children with a glucokinase defect and thereby a decrease in insulin, have a low birthweight.[13] This was particularly apparent in children of diabetic mothers, since these children would be expected to have a high birthweight as a consequence of high glucose passing the placenta and thereby stimulating the fetal pancreas to produce increasing amounts of anabolic insulin.

## Search for thrifty genes

Two major approaches are being used in the search for thrifty genes, or genes predisposing to (abdominal) obesity. The *candidate gene approach* aims at the identification of genes based upon information of their function. Although this approach has been successful in a number of monogenic disorders with known biochemical defects (for example, phenylketonuria), our knowledge about the underlying defects causing type 2 diabetes is limited. It is therefore not surprising that the candidate gene approach has not been very successful for the identification of thrifty genes.

The *random gene search*, also referred to as *positional cloning*, assumes no knowledge of the underlying defects. Instead, positional cloning aims at localizing the disease gene on the basis of its position in the genome.[14] If a chromosomal region has been linked to the disease, the next step would be the search for attractive candidate genes in the region or narrowing the region by linkage disequilibrium mapping. This approach has been successful in a number of monogenic disorders where the relationship between genotype and penetrance of the phenotype is more straightforward than for type 2 diabetes. It can be assumed that common variants in a number of genes will increase susceptibility to type 2 diabetes and that these genes will act in concert with a number of environmental factors.

## Candidate genes for the metabolic syndrome and type 2 diabetes

The thrifty gene hypothesis proposes that efficient storage of energy could have been associated with survival advantage during the evolution.[3,11] Efficient storage of energy must include storage of fat and weight gain. Given the scenario presented earlier, obesity genes could predispose to the metabolic syndrome and thereby to type 2 diabetes. Despite large fluctuations in food intake and energy expenditure, body fat is tightly regulated in humans. A powerful feedback system (also referred to as the *lipostat hypothesis*) between fat and a satiety/energy expenditure centre in the hypothalamus has been postulated, since damage to this region causes morbid obesity.

There are several candidate genes for the metabolic syndrome, including the genes for the $\beta_2$, $\beta_3$-adrenergic receptor, lipoprotein lipase, hormone sensitive lipase, peroxisome proliferator-activated receptor $\gamma$ (**PPAR-$\gamma$**), insulin receptor substrate (**IRS-1**), glycogen synthase etc. (Fig. 4).

### $\beta_3$-adrenergic receptor gene

Catecholamines stimulate lipolysis through the $\beta$-adrenergic receptors and inhibit lipolysis through $\alpha$-adrenergic receptors. The

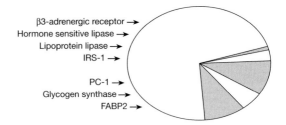

**Fig. 4** Common variants in candidate genes as cause of the metabolic syndrome.

$\beta_2$-adrenergic receptor ($\beta_2$-AR) is expressed in several tissues including the lung and fat tissue. The $\beta_3$-AR is expressed in brown adipose tissue of rodents and considered responsible for thermogenesis. In humans it is expressed in visceral fat. Catecholamine-induced lipolysis is increased in visceral fat from subjects with abdominal obesity due to increased $\beta_3$-AR function.

A few years ago a mutation in the first intracellular loop of the receptor changing a tryptophan in position 64 to arginine was reported.[15] Mutation carriers showed more abdominal obesity, higher insulin concentrations, more insulin resistance and higher blood pressure than individuals homozygous for the wild type (Trp64Trp), that is, all features of the metabolic syndrome. Furthermore, they had a lower metabolic rate and lower resting sympathetic nervous system activity, all features one would expect of a 'thrifty' gene.

### Hormone sensitive lipase

The breakdown of triglycerides is regulated by several lipases including the hormone sensitive lipase (**HSL**) in adipose tissue, the endothelial lipoprotein lipase (LPL) and hepatic lipase. The genes encoding for these lipases have been widely studied as putative candidate genes for human obesity and the metabolic syndrome. A polymorphism in the HSL gene was associated with type 2 diabetes characterized by the metabolic syndrome.[16] Importantly, this variant was in a transmission disequilibrium test more often transmitted from heterozygous parents to abdominally obese offspring.

### PPAR-$\gamma$

There are three forms of PPAR receptors, $\alpha$, $\beta$ and $\gamma$, which heterodimerize with the retinoid X receptor (RXR) to induce transcription of a number of target genes in adipose tissue. Fatty acids or their derivatives are naturally occurring ligands in addition to drugs like thiazolidinediones (PPAR-$\gamma$) and fibrates (PPAR-$\alpha$). Two dominant negative mutations in the PPAR-$\gamma$ gene (P467L and V290M) have been described in two families with severe insulin resistance, early onset diabetes and hypertension.[17] Another more common Pro12Ala variant has been associated with low BMI and increased insulin sensitivity.[18] *In vitro*, this mutation leads to decreased PPAR-$\gamma$ activity. This variant is associated with a 15 per cent risk reduction for type 2 diabetes.[19]

### Glycoprotein PC-1

The membrane glycoprotein PC-1 was isolated from a patient with extreme insulin resistance and found to inhibit insulin receptor tyrosine kinase activity. An A121C variant in exon 4 of the PC-1 gene (Glu→Lys) has been associated with insulin resistance and features of the metabolic syndrome. *In vitro*, this variant is associated with impaired autophosphorylation of the insulin receptor tyrosine kinase.[20]

## IRS-1

The docking protein IRS-1 links the tyrosine phosphorylated insulin receptor to the downstream part of the insulin signalling pathway. IRS-1 is phosphorylated on multiple tyrosine residues, and could be a candidate for genetic insulin resistance. Two aminoacid polymorphisms were described in the IRS-1 gene.[21] These aminoacid substitutions, which were located close to the tyrosine phosphorylation site, were slightly more frequent in type 2 diabetic patients than in control subjects. In obese non-diabetic Danish subjects, the presence of the 972 polymorphism was associated with insulin resistance. The 972 variant of the IRS-1 gene seems to be predominantly increased in type 2 diabetic patients with the metabolic syndrome. Later on several other insulin receptors substrates (IRS-2, IRS-3 and IRS-4) have been discovered but no consistent variations in these genes have been found.

## Glycogen synthase

Impaired stimulation of glycogen synthesis by insulin is a hallmark of type 2 diabetes and IGT. Glycogen synthase, the key enzyme of this pathway, could therefore be an important candidate for a genetic defect causing insulin resistance. An XbaI polymorphism of the glycogen synthase gene has been associated with type 2 diabetes and insulin resistance, particularly impaired insulin-stimulated glycogen synthesis in skeletal muscle.[22] We recently applied the discordant sib-pair approach to explore this association further. The sibling with the rare A2 allele had more features of the metabolic syndrome and an increased risk of myocardial infarction compared to siblings with the A1 allele.[23]

Of note, the relative contribution of variations in these genes to the common form of type 2 diabetes is not known. The prevalence varies markedly between different populations, for example, in Scandinavia the Arg64 allele frequency of the $\beta_3$-adrenergic receptor gene is about 10 per cent but in Japan 30 per cent. It is assumed that a single variant is not sufficient to cause type 2 diabetes, the interaction between several variants and a hostile environment is needed to trigger the events leading to type 2 diabetes.

## Genome-wide scan

The advantage of the genome-wide scan approach is that it does not assume any knowledge about the pathophysiological mechanisms leading to the metabolic syndrome, the disadvantage(s) is that it requires large family resources and that it encompasses a high risk of false positive results. Several genome wide scans have been carried out with type 2 diabetes as phenotype.

Linkage has been reported to several regions 2q,[24] 12q[25] and 20q[26] being the most promising ones. For NIDDM-1, it seems likely that the linkage is due to an intronic variant in a novel gene, *calpain 10*,[27] emphasizing the problems with identifying the genetic causes of polygenic diseases.

# Other specific types
## Genetic defects of $\beta$-cell function

Several monogenic forms of diabetes with impaired $\beta$-cell function have been described in the past years.[28–30] These include the different forms of maturity onset diabetes of the young (**MODY**) mitochondrial diabetes with deafness (**MIDD**) and other types. MODY is inherited in an autosomal dominant fashion and the disease usually becomes manifested before 25 years of age. MODY-1 is rare and due to mutations in a liver transcription factor, HNF-4α on chromosome 20. MODY-2 is due to several mutations in the glucokinase gene on chromosome 7. The disease is characterized by mild elevations in blood glucose, complications are rare or absent. MODY-3 is the most common form of MODY and due to mutations in another hepatocyte nuclear factor, HNF-1α on chromosome 12. Patients with MODY-1 and MODY-3 are susceptible to microangiopathic but not to macroangiopathic complications. One reason could be that they display almost normal insulin sensitivity. MODY-4 is caused by heterozygous mutations in the insulin transcription factor, IPF-1. In its homozygous form the mutation causes complete agenesis of the pancreas. In its heterozygous form, it predisposes to early-onset type 2 diabetes, but its penetrance is much less than the other forms of MODY. MODY-5 is due to mutations in the HNF-1$\beta$ gene, the heterodimer of HNF-1α. These patients usually display severe kidney disease with cystic deformations.

Mutations in mitochondrial DNA have been found in diabetic patients with deafness (MIDD). As mitochondrial DNA is only inherited from the mother, the disease has a maternal transmission. The most common mutation occurs at position 3243 in the transfer RNA leucine gene. The same mutation can cause a number of neurological disorders like the MELAS syndrome (mitochondrial myopathy, encephalopathy, lactic acidosis and stroke-like syndrome).[31]

## Heterogeneity of diabetes

The extent of heterogeneity in diabetes has exceeded all expectations. In Northern Europe about 10–15 per cent have classical type 1 diabetes, 10 per cent slowly progressing type 1 diabetes or LADA; this means that about 25 per cent of all patients have an autoimmune form of diabetes (Fig. 5). In addition, 3–5 per cent have MODY or MIDD. About

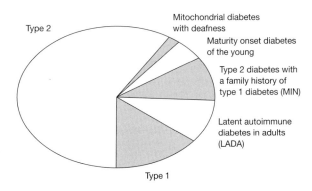

**Fig. 5** The spectrum of diabetes.

10 per cent come from mixed multiplex families, in which the type 2 diabetic patients tend to have a more severe disturbance in insulin secretion than commonly seen in type 2 diabetes. The majority of patients represent type 2 diabetic patients with the metabolic syndrome (60–70 per cent). These figures are quite different in other parts of the world. In Japan classical early-onset type 1 diabetes is rare (about 1 per cent) and LADA is the most common form of autoimmune diabetes. The clinical picture of type 2 diabetes also seems to differ from other parts of the world, obesity is less pronounced and impaired $\beta$-cell function is more predominant than in other parts of the world.

Heterogeneity is also seen within pedigrees and families. Both type 1 and type 2 diabetes and MODY can occur in the same families. MODY and MIDD are seen in about 15–20 per cent of familial early-onset (lesser than 40 years of age) diabetes.[30] Notably, the common form of type 2 diabetes can also present early; bilineality (diabetes in both parents) is often associated with early-onset diabetes. These young patients usually present with childhood obesity.

## Changes in the incidence of type 2 diabetes

The worldwide prevalence of type 2 diabetes has been predicted to increase by approximately 40 per cent over the next 10 years from 150–210 million patients.[2] Of note, these figures are based upon estimations, not upon real figures. They, however, clearly demonstrate that an epidemic of type 2 diabetes is occurring across the world and seems to particularly affect developing countries and migrants from developing countries. This will impose a tremendous burden on the health care system worldwide. Several potential causes for this epidemic have been named including enrichment of thrifty genes and their incompatibility with the affluent westernized society. There are also alternative explanations like intrauterine malnutrition (thrifty phenotype) or simply that energy intake exceeds energy expenditure. Regardless of the cause, it has been shown that diet plus exercise can prevent type 2 diabetes and its cardiovascular complications. Therefore, preventive programs at the community level are urgently needed to halt this epidemic of type 2 diabetes.

## References

1. Alberti K, Zimmet P, Consultation W. Definiton,diagnosis and classification of diabetes mellitus and its complications. Part 1: Diagnosis and classification of diabetes mellitus, provisional report of a WHO consultation. *Diabetic Medicine*, 1998; **15**: 539–53.

2. Zimmet P. Diabetes epidemiology as a tool to trigger diabetes research and care. *Diabetologia*, 1999; **42**: 499–518.

3. Groop L, Tuomi T. Non-insulin-dependent diabetes mellitus – a collision between thrifty genes and an affluent society. *Annals of Medicine*, 1997; **29**: 37–53.

4. Isomaa B, Almgren P, Henricssson M, Taskinen M-R, Sarelin L, Groop L. Chronic complications in patients with slowly progressing autoimmune type 1 diabetes (LADA). *Diabetes Care*, 1992; **22**: 1347–53.

5. Tuomi T, Groop L, Zimmet P, Rowley M, Knowles W, Mackay I. Antibodies to glutamic acid decarboxylase (GAD) identify latent IDDM in patients with onset of diabetes after the age of 35 years. *Diabetes*, 1993; **42**: 359–62.

6. Tuomi T, Carlsson Å-L, Li H, Cano L, Isomaa B, Miettinen A *et al.* Clinical and genetic characteristics of type 2 diabetes with and without GAD antibodies. *Diabetes*, 1999; **48**: 150–7.

7. Isomaa B *et al.* Cardiovascular morbidity and mortality associated with the metabolic syndrome. *Diabetes Care*, 2001; **24**: 683–9.

8. Groop L *et al.* Metabolic consequences of a family history of NIDDM (The Botnia Study). *Diabetes*, 1996; **45**: 1585–93.

9. Beck-Nielsen H, Groop L. Metabolic and genetic characterization of prediabetic states. Sequence of events leading to non-insulin-dependent diabetes mellitus. *Journal of Clinical Investigation*, 1994; **94**: 1714–1721.

10. Bouchard C. Genetics of body fat content. In: Angel H, Anderson H, Bouchard C, Lau D, Leiter L, Mendelson R, editors. *Progress in Obesity Research 7*. London: John Libbey, 1996: 33–41.

11. Neel V. Diabetes mellitus: a 'thrifty' genotype rendered detrimental by progress? *American Journal of Human Genetics*, 1962; **14**: 352–62.

12. Hales C, Barker D. Type 2 diabetes mellitus: the thrifty phenotype hypothesis. *Diabetologia*, 1992; **35**: 595–601.

13. Hattersley A, Beards F, Ballantyne E, Appleton M, Harvey R, Ellard S. Mutations in the glucokinase gene of the foetus result in reduced birth weight. *Nature Genetics*, 1998; **19**: 268–270.

14. Lander E, Kruglyak L. Genetic dissection of complex traits: guidelines for interpreting and reporting linkage results. *Nature Genetics*, 1995; **11**: 241–7.

15. Widèn E, Lehto M, Kanninen T, Walston J, Shuldiner A, Groop L. Association of a polymorphism in the beta-3-adrenergic-receptor gene with features of the insulin resistance syndrome in Finns. *New England Journal of Medicine*, 1995; **333**: 348–51.

16. Klannemark M *et al.* The putative role of the hormone sensitive lipase gene in the pathogenesis of the metabolic syndrome. *Diabetologia*, 1998; **41**: 1515–22.

17. Barroso I *et al.* Dominant negative mutations in the human PPARgamma associated with severe insulin resistance, diabetes mellitus and hypertension. *Nature*, 1999; **402**: 880–3.

18. Deeb S *et al.* A Pro12Ala substitution in PPARgamma2 associated with decreased receptor activity, lower body mass index and improved insulin sensitivity. *Nature Genetics*, 1998; **20**: 284–7.

19. Altshuler D *et al.* The common PPAR$\gamma$ Pro 12Ala polymorphism is associated with decreased risk of type 2 diabetes. *Nature Genetics* 2000; **26**: 76–80.

20. Pizzuti A *et al.* A polymorphism (K12Q) of the human glycoprotein PC-1 gene coding region is strongly associated with insulin resistance. *Diabetes*, 1999; **48**: 1881–4.

21. Almind K, Bjoerbaek C, Vestergaard H, Hansen T, Echwald S, Pedersen O. Aminoacid polymoprhism of the insulin receptor substrate-1 in non-insulin-dependent diabetes mellitus. *Lancet*, 1993; **342**: 828–32.

22. Groop L *et al.* Association between polymorphism of the glycogen synthase gene and non-insulin-dependent diabetes mellitus. *New England Journal of Medicine*, 1993; **328**: 10–14.

23. Orho-Melander M, Almgren P, Kanninen T, Forsblom C, Groop L. A paired sibling analysis of the XbaI polymorphism in the muscle glycogen synthase gene. *Diabetologia*, 1999; **42**: 1138–45.

24. Hanis C *et al.* A genome-wide search for human non-insulin-dependent (type 2) diabetes genes reveals a major susceptibility locus on chromosome 2. *Nature Genetics*, 1996; **13**: 161–6.

25. Mahtani MM *et al.* Mapping of a gene for type 2 diabetes associated with an insulin secretion defect by a genome scan in Finnish families. *Nature Genetics*, 1996; **14**(1): 90–4.

26. Zouali H *et al.* A susceptibility locus for early-onset non-insulin dependent (type 2) diabetes mellitus maps to chromosome 20q, proximal to the phosphoenolpyruvate carboxykinase gene. *Human Molecular Genetics*, 1997; **6**: 1401–8.

27. Horikawa Y *et al.* Genetic variation in the calpain 10 gene (CAPN10) is associated with type 2 diabetes mellitus. *Nature Genetics*, 2000; **26**: 1–13.

28. Froguel P *et al.* Familial hyperglycemia due to mutations in the glucokinase gene. *New England Journal of Medicine*, 1993; **328**: 697–702.

29. **Yamagata K** *et al.* Mutations in the hepatocyte nuclear factor-1alpha gene in maturity-onset diabetes of the young (MODY3). *Nature*, 1996; **384**: 455–8.

30. **Lehto M** *et al.* High frequency of MODY and mitochondrial gene mutations in Scandinavian families with early-onset diabetes. *Diabetologia*, 1999; **42**: 1131–7.

31. **Kadowaki T** *et al.* A subtype of diabetes mellitus associated with a mutation of mitochondrial DNA. *New England Journal of Medicine*, 1994; **330**: 962–8.

# 4 The treatment of type 1 diabetes mellitus

## Baiju R. Shah and Bernard Zinman

## Introduction

The therapy for type 1 diabetes mellitus must focus on correcting the metabolic abnormalities and long-term consequences of insulin deficiency, resulting from autoimmune destruction of the pancreatic $\beta$-cells. This seemingly straightforward task of hormone replacement has been particularly difficult because of the complexity of physiological insulin secretion, and has eluded scientists for more than 75 years.[1]

The healthy functioning pancreas secretes insulin in response to the daily variations in nutrient intake and exercise (Fig. 1). Polonsky *et al.* carefully documented endogenous insulin secretion in normal subjects.[2] They found insulin secretion can be divided into components representing basal secretion and meal requirements. Basal secretion, which represents one-half of total daily secretion, limits endogenous glucose production; while postprandial peaks, which can reach up to five times the baseline level, enhance tissue uptake and storage of glucose. This pattern of insulin release is further characterized by a repetitive pulsatile pattern superimposed on the larger secretory profiles.

Exercise also modulates insulin secretion. Since glucose utilization and insulin sensitivity increase for most intensities of exercise,

euglycaemia can be preserved by a reduction in pancreatic insulin secretion.[3]

## General principles of treatment

The principal clinical goals for the management of type 1 diabetes are to avoid symptoms of hyper- and hypo-glycaemia, and to prevent the development of long-term complications.

The paradigm for diabetes care has changed significantly in recent years. Patients are now encouraged to accept day-to-day responsibility for their diabetes, including making treatment regimen decisions related to meals, exercise, and insulin dose adjustments. The nature and goals of diabetes education provided to patients must focus on problem solving in the context of day-to-day lifestyle issues. To aid in the acquisition of the necessary skills, multidisciplinary diabetes health care teams are essential. The team is centred around the patient and his or her family, and includes the patient's primary care physician, diabetes specialist physician, nurses specially trained in diabetes education, and dietitians. Other personnel attached to the team include other medical specialists (such as ophthalmologists, nephrologists, cardiologists), pharmacists, social workers, podiatrists, and psychologists.

## Lifestyle factors

### Diet

Dietary modification is the oldest treatment prescribed for diabetes, described over 3500 years ago. Today, the philosophy for dietary management of type 1 diabetes has changed. Rather than modifying the diet to suit the pharmacological management, the insulin therapy is adjusted in response to the food consumed. To start, regularly timed meals and snacks with known carbohydrate composition will facilitate management. However, with increased knowledge and confidence, insulin dose adjustments based on anticipated nutrient intake, using such techniques as carbohydrate counting, provide the most successful outcome.

All patients with diabetes should be counselled by a dietitian on the effects of diet on glucose control, and how to modify insulin doses in response to dietary choices. Snacks between meals or at bedtime may be required to prevent hypoglycaemia but this will

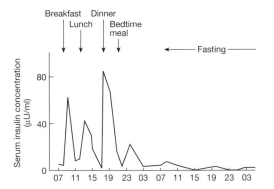

**Fig. 1** Insulin secretion in response to meals and the overnight fasted state. (Reproduced from Lee WL, Zinman B. From insulin to insulin analogues: progress in the treatment of type 1 diabetes mellitus. *Diabetes Reviews*, 1998; **6**: 73–88.)

depend on the insulin regimen being used. Caloric intake should be targeted to attain or maintain the patient at ideal body weight. Requirements vary depending on the patient's age, sex and activity level, and are no different for patients with diabetes than those without it. Since many patients with type 1 diabetes are children or adolescents, energy intake must be adequate to maintain normal growth and development. The distribution of these calories is important to maintain good nutrient balance emphasizing healthy heart principles:

- *Carbohydrates* should account for up to 60 per cent of the calories. Studies suggest that the intake of soluble fibre lowers postprandial blood glucose. However, controversy persists as to the impact of simple carbohydrates on overall glucose control.

- *Protein* requirements for patients with well-controlled diabetes are identical to those for non-diabetic people. The recommended daily allowance for protein is also no different – at least 0.8 g/kg body weight. However, low-protein diets may be valuable for patients with renal failure.

- *Fat* consumption should be limited to less than 30 per cent of total caloric intake. In particular, saturated fatty acids should be reduced, as they have been implicated in raising cholesterol levels.

Anticipated changes from a patient's usual dietary routine can be compensated for by adjusting the dose of insulin before the meal. In general, an extra 10 g of carbohydrate requires approximately one extra unit of insulin; however responses vary between patients and even between meals, and must be determined individually. With experience, patients can become adept at predicting their response to dietary changes, and can modify their insulin dose appropriately. This technique is called 'carbohydrate counting', and is an important part of an intensive diabetes management program.

## Exercise

As in non-diabetic individuals, peripheral glucose uptake and insulin sensitivity are increased following most intensities of exercise in patients with diabetes. To maintain euglycaemia, a physiological decrease in insulin secretion occurs in normal $\beta$ cells. However, patients with diabetes lose their ability to regulate $\beta$-cell function, so unless preventative steps are taken, hypoglycaemia may develop.

Patients must be cautioned that any exercise or activity which increases energy expenditure has potential consequences on glycaemic control. Exercise should be anticipated with an increased carbohydrate intake or a reduced dose of administered insulin. Careful monitoring of glucose levels is essential to guide insulin treatment adjustments. Patients who begin a regular exercise programme often require permanent adjustments to their insulin dose while engaging in the programme. However, with adequate monitoring and management, people with diabetes can participate in the same recreational and competitive physical activities as their non-diabetic peers.[4]

Eating an extra carbohydrate snack before exercising is usually unnecessary if insulin doses are changed appropriately. To adjust doses for exercise, patients should consider the intensity and duration of the planned exercise. Longer-duration exercise, where the injected insulin's peak action occurs while the patient is still exercising, requires a larger reduction in insulin dose than short-duration low-intensity exercise. Pre-meal insulin doses should be reduced by

approximately 50 per cent for moderate postprandial exercise. Patients should also increase the frequency of blood glucose monitoring around the time of exercise to determine their response to the adjustment for the future. Short bursts of high intensity exercise may result in hyperglycaemia due to excessive catecholamine release. Additionally, exercise can cause prolonged hypoglycaemia, up to 24 hours after the activity is completed. Therefore, subsequent insulin doses and/or nutrient intake may have to be adjusted.

# Insulin replacement therapy

Insulin has remained an essential component of therapy for type 1 diabetes since its isolation by Banting, Best, Collip, and Macleod, and its first clinical use on January 11, 1922. Subsequently, technology has allowed the creation of several different types of insulin from several different sources.

## Types of injectable insulins

The different types of insulin currently available are listed in Table 1.[5] Because it has a rapid onset and short period of action, regular insulin – also known as crystalline zinc insulin or soluble insulin – is used as a meal insulin to simulate the physiological postprandial insulin pulse, thereby minimizing blood glucose excursions. The basal insulins are formed by the addition of protamine in neutral protamine Hagedorn (NPH) and zinc in the lente series. These additions place these insulins into suspension and delay their absorption from subcutaneous tissues, prolonging their onset and duration of action.

Each of the insulin types is available from several different species. Beef and pork insulins are extracted from the pancreas of cows and pigs. In contrast, human insulin produced by recombinant DNA techniques has been available since the 1980s. Because these proteins are identical to normal human insulin, antibody development, allergy and contamination are rare. In fact, since recombinant insulin is also now cheaper to produce than animal insulins, most manufacturers have stopped marketing animal insulin.

## Insulin analogues

One of the limitations of insulin therapy is that insulin monomers tend to aggregate into hexamers when in high concentrations.

**Table 1** Pharmacokinetics of commercially available insulins

| Insulin | Action (h) | | |
|---|---|---|---|
| | Onset | Peak | Duration |
| Meal insulin | | | |
|   Soluble | ½ | 2–5 | 6–8 |
|   Fast-acting analogue | ¼ | ½ | 2–4 |
| Basal insulin | | | |
|   NPH | 1–2 | 4–12 | 18–26 |
|   Lente | 1–3 | 6–15 | 18–26 |
|   Ultralente | 4–6 | 8–30 | 24–36 |

Absorption of these complexes from the subcutaneous tissue is limited, requiring first their dissociation into dimers and monomers. As a result, insulin absorption profiles are non-physiological, even if administered as recommended, which is half hour before a meal. This delayed absorption and prolonged action of subcutaneously injected regular insulin results in immediate postprandial hyperglycaemia with the risk of subsequent hypoglycaemia.

Meal insulin analogues have been developed by creating amino acid substitutions in the B-chain of insulin, changing the ultrastructure of the insulin molecule, resulting in more rapid absorption and action of insulin.[6] The first of these analogues, Insulin lispro, became commercially available in 1996.[7] The 28th and 29th amino acids in the B-chain of regular insulin, proline and lysine, are reversed. This exchange causes a conformational change in the protein which reduces dimer formation by a factor of 300 compared to regular insulin. Hence, lispro has a more rapid onset of activity, rapid time to peak activity, higher peak of activity, and shorter duration of activity than regular insulin. The practical advantage of these pharmacokinetics is that lispro can be administered immediately before a meal, rather than 30–45 min before eating as with regular insulin. The use of lispro has resulted in improved postprandial glucose control and decreased hypoglycaemic episodes.[8] A second, similar analogue, Insulin aspart, is also now available.[9]

An example of an insulin analogue for basal insulin replacement is Insulin glargine. The amino acid substitutions in this analogue slow its absorption and give it a smoother profile than NPH.[10] Insulin glargine is only recently commercially available and its optimal usage remains to be determined. The development of a series of insulin analogues with improved pharmacokinetic profiles can be expected in the next few years, improving our ability to replace insulin more appropriately.

## Insulin treatment regimens

The initiation of insulin therapy in a patient with newly developed type 1 diabetes corrects the initial hyperglycaemia and ketosis resulting from insulin deficiency. It also reverses the peripheral insulin resistance caused by hyperglycaemia itself. By improving insulin sensitivity, the minimal residual function of the $\beta$ cells may be adequate to prevent hyperglycaemia and keto-sis. This 'honeymoon phase' may last weeks to several months, dur-ing which time the patient may not require insulin therapy. However with time, the $\beta$ cells continue to fail and the patient becomes dependent on exogenous insulin. Interruption of insulin therapy during the honeymoon phase is not recommended, since maintenance of glycaemic control with exogenous insulin appears to promote longer survival of endogenous $\beta$-cell secretion and thus improved control.[11]

As already stated, physiological insulin secretion requires a basal level of insulin in the fasting state, with large episodic bursts of insulin secretion in response to meals. Therefore, insulin replacement should mimic this pattern: basal insulin replacement with meal boluses. In general, most patients' total required daily dose of insulin is approximately 0.7 units per kg of body weight. This dose can be administered in several different strategies in an attempt to duplicate normal insulin physiology.

## Intensive therapy

Intensive therapy mimics, as closely as possible, the normal function of the $\beta$ cells. Several small trials, culminating in the large Diabetes Control and Complications Trial (DCCT) showed conclusively that with multiple daily injections (MDI) of insulin or with continuous subcutaneous insulin infusion (CSII), together with frequent monitoring of blood glucose, the risk and progression of the microvascular complications of diabetes, such as retinopathy, nephropathy or neuropathy, can be reduced.[12] Intensive therapy may also be beneficial for macrovascular disease, although this remains to be established conclusively.[13]

MDI requires the administration of four injections of insulin per day. Prior to eating, meal insulins like regular or lispro are administered to control excursions of plasma glucose postprandially. These injections emulate the physiological pulses in insulin secretion accompanying meals in normal individuals. Because of its slower onset of action, regular insulin should be administered about 30 min before eating; lispro can be administered immediately prior to the meal, and results in superior meal glycaemic control. Basal insulins, such as NPH, lente or ultralente, are administered before bedtime to simulate overnight secretion.

About one quarter of patients treated with lispro for meals require a second injection of basal insulin before breakfast to prevent hyperglycaemia before the evening meal.[14] This effect appears to be independent of the type of insulin used for bedtime basal replacement.

When initiating MDI, approximately 40 per cent of the total daily dose is given as the basal insulin at bedtime. The remaining insulin is divided as meal insulin before each meal; requirements before lunch are usually less than those before the other two meals (Box 1). The meal insulin doses can be adjusted for each meal, depending on three variables:

- the *preprandial glucose level*, as measured using a capillary monitor,
- the *carbohydrate content* of the meal, and
- the level and timing of *exercise* the patient anticipates after the meal.

CSII uses a small pump, which can be kept under clothing or attached to a belt. The pump contains the supply of insulin which is delivered by a cannula into the subcutaneous tissue. Lispro is the preferred insulin for CSII, since it results in improved control with lower rates of hypoglycaemia.[15] The pumps are programmed by the patient to deliver different basal rates at different times of day. When eating, the patient then delivers an extra bolus of insulin to control the blood glucose postprandially. One of the major advantages of pump therapy is that it gives patients flexibility in the timing of meals – the basal rate of insulin is always being infused, and thus a meal can safely be delayed or skipped without deterioration in control. This can sometimes also be achieved in MDI especially where the basal insulin is given as two roughly equal injections, on rising and at bedtime, but CSII delivers this facility most reliably. The basal rate in CSII can be adjusted depending on activity level and the size of the pre-meal bolus can vary depending on the meal. Some individuals require increasing doses in the early waking hours (0500–0800) to counteract the 'dawn phenomenon', which is due to counterregulatory hormone release. CSII uniquely provides the flexibility to adjust the basal rate under these circumstances.

**Box 1**   **Initiation of intensive therapy**

◆ Step 1   Determine total daily dose

Sum of current insulin doses *or* 0.5 units × body weight (kg)

*For example, a patient weighing 72 kg: 0.5 × 72 = 36 units per day*

◆ Step 2   Determine basal requirements

40% of total daily dose

| MDI | CSII |
|---|---|
| Given as basal insulin at bedtime | Given divided over 24 hours |
| *NPH 14 units at bedtime* | *Fast-acting analogue 0.6 units/h* |

◆ Step 3   Determine meal requirements

35% of remaining insulin before breakfast, 30% before lunch, 35% before dinner

| MDI | CSII |
|---|---|
| Given as meal insulin before meals | Given as boluses via infusion |
| *Fast-acting analogue 8 units before breakfast* | *Fast-acting analogue 8 units bolus before breakfast* |
| *Fast-acting analogue 6 units before lunch* | *Fast-acting analogue 6 units bolus before lunch* |
| *Fast-acting analogue 8 units before dinner* | *Fast-acting analogue 8 units bolus before dinner* |

Patients starting on infusion pump may need a small reduction from their previous total daily insulin dose. Approximately 40 per cent of the insulin is administered as the basal infusion rate, from 0.6–1.2 units/h. The remainder is given as boluses before meals, with larger boluses before breakfast and dinner (Box 1).

Many pumps have safety features to minimize the risk of a prolonged severe hypoglycaemic episode. If there is no interaction with the pump for several hours, the pump sounds an alarm and stops the insulin infusion. However, malfunction of the pump or air in the infusion system can lead to interrupted insulin delivery with rapid increases in blood glucose and possible ketosis. The cannula must be replaced in a new location every two days by the patient to prevent subcutaneous cellulitis or abscesses. At this time, the expense of the pump and supplies limits their widespread use, although there were approximately 60 000 CSII users in the United States in 1998.

While intensive therapy has been shown to improve glucose control and reduce complications of diabetes, the DCCT also showed that tight regulation of blood glucose results in a higher frequency of severe hypoglycaemic episodes. Thus, the glycaemic targets for patients on intensive therapy may have to be adjusted to reduce the frequency of unacceptable severe hypoglycaemia. While not suitable for all patients, intensive therapy is the preferred regimen to control type 1 diabetes.

## Conventional therapy

Intensive insulin therapy has been conclusively shown to reduce the progression and development of the microvascular complications of diabetes. However, a large number of patients with type 1 diabetes are unable or unwilling to master the skills that intensive therapy requires.

For these patients, a conventional 'split-mixed' regimen of twice-daily injections of a mixture of basal (NPH, lente or ultralente) and meal (lispro or regular) insulins is the most frequent regimen used.

The insulin is administered before breakfast and before dinner. The meal insulin component of each injection prevents post-meal hyperglycaemia. The basal insulin component administered before breakfast controls glycaemia over the lunch period, but can cause mid-afternoon hypoglycaemia. The basal component of the pre-dinner injection often reaches peak activity in the middle of the night, leading to nocturnal hypoglycaemia. Should this become intolerable, patients should be encouraged to divide their evening insulin dose, giving the meal component before dinner and delaying the basal insulin component until bedtime, so that its peak would be delayed until the following morning. This hybrid thrice-daily injection regimen is better than conventional therapy, but inferior to full scale intensive therapy.

To start a patient on twice-daily insulin therapy, approximately two-thirds of the total daily dose is administered in the morning, and one-third in the evening; of each dose, approximately two-thirds is given as basal, and one-third as meal insulin. Fixed or pre-mixed insulins, such as 30/70, are not recommended for patients with type 1 diabetes, but are more appropriate for patients with type 2 diabetes where daily insulin dose adjustments are not generally required.

What these regimens gain in convenience over intensive therapy, they lose in flexibility. Adjusting insulin doses to match activity level and dietary content is difficult with only two or three injections per day. Patients following conventional therapy must be more rigid in timing their lunch and dinner after the morning insulin injection, and must maintain the carbohydrate content of each meal fairly consistently from day to day. In general, their ability to reach recommended treatment glycaemic goals is severely compromised.

# Insulin administration

The most common method of insulin delivery is using disposable syringes. Insulin is supplied in multiple-dose vials. Insulins in suspension, such as NPH, lente or ultralente, must be gently mixed prior to being drawn up, to ensure that the suspension is evenly distributed. The patient draws up the required amount of insulin from the vial. When two types of insulin are to be mixed in the same injection, the patient draws up the meal insulin first, then the suspended insulin. If patients are unable to draw up insulin themselves, syringes can be prefilled by a caregiver or pharmacist. The insulin is injected subcutaneously.

An alternative device for administering insulin is the pen-cartridge. Each cartridge contains a reservoir of insulin, and the patient can dial the amount to be administered. The needle of the pen is then inserted subcutaneously, and a plunger is depressed to deliver the insulin. These devices are the method of administration of choice for MDI, because they improve accuracy of delivery and make insulin administration more convenient, especially in public places. Shaking of the pen cartridge mixes insulins less effectively than shaking a multiple-dose vial and patients using isophane or lente insulins in pens must be instructed accordingly.[17]

Jet injectors, which inject insulin through the skin under pressure without needles, are also available. These injectors are often associated with subcutaneous bruising and are awkward to use, so are generally reserved for patients with needle phobia.

Insulin preparations are fairly chemically stable. Once a vial is opened, it can be stored at room temperature for 6–8 weeks.

Insulin is best injected into areas of the body with adequate subcutaneous fat – the abdomen, buttock, thigh and upper arm can be used. Absorption is variable between sites; the abdomen is the preferred site of injection since absorption is rapid and more consistent. Massage, exercise and warm temperatures can accelerate absorption. To prevent cutaneous complications of insulin administration, patients should rotate injections within the same general body area: for example using the full abdomen, not just the periumbilical region.

# Monitoring glucose control

Once a patient begins insulin therapy, the effectiveness of treatment must be evaluated. The outcomes which should be monitored include short-term variables, such as day-to-day blood glucose values and frequency of hypoglycaemic side-effects; intermediate-term variables, such as glucose control as reflected by haemoglobin $A_{1c}$ level; and long-term variables, such as progression to microvascular and macrovascular complications.

## Capillary blood glucose monitoring

Capillary blood glucose monitoring is essential usually for patients to manage their diabetes actively.[18] A drop of blood, obtained from a fingertip using a spring-loaded lancet, is placed onto a test strip. Older techniques use a chemically-induced colour change to indicate a range of blood or plasma glucose concentrations. More accurate modern meters determine the glucose concentration of the blood using electrochemical methods. By recording their blood glucose concentrations at different times of the day, patients can create a 'log book', profiling the outcome of their insulin treatment. Many meters also have memory capabilities and computer software to present multiple displays of the monitor's results, helping to identify glycaemic patterns.

Frequency of monitoring depends on the patients' needs, abilities and motivation. Patients on intensive insulin therapy must check blood glucose levels four times per day, before each insulin administration. They are taught to adjust their insulin dose depending on the pre-dose glucose concentration. Patients striving for tight control can also check glucose levels after meals to examine the adequacy of their insulin dose in preventing postprandial hyperglycaemia, and during the night to uncover nocturnal hypoglycaemia. Even if patients are unwilling to check glucose concentrations so frequently, they should be instructed either to monitor capillary glucose more frequently at scheduled intervals, or to vary the time of day when they monitor, thereby creating a profile of blood glucose at different times of the day. This profile allows patients and their health care providers to make appropriate adjustments to the overall insulin regimen.

Urine glucose monitoring should not be used for patients with type 1 diabetes who are willing and able to monitor blood glucose, since it is unable to detect hypoglycaemia and does not provide useful data for insulin dose adjustment.

## Glycosylated haemoglobin

Circulating glucose molecules are non-enzymatically and irreversibly bound to haemoglobin A molecules forming the electrophoretically fast haemoglobins $A_{1a}$, $A_{1b}$ and $A_{1c}$. For technical reasons, most clinical laboratories measure only haemoglobin $A_{1c}$ – the proportion of haemoglobin molecules which is glycosylated is a function of the plasma glucose concentration over time. Thus, the haemoglobin $A_{1c}$ is an accurate reflection of the glucose control over the preceding two to three months – the average lifespan of the red blood cells – and should be measured every three months in patients with diabetes.

Elevated haemoglobin $A_{1c}$ indicates poor glycaemic control and the need to adjust the patient's treatment regimen. However, capillary blood glucose self-monitoring results are required to make specific adjustments in individual components of the treatment plan.

Haemoglobin $A_{1c}$ may be reduced in people with haemoglobinopathies, as glycosylation of the abnormal haemoglobin molecule may be impaired. Falsely elevated haemoglobin $A_{1c}$ levels may occur in the presence of carbamylated haemoglobin in uraemia, acetaldehyde-bound haemoglobin in alcoholics or fetal haemoglobin in haematic derangements of pregnancy. Failing these circumstances, an elevated haemoglobin $A_{1c}$ value despite excellent capillary self-monitoring records usually reflects patient inaccuracies or falsified capillary results.

Haemoglobin $A_{1c}$ is known to correlate with the development of long-term microvascular complications of diabetes, and a 10 per cent reduction of haemoglobin $A_{1c}$ concentration results in a 45 per cent relative risk reduction for retinopathy.[19] 'Optimal glucose control'[20] with fasting plasma glucose concentration 4–7 mmol/l and a haemoglobin $A_{1c}$ less than 115 per cent of the upper limit of normal (Table 2) is associated with a low risk of developing long-term complications. However, this degree of control was achieved in only

**Table 2** Targets of glucose control

|  | Ideal (non-diabetic) | Optimal | Suboptimal | Inadequate |
|---|---|---|---|---|
| Fasting glucose level (mmol/l) | 3.8–6.1 | 4–7 | 7.1–10 | >10 |
| Haemoglobin A₁c (% of upper limit) | ≤100 | ≤115 | 116–140 | >140 |

From: 1998 Clinical practice guidelines for the management of diabetes in Canada, *Canadian Medical Association Journal*, 1998; **159**: S1–29.

50 per cent of the patients in the intensive therapy group of the DCCT. It should be noted that the true definition of good control includes not just the optional haemoglobin HbA₁c but also a lack of problematic hypoglycaemia.

# Complications of insulin treatment

## Hypoglycaemia

The most common and potentially life-threatening acute complication of insulin therapy is hypoglycaemia. Most patients with type 1 diabetes who are trying to maintain a tighter glucose control, will experience hypoglycaemia from time to time. In the DCCT, for every 10 per cent reduction in haemoglobin A₁c, the risk of severe hypoglycaemia increased 18 per cent.[12] Not all trials of intensified insulin therapy share this experience[16] but it is the common finding.

The maintenance of adequate blood concentrations of glucose is critical, because unlike other tissues, the brain has an absolute need for glucose under most circumstances. Low plasma glucose will result in the secretion of glucagon, adrenaline, cortisol and growth hormone and stimulation of the sympathetic nervous system. Glucagon and adrenaline are the most important counterregulatory hormones against hypoglycaemia.

While extremely variable, most patients develop symptoms of hypoglycaemia when the blood glucose is lower than 4.0 mmol/l. Symptoms are both adrenergic and neuroglycopenic, although in most patients adrenergic symptoms occur earlier as blood glucose is falling. Release of counterregulatory catecholamines causes sweating, tachycardia, anxiety, pallor, nausea and hunger. An inadequate supply of glucose for brain metabolism, on the other hand, causes headache, blurred vision, paresthesiae, changes in mental status, cognitive impairment, aphasia, seizures and coma.

While either glucagon or adrenaline on their own could raise blood glucose in response to hypoglycaemia, patients with type 1 diabetes may have impaired secretion of both. Glucagon is usually the first affected, with impaired release in nearly all patients with type 1 diabetes of at least five years' duration. Later, adrenaline responses can become blunted, and patients may develop hypoglycaemia unawareness as the adrenergic warning symptoms fade. Unawareness occurs most commonly in patients who have had frequent hypoglycaemic episodes. It can be reversed if hypoglycaemia is strictly avoided, which may require upward adjustment of glycaemic targets.

Most hypoglycaemic reactions are mild. Once aware of the symptoms, patients can self-treat hypoglycaemia by ingesting a source of glucose, either as food or in a tablet. Severe episodes are those where the patient requires the help of someone else for treatment, either family members or emergency medical services, because the patient is confused, in a coma or having a seizure. Family members should be taught how to use glucagon subcutaneous injection kits for instances where the hypoglycaemic patient is unable to ingest carbohydrates.

## Ketoacidosis

Insulin plays a critical role in preventing hepatic gluconeogenesis and ketogenesis by antagonizing the effects of glucagon on the liver. It also has anti-lipolytic effects, by preventing conversion of triglyceride into non-esterified fatty acids. Patients with type 1 diabetes may become insulin deficient in absolute terms or as a consequence of an intercurrent illness which increases secretion of counterregulatory hormones.

The metabolic consequences of inadequate insulin are hyperglycaemia and ketosis with anion gap metabolic acidosis. The hyperglycaemia and resultant glycosuria can cause an osmotic diuresis which may lead to profound volume contraction. The diuresis may cause significant total-body potassium depletion, and with insulin treatment, life-threatening hypokalaemia may develop. Symptoms of ketoacidosis include nausea, vomiting, polyuria, abdominal pain and changes in the level of consciousness. Laboratory investigations reveal an anion gap metabolic acidosis. The initial treatment of ketosis corrects the life-threatening complications with fluid repletion, potassium replacement and sodium bicarbonate in severe acidosis. Infusion of insulin is required to counteract the effect of glucagon. Should the glucose concentration normalize before the anion gap is cleared, the insulin infusion should be maintained, with intravenous dextrose to maintain euglycaemia.

The occurrence of ketoacidosis can be avoided by the appropriate management of sick days, as outlined below.

## Local cutaneous reactions

Repeated injection of insulin into the same site may cause lipohypertrophic deposition in the subcutaneous fat. It is probably caused by a direct effect of insulin on the subcutaneous tissues, promoting lipogenesis.[21] The problem is accentuated in areas with decreased pain sensitivity, since patients favour these sites for injection. Absorption of insulin from these hypertrophied areas is variable, leading to unpredictable glycaemic control. For this and for cosmetic reasons, patients are encouraged to rotate their injection sites. Avoiding further insulin injections into the hypertrophied area will usually allow the tissue to regress.

# Management during illness or surgery

Even when not eating, patients with type 1 diabetes cannot stop taking insulin. Counter-regulatory hormones released in response to physiological stress or intercurrent illness often cause hyperglycaemia despite decreased caloric intake. Since β-cell function in these patients is negligible, they have inadequate endogenous insulin release to prevent ketosis. Failure to provide exogenous insulin in adequate amounts will result in diabetic ketoacidosis.

Patients should be instructed to monitor their blood glucose levels every four hours when sick, and to test their urine for the presence of ketones. If blood glucose is elevated, insulin doses are increased with supplemental injections. One regimen for significant hyperglycaemia includes the administration of boluses of subcutaneous soluble insulin, equivalent to half the usual meal-time dose, every 2–4 h, until the blood glucose begins to fall. If blood glucose levels are low, insulin doses should be reduced by up to 50 per cent, but never stopped. If nauseated or unable to eat, patients should substitute a sugar-rich fluid diet to maintain serum glucose levels. If this is not tolerated, patients may require intravenous glucose. The presence of significant ketonuria also indicates a need for parenteral therapy.

When a patient is clearly going to be unable to eat for a long period of time, such as peri-operatively, an intravenous insulin infusion should be started. The infusion should deliver, over 24 h, approximately 50–100 per cent of the usual daily subcutaneous dose. Capillary blood glucose testing should be performed every hour initially to ensure the glucose is being maintained at a safe level. A common regimen includes administration of intravenous glucose solutions (5–10 per cent) containing potassium, with simultaneous infusion of regular insulin delivered intravenously by adjustable infusion pump. The insulin dose is adjusted according to the measured blood glucose, aiming for levels of 4–9 mmol/l. If the patient is unable to take food orally for several days, these regimens do not provide adequate nutrition and should be replaced with parenteral feeding. Because the half-life of intravenous insulin is only a few minutes, the infusion cannot simply be stopped without risking ketoacidosis. Instead, a subcutaneously injected dose of meal insulin is given, and the infusion can then be safely stopped 2–3 h later as the biological action of the subcutaneous dose begins.

## New approaches to treatment

### Alternate routes of insulin delivery

Several alternate methods of delivering insulin have been explored to replace the traditional subcutaneous routes.[22]

Use of intranasal insulin is limited by large variation in insulin absorption and hence bioavailability, with inflammation of the mucosa or climatic change, causing erratic glycaemic control. Inhaled insulin is more attractive, because absorption is excellent across the alveoli. Unfortunately, bioavailability remains low, and the administration of the dose must be accurately timed with inhalation. Relatively large doses of insulin are administered.[23]

Patients frequently wonder whether oral insulin preparations are available. To date, efforts have not been successful because the insulin molecule is digested. However, attempts are being made to encapsulate insulin into microspheres and use other techniques to make this molecule traverse mucosal membranes.

The ultimate goal of insulin delivery is the development of an 'artificial pancreas', which would sense ambient glucose concentrations, and respond with an appropriate release of insulin. Developing an adequate clinically useful glucose sensor has remained a difficult challenge.

### Pancreatic transplant

The first pancreas transplant was performed in 1966; however, only recently has the number of transplants begun rapidly increasing.[24] Transplant is the only available therapy which is curative of type 1 diabetes: patients retain a euglycaemic state independent of exogenous insulin, and have a normal glycosylated haemoglobin concentration.

Success rates are high: the patient survival rate following transplant is 94 per cent at one year, 90 per cent at three; the graft survival rate is 81 per cent at one year and 72 per cent at three.[25]

The primary difficulty with transplantation is that, to maintain graft survival, patients must be placed on anti-rejection medications which have their own toxicities and complications. Therefore, the majority of pancreatic transplants occur in patients who are simultaneously receiving or have previously received renal transplants. Infrequently, transplants will be offered to patients in whom the side effects of anti-rejection drugs are less serious than the consequences of ongoing diabetes. The medications to combat rejection also protect the graft from the autoimmune process which destroyed their native $\beta$-cells in the first place.

Studies have demonstrated that transplantation may also arrest the progression of the complications of diabetes. Diabetic neuropathy stabilizes or improves following transplant in most patients. Advanced retinopathy may stabilize. Early nephropathy in patients without renal transplants may regress, and renal function may stabilize, although the cyclosporine used for immunosuppression is nephrotoxic. Unfortunately, there is no evidence that macrovascular disease is influenced by transplantation.

Since transplant is infrequently used to correct exocrine pancreatic function, attempts have been made to transplant only insulin-producing islet cells. In most cases, success rates have been much lower than those for transplanting intact organs.[26] However, a recent protocol has been developed with a novel mechanism for isolating and purifying islet cells and a unique immunosuppressive regimen.[27] Although only a handful of patients have been reported so far, all were free of insulin injections after one year of follow-up. Confirmation of these results is underway.

## References

1. **Zinman B.** The physiologic replacement of insulin: an elusive goal. *New England Journal of Medicine*, 1989; **321**: 363–70.

2. **Polonsky KS, Given BD, van Cauter E.** Twenty-four-hour profiles and pulsatile patterns on insulin secretion in normal and obese subjects. *Journal of Clinical Investigation*, 1988; **81**: 442–8.

3. **Levitt NS, Hirsch L, Rubenstein AH, Polonsky KS.** Quantitative evaluation of the effect of low-intensity exercise on insulin secretion in man. *Metabolism: Clinical and Experimental*, 1993; **42**: 829–33.

4. **Giacca A, Groenewoud Y, Tsui E, McClean P, Zinman B.** Glucose production, utilization, and cycling in response to moderate exercise in obese subjects with type 2 diabetes and mild hyperglycaemia. *Diabetes*, 1998; **47**: 1763–70.

5. **Burge MR, Schade DS.** Insulins. *Endocrinology and Metabolism Clinics of North America*, 1997; **26**: 575–98.

6. **Lee WL, Zinman B.** From insulin to insulin analogues: progress in the treatment of type 1 diabetes mellitus. *Diabetes Reviews*, 1998; **6**: 73–88.

7. **Holleman F, Hoekstra JBL.** Insulin lispro. *New England Journal of Medicine*, 1997; **337**: 176–83.

8. **Garg SK et al.** Pre-meal insulin analogue insulin lispro vs humulin R insulin treatment in young subjects with type 1 diabetes. *Diabetic Medicine*, 1996; **13**: 47–52.

9. **Home PD, Lindholm A, Hylleberg B, Round P.** Improved glycemic control with insulin aspart: a multicenter randomized double-blind crossover trial in type 1 diabetic patients. UK Insulin Aspart Study Group. *Diabetes Care*, 1998; **21**: 1904–9.

10. **Rosskamp RH, Park G**. Long-acting insulin analogs. *Diabetes Care*, 1999; **22**(suppl. 2): B109–13.

11. **The Diabetes Control and Complications Trial Research Group**. Effect of intensive therapy on residual beta-cell function in patients with type 1 diabetes in the Diabetes Control and Complications Trial. *Annals of Internal Medicine*, 1998; **128**: 517–23.

12. **Diabetes Control and Complications Trial Research Group**. The effect of intensive treatment of diabetes on the development and progression of long-term complications in insulin-dependent diabetes mellitus. *New England Journal of Medicine*, 1993; **329**: 977–86.

13. **Lawson ML, Gerstein HC, Tsui E, Zinman B**. Effect of intensive therapy on early macrovascular disease in young individuals with type 1 diabetes. *Diabetes Care*, 1999; **22**: B35–9.

14. **The Canadian Lispro Study Group**. Effectiveness of human ultralente versus NPH insulin in providing basal insulin replacement for an insulin lispro multiple daily injection regimen. *Diabetes Care*, 1999; **22**: 603–8.

15. **Zinman B, Tildesley H, Chiasson JL, Tsui E, Strack T**. Insulin lispro in CSII: results of a double-blind crossover study. *Diabetes*, 1997; **46**: 440–3.

16. **Muller UA** *et al.* Intensified treatment and education of type 1 diabetes as clinical routine. A nationwide quality-circle experience in Germany. ASD (the Working Group on Structured Diabetes Therapy of the German Diabetes Association). *Diabetes Care*, 1999; **22**(suppl. 2): B29–34.

17. **Jehle PM, Micheler C, Jehle DR, Breitig D, Boehm BO**. Inadequate suspension of neutral protamine Hagedorn (NPH) insulin in pens. *Lancet*, 1999; **354**: 1604–7.

18. **Terent A, Hagfall O, Cederholm U**. The effect of education and self-monitoring of blood glucose on glycosylated haemoglobin in type I diabetes: a controlled 18-month trial in a representative population. *Acta Medica Scandinavica*, 1985; **217**: 47–53.

19. **Diabetes Control and Complications Trial Research Group**. The relationship of glycemic exposure (HbA$_{1c}$) to the risk of development and progression of retinopathy in the Diabetes Control and Complications Trial. *Diabetes*, 1999; **44**: 968–83.

20. **Meltzer S** *et al.* 1998 clinical practice guidelines for the management of diabetes in Canada. *Canadian Medical Association Journal*, 1998; **159**: S1–29.

21. **Renold AE, Marble A, Fawcett DW**. Action of insulin on deposition of glycogen and storage of fat in adipose tissue. *Endocrinology*, 1950; **40**: 55–66.

22. **Saudek CD**. Novel forms of insulin delivery. *Endocrinology and Metabolism Clinics of North America*, 1997; **26**: 599–610.

23. **Skyler JS** *et al.* Efficacy of inhaled human insulin in type 1 diabetes mellitus: a randomised proof-of-concept study. *Lancet*, 2001; **357**: 324–5.

24. **Sutherland DE, Gruessner AC, Gruessner RW**. Pancreas transplantation: a review. *Transplantation Proceedings*, 1998; **30**: 1940–3.

25. **United Network for Organ Sharing**. Critical data, pancreatic transplant registry data. From UNOS web site, http://www.unos.org. Data as of 2000 June 30.

26. **Lacy PE**. Status of islet cell transplantation. *Diabetes Care*, 1993; **1**: 76.

27. **Shapiro AMJ** *et al.* Islet transplantation in seven patients with type 1 diabetes mellitus using a glucocorticoid-free immunosuppressive regimen. *New England Journal of Medicine*, 2000; **343**: 230–8.

# 5 Treatment of type 2 diabetes

*Tara Wallace and D.R. Matthews*

## Aims of treatment

The strategy for the treatment of type 2 diabetes mellitus is based on our understanding of its cause and pathology. The short-term aims are to ameliorate the acute symptoms of hyperglycaemia such as thirst, polyuria and tiredness. The strategic plan, however, must be aimed at restoring well-being and prevention of long-term complications, namely cardiovascular, cerebrovascular and peripheral vascular disease, retinopathy, nephropathy and neuropathy.

Obesity and sedentary lifestyles are clearly associated with the increased prevalence of diabetes and so diet and an exercise plan are necessary. Metformin may prevent weight increase and gastrointestinal enzyme modifiers can act to decrease nutrient absorption. Decreased $\beta$-cell function is a consistent finding and methods for treating this include sulphonylureas and insulin. Insulin resistance can be ameliorated by weight loss and by thiazolidinediones. There is also a quest for agents which slow glycosylation of proteins.

Since atherosclerotic processes play such a major role in the morbidity of diabetes it is of paramount importance that other risks for them are minimized. This involves the cessation of smoking, the reduction of blood pressure and strict attention to maintaining normal lipid levels (Table 1).

Finally, in strategic terms, there is a necessity to take a very long-term view. The United Kingdom Prospective Diabetes Study (UKPDS) provided evidence that intensive glucose control and tight blood pressure control were beneficial. The study lasted for 20 years and the benefits emerged over 10 years. The lesson from this is that therapy, advice, care, and encouragement are needed by committed professionals over many years and that there are no quick fixes.

## Targets for glycaemic control

The UKPDS – the largest ever prospective study of type 2 diabetes – demonstrated that patients in an intensively treated group had a 12 per cent reduction in any diabetes endpoint ($p = 0.029$) and a 25 per cent reduction in microvascular endpoints ($p = 0.0099$) compared to a parallel patient group on conventional therapy.[1] Intensive therapy achieved a median glycated haemoglobin ($HbA_{1c}$) of 7.0 per cent at 10 years compared, to 7.9 per cent. However 7.0 per cent $HbA_{1c}$ cannot be regarded as a target – in the UKPDS it was simply the median value achieved in the intensively treated group. The target in this group was for fasting plasma glucose of 6 mmol/l but was constrained by the need for the UKPDS to address the question of monotherapy – therapy was not always modified if the target was exceeded. However the UKPDS epidemiology study[2] was concordant with the trial data. This showed that diabetic complications were a function of updated (pre-existing) $HbA_{1c}$ – a 1 per cent decrease in $HbA_{1c}$ resulted in a 21 per cent reduction in endpoint events.[1] This applied across the whole range of $HbA_{1c}$ values, indicating a log-linear relationship between the hazard ratio and $HbA_{1c}$. The lack of any discernible threshold at which the beneficial effects of improved glycaemic control become apparent strongly suggests that there is the potential for clinical gain at any level of glycaemia.

The aim of treatment should therefore be to lower the glucose levels to as near to those of the normal population as possible – any improvement in $HbA_{1c}$ would dramatically reduce the risk of diabetic complications. In practice normal $HbA_{1c}$ is almost impossible to achieve except very early in the course of the disease. Over-enthusiastic lowering of $HbA_{1c}$ leads to unacceptable risks of hypoglycaemia. In clinical practice a target of $HbA_{1c}$ of 7 per cent might be ideal, but pragmatically it may not always be possible nor practical to achieve.

**Table 1** Treatment of type 2 diabetes: aims and therapies

| Strategic aim | Tactical aim | Treatment |
|---|---|---|
| Prevention of tissue damage | Prevention of hyperglycaemic symptoms | Sulphonylureas, repaglinide *Increase insulin secretion* |
| | | Insulin |
| | | Metformin |
| | | Acarbose *Delays carbohydrate absorption* |
| | | Thiazolidinediones *Decrease insulin resistance* |
| | Treatment of hypertension | Choice of drug less important than achieving normotension |
| | Cessation of smoking | |
| | Treatment of dyslipidaemia | Statin (hypercholesterolaemia) Fibrate (hypertriglyceridaemia) |

# Lifestyle modification

## Diet

Diet is the mainstay of treatment of type 2 diabetes. Many people with type 2 diabetes are overweight at diagnosis: the mean body mass index of patients at entry to the UKPDS was 27.5 kg/m$^2$.[1] Calorie restriction to achieve normal weight is important and this, together with restricting rapidly absorbable sugars and increasing fibre, will often allow rapid amelioration of symptoms. The UKPDS showed that a dramatic reduction of weight was possible in the first three months of treatment and that glycaemia rapidly improved.

The basis of dietary advice is that at least 55 per cent of the total energy content of diet should be in the form of carbohydrate, total fat intake should be restricted to less than 30 per cent (saturated fat less than 10 per cent) and protein intake should be in the order of 10–15 per cent. Sucrose intake should be limited to less than 50 g a day. Patients should be advised to eat regular meals and aim to eat five portions of fruit or vegetables every day. The manipulation of the diet, apart from caloric restriction to achieve optimal weight loss, is designed to provide slow, moderate increments in blood glucose concentration and avoid rapid large increments, with which the failing pancreas is unable to cope. For these reasons, the mainstay of the diet is regular intake of slowly absorbed, complex carbohydrates, as in starchy foods. There is no place for commercial 'diabetic' foods – in addition to being high in fat content and calories, these foods contain bulk sweeteners (fructose, sorbitol and isomalt) which raise blood glucose levels. The use of non-caloric sweeteners such as aspartame and saccharin are acceptable whereas sorbitol and fructose should be avoided because of their caloric content.

Although intensive treatment with sulphonylureas or insulin is associated with weight gain, the UKPDS provides evidence that the benefits of tight glycaemic control outweigh the risks associated with weight gain.[1] However, patients and physicians need to address the problem pro-actively: patients should be told to reduce their insulin if they get recurrent hypoglycaemia rather than increase food intake; snacks should be discouraged in those on long-acting insulin alone and additional dietetic advice about reduction of total calorie intake may be necessary.

## Exercise

Acute exercise lowers plasma glucose in diabetic subjects by enhancing the effect of insulin on glucose entry into skeletal muscle, that is it improves insulin sensitivity.[3] When training is discontinued, the increased insulin sensitivity is lost within a few days.[4] Exercise also produces beneficial effects on the cardiovascular system and helps to achieve and maintain an ideal body weight. Although difficult to substantiate scientifically, it is observable in clinical practice that those who continue to maintain their physical fitness develop less complications. The association is not robust, however, since those who develop complications are likely to reduce their exercise.

# Drug treatment of type 2 diabetes

The UKPDS has shown that good glycaemic and blood pressure control are of paramount importance in the prevention of the development of long-term complications. The study demonstrated that an intensive glycaemic treatment policy was associated with a 12 per cent reduction in any diabetes endpoint ($p = 0.029$) and a 25 per cent reduction in microvascular endpoints ($p = 0.0099$).[1] In order to halt the inexorable rise in blood glucose it is essential to appreciate the fact that $\beta$-cell failure is a progressive process. The UKPDS showed a reduction in $\beta$-cell function from a mean of 50 per cent at diagnosis to 25 per cent at five years.[5] The fasting plasma glucose rose at a rate of approximately 0.2 mmol/year[5] and the HbA1c at 0.2 per cent per year (Fig. 1). However in the Belfast study,[6] this relatively slow rate of increase occurred only in those patients with the lowest mean fasting plasma glucose at diagnosis (7.5 mmol/l) and half of the patients in that study deteriorated at the significantly faster rate of 1.5 mmol/l/year. There is no currently available therapy that stops the decline in $\beta$-cell function, hence it is necessary to intensify treatment regularly in order to maintain a given level of glycaemic control.

## Drugs increasing insulin levels

### Sulphonylureas

Sulphonylureas are chemically related to sulphonamides; their hypoglycaemic actions were discovered in 1942 when it was noticed that two patients with typhoid being treated with a sulphonamide derivative died of hypoglycaemia. Sulphonylureas bind to sulphonylurea receptors on the $\beta$-cell plasma membrane, causing closure of ATP-sensitive potassium channels (Kir) leading to depolarization of the cell membrane. This in turn opens voltage-gated calcium channels, allowing influx of calcium ions and subsequent secretion of insulin (Fig. 2).

The first generation sulphonylurea, chlorpropamide, has a relatively long half-life and can be given once daily. Its long half-life makes it less popular in those prone to hypoglycaemia, particularly the elderly. Some patients may experience facial flushing following the ingestion of alcohol while taking chlorpropamide and it enhances the action of antidiuretic hormone and may rarely result in hyponatraemia. In the UKPDS it was found that treatment with chlorpropamide was associated with significantly higher blood pressure than treatment with glibenclamide, metformin or insulin[1] and did not prevent retinopathy. Tolbutamide has the potential advantage of being metabolized by the liver and not excreted renally, hence allowing its use in early renal impairment. However, its safety profile was questioned in the

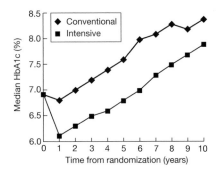

**Fig. 1** A comparison of HbA1c against time from randomization in the UKPDS conventionally and intensively treated groups.

UGDP (University Group Diabetes Program) trial[7] and, although the risks of its use have never been substantiated, it still carries a US government prescription warning. The so-called 'second-generation' sulphonylureas, namely gliclazide, glibenclamide, glipizide and gliquidone, have shorter plasma half-lives and have generally been given twice daily. There is growing evidence that this is unnecessary, since their effects depend on their receptor binding which lasts much longer than their plasma phase. These agents are more likely to be given once daily in the future (Table 2).

Sulphonylureas are generally well tolerated but hypoglycaemia and weight gain are notable side effects, and patients may experience mild gastrointestinal disturbances and headaches. Hypersensitivity reactions are uncommon but may occur in the first 6–8 weeks of therapy and include transient rashes (which may rarely proceed to erythema multiforme and exfoliative dermatitis), fever, and jaundice. Blood disorders are rare but include thrombocytopaenia, agranulocytosis and aplastic anaemia.

Despite previous concerns about the possibility of tolbutamide playing a role in preventing ischaemic preconditioning,[7] no deleterious effect of sulphonylureas was seen on macrovascular endpoints in the UKPDS.[1]

### Repaglinide

Repaglinide is a new insulin secretagogue that differs from sulphonylureas in its chemical structure. It acts on $\beta$-cell receptors to stimulate insulin secretion, via a binding site on the ATP-sensitive potassium channel possibly distinct from that of the sulphonylurea receptor. Due to its rapid absorption and short plasma half-life (approximately one hour) it acts as a postprandial glucose regulator. It is excreted predominantly via the bile with only about 6 per cent being excreted via the kidneys,[8] which makes it an attractive option for patients with impaired renal function. Repaglinide is taken about 15 min before a meal starting at a dose of 0.5 mg once daily and titrating the dose up to a maximum of 4 mg four times daily.

In short-term trials, studying small numbers of patients, repaglinide has been shown to lower mean $HbA_{1c}$ by 1.8 per cent, mean fasting plasma glucose by 2.4 mmol/l and mean postprandial plasma glucose by 3.1 mmol/l.[9] Repaglinide appears to be well tolerated; the most commonly reported side effect is hypoglycaemia which is most likely to occur during dose titration.[9] Overall the hypoglycaemia rate is likely to be lower than that found with other sulphonylureas. It has proved efficacious and safe in the short term when used in combination with metformin.[10] Another new agent with a similar time course of action is nateglinide. Further clinical trials are necessary to establish the role of these agents in our clinical armamentarium.

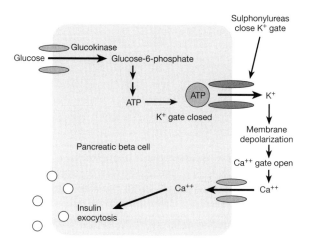

**Fig. 2** The mechanism of action of sulphonylureas.

**Table 2** Pharmacokinetics of some sulphonylureas

| Drug | Dose | Metabolism | Comments |
|---|---|---|---|
| Chlorpropamide | 125–500 mg | Hepatic<br>~20% excreted unchanged in urine | ?adverse effects on blood pressure |
| Tolbutamide | 0.5–2 g | Hepatic<br><20% excreted unchanged in urine | Concerns raised over possible increase in cardiovascular risk in UDPG |
| Glibenclamide | 2.5–15 mg | Hepatic (~100%)<br>Metabolites excreted in bile (50%) and urine (50%) | Risk of hypoglycaemia early in treatment |
| Gliclazide | 40–320 mg | Hepatic<br><5% excreted unchanged in urine | Useful first line treatment |
| Glipizide | 2.5–40 mg | Hepatic<br><10% excreted unchanged in urine | |
| Glimepiride | 1–6 mg | Hepatic | |
| Repaglinide | 4–16 mg | Hepatic<br>Excreted in bile (6% in urine) | Given preprandially |

### Sulphonylurea failure versus sulphonylurea inadequacy

$\beta$-cell failure is a progressive process and there is no currently identified treatment capable of stopping this. A distinction needs to be drawn between inadequate treatment and treatment failure. The former is the result of failing to recognise the need to intensify treatment regularly in order to maintain a given level of glycaemia. The latter is due to the eventual inability of the $\beta$-cell to secrete adequate insulin even with augmentation by sulphonylureas. In the UKPDS, failure of sulphonylurea therapy was significantly faster in those who had a higher fasting plasma glucose at diagnosis. Sixty one per cent of those who had fasting glucose greater than or equal to 10 mmol/l at randomization required additional therapy at six years compared to 23 per cent of those with a fasting glucose less than 7.8 mmol/l ($p = 0.00001$).[11]

## Drugs reducing insulin resistance/suppressing excessive hepatic glucose production

### Biguanides

Metformin and phenformin were introduced in the late 1950s. Phenformin was subsequently withdrawn from clinical use when an association with lactic acidosis was noted in the late 1970s.

Metformin (dimethylbiguanide) lowers blood glucose levels by increasing peripheral uptake of glucose and decreasing gluconeogenesis. It has no effects on insulin secretion and clinical hypoglycaemia is rare. Metformin can be expected to lower fasting plasma glucose by approximately 2 mmol/l and HbA1c by approximately 1 per cent.[12]

In contrast to other treatments, metformin does not cause weight gain[13] and may promote weight loss.[12] On starting metformin, approximately one third of patients will have transient nausea, anorexia or diarrhoea, which can be attenuated by starting with a low dose (500 mg daily) and gradually increasing the dose up to a maximum of 850 mg thrice daily. It can be used as monotherapy, particularly in overweight patients, or in combination with sulphonylureas.

Metformin is excreted unchanged via the kidneys by a combination of glomerular filtration and tubular secretion.[14] It is contraindicated in those with impaired renal or hepatic function, cardiac failure or a history of alcohol abuse as the presence of these conditions increases the risk of developing lactic acidosis. Renal function must be monitored regularly while patients continue on metformin, with a deterioration in plasma creatinine indicating the need to discontinue the drug.

#### Lactic acidosis

Lactic acidosis is a rare but serious adverse effect associated with metformin use and is estimated to have an incidence of 0.03 per 1000 patient years.[14] Most cases of metformin associated lactic acidosis arise in patients in whom the presence of contraindications has been overlooked and is not necessarily due to metformin accumulation.[15] In the event of accumulation, metformin can be removed by dialysis.[16] The mortality rate is about 50 per cent: the prognosis being dependent on the severity of the underlying condition.[15] The risk of death from lactic acidosis in metformin-treated patients is similar to that of hypoglycaemia in sulphonylurea-treated patients.[17]

### Thiazolidinediones

The thiazolidinediones are a new class of agents introduced in 1997. They have direct effects on insulin resistance by selectively binding to nuclear peroxisome proliferator activator receptors (PPAR$\gamma$) which improve peripheral actions of insulin. The first agent on the market was troglitazone which, used as monotherapy, caused a 0.8–1.3 per cent reduction in HbA1c after 1–4 weeks for an initial response, reaching a maximum response at 8–12 weeks. However a small number of patients experienced capricious effects of hepatotoxicity and the drug was withdrawn in the UK late in 1998. It continued to be prescribed in the US, and was used in the Diabetes Prevention Program with the caveat that regular liver-function testing would be necessary. Despite this caution at least one person died of fulminant hepatic failure. Newer thiazolidinediones (rosiglitazone and pioglitazone) have no reported hepatotoxicity and are likely to be used more widely in clinical practice. Both rosiglitazone and pioglitazone are licensed for monotherapy in the USA but only for combination therapy (i.e. with either sulphonylurea *or* metformin) in Europe. Rosiglitazone causes a rise in LDL cholesterol early in its use, whereas pioglitazone reduces LDL. Both drugs increase HDL cholesterol. Results from outcome studies are not yet available. The thiazolidinediones are associated with marked weight gain within a few months of initiation of therapy.

## Drugs affecting absorption of nutrients

A variety of drugs have been developed which alter the absorption of food from the gastrointestinal tract. All these drugs cause side effects related to the retention of these nutrients in the gut and it is a better option to encourage patients to make appropriate dietary changes.

### Acarbose

Acarbose is a complex oligosaccharide that reversibly inhibits $\alpha$-glucosidase enzymes in the small intestine when administered orally. It has an affinity 10–100 000 times that of sucrose for $\alpha$-glucosidase. It delays the cleavage of oligo- and disaccharides to monosaccharides and this results in delayed absorption of carbohydrate and lower peak postprandial blood glucose levels. The resultant undigested carbohydrate in the lower gastrointestinal tract accounts for the most common side effects of flatulence, diarrhoea, and cramping. The side effects lessen with time and can be attenuated by titrating the dose up gradually from 50 mg once daily to a maximum dose of 100 mg thrice daily. In practice the maximum dose is often limited by gastrointestinal side effects. In order to be effective, acarbose must be taken with the first mouthful of a meal. Acarbose may induce elevation of hepatic transaminases which is reversible on withdrawal of treatment. Liver transaminases should be monitored for the first year of treatment.

Less than 2 per cent of intact acarbose is absorbed but it is metabolised in the intestinal tract and approximately one-third of inactive metabolites are absorbed and subsequently excreted in the urine. Acarbose results in a mean fall in fasting plasma glucose of 1.22 mmol/l,[18] a mean decrease in postprandial blood glucose of 2.8 mmol/l[18] and a mean decrease in HbA1c of 0.73–1.1 per cent.[19] When used as monotherapy, acarbose does not cause hypoglycaemia but if hypoglycaemic episodes occur in patients on combination therapy it is important to treat this with glucose not sucrose, since sucrose absorption is impaired by the drug.

### Guar gum

Guar, a gum extracted from plant sources, may be used as a supplement to soluble fibre in the diet. It reduces postprandial glycaemia by slowing intestinal glucose absorption. The recommended dose is 5 g three times a day, either sprinkled on food or stirred into 200 ml of fluid. Side effects include flatulence, abdominal distension and gastrointestinal obstruction.

### Orlistat

Orlistat is an antiobesity agent that acts by inhibition of pancreatic lipase. When taken orally, with meals, it results in a dose dependent reduction (of up to 30 per cent) in dietary fat absorption. Although orlistat promotes weight loss, gastrointestinal side effects occur in approximately 80 per cent of patients[20] which may limit its use in clinical practice. However it represents a potential pharmacological agent for use in the treatment of obesity.

### Agents not commercially available

Glucagon-like peptide (GLP-1) is a peptide hormone produced as a result of post-translational processing of pro-glucagon. It is secreted by enteroglucagon-producing cells in the lower gut, i.e. distal jejunum, ileum, colon and rectum, and has a plasma half-life of about 15 min.[21] GLP-1 causes glucose-dependent stimulation of insulin secretion[22] and also inhibits glucagon secretion.[23] The latter is also a glucose-dependent process and so the glucagon response to hypoglycaemia is preserved. GLP-1 delays gastric emptying following liquid meals and may have similar effects following solid meals. It is also thought to suppress appetite via effects on the central nervous system[24] and possibly to accelerate pro-insulin synthesis. Although GLP-1 exerts a variety of antidiabetic actions, in trials it has been necessary to administer GLP-1 either as a continuous intravenous infusion or as subcutaneous injections every two hours which is clearly not acceptable in clinical practice. If GLP-1 is to be put to therapeutic use, other methods of administration or sustained release formulations will need to be developed.

Pramlintide is a synthetic analogue of amylin, also known as islet associated polypeptide (IAPP). It is a 37 amino acid polypeptide that is synthesized and secreted by pancreatic $\beta$-cells.[25] IAPP concentrations are markedly reduced in type 1 diabetes and perhaps increased in type 2. The $\beta$-pleating of multiple chains of IAPP causes the amyloidosis seen in $\beta$-cells in man and this may be one of the causes of progressive deterioration of $\beta$-cell function. Pramlintide has been shown to slow gastric emptying[26] and it causes a reduction in postprandial glucose excursions. Documented side effects include nausea. In studies it has been administered either as an intravenous infusion or as thrice-daily subcutaneous injections that would limit its use should it be introduced into clinical practice.

## Insulin

Insulin is indicated for the treatment of type 2 diabetes when oral therapy and diet have failed to provide adequate glycaemic control. It can be used as monotherapy or in combination with oral agents. The UKPDS demonstrated its successful use as a first-line therapy after diet failure,[1] but in practice most physicians continue to use it after failure of oral therapies.

### Insulin regime

Once daily nocturnal isophane insulin aims to normalize fasting plasma glucose and is used in combination with sulphonylureas and metformin. It may be the most appropriate regime for very elderly patients, those in whom the aim of treatment is merely to provide symptomatic relief, and in patients unable to give their own injections (in which case it may be more practical to give the insulin in the morning). It may also be an effective way of introducing the idea of insulin to a reluctant patient and can provide adequate control for prolonged periods.

Most patients, however, require twice daily insulin in the form of pre-mixed insulins consisting of a mixture of soluble (rapid acting) and isophane (intermediate duration) insulin, for example, 30 per cent soluble and 70 per cent isophane insulin. With this regimen, sulphonylureas should be discontinued, although it makes sense to continue metformin therapy in overweight patients in an attempt to offset the inevitable weight gain associated with intensifying therapy.

Basal bolus regimes consisting of preprandial soluble insulin with nocturnal isophane are not usually required in the treatment of type 2 diabetes, but may allow patients greater flexibility in their lifestyles. With growing interest in the potential influence of postprandial glucose control in the prognosis for type 2 diabetes, the use of pre-meal injections of short acting insulins is being re-explored but there are no data on which to base a change in practice at the time of writing.

### Dose

The average insulin dose requirement is in the order of 0.5 units/kg/day but varies hugely between patients, some needing as much as 400 units daily. Overweight patients usually require higher doses, for example, 1–2 units/kg/day. The logical approach to starting insulin is to start with a low dose, for example, 14 units a day and titrate upwards over a few weeks, guided by blood test results.

### Atherogenicity

As many people with type 2 diabetes are overweight[1] and insulin resistant,[27] they often require high doses of insulin. This has led to concerns about possible atherogenic effects of insulin.[28] The UKPDS showed no increase in myocardial infarction rates in the intensively treated group and no difference in macrovascular endpoints between the intensively and conventionally treated groups. A 16 per cent risk reduction in myocardial infarction with intensive treatment was of borderline significance ($p = 0.052$). This may reflect the relatively short follow up time of 10 years, compared to the median life expectancy, at diagnosis, of 20 years.[1] The benefits conferred by good control outweigh any theoretical and unsubstantiated disadvantages of insulin therapy.

## Combination therapy

Combination therapy with more than one oral agent is standard practice. Metformin monotherapy is used as a first line treatment in overweight patients but can usefully be supplemented with sulphonylureas. This therapy is a rational approach addressing the problems of increased insulin resistance and reduced insulin secretion. Thiazolidinediones and sulphonylureas are an equally logical combination. Triple oral therapy using secretagogues, insulin resistance

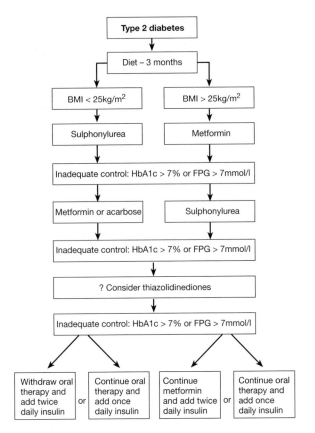

**Fig. 3** Algorithm for the treatment of glycaemia in type 2 diabetes.

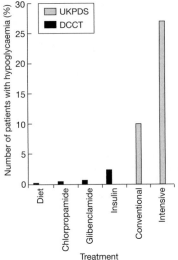

**Fig. 4** Number of patients experiencing one or more severe hypoglycaemic episodes per year in the UKDPS intensively treated group and the DCCT.

modulators and acarbose have been reported and show some success. In view of the progressive nature of $\beta$-cell failure it is essential to reassess the adequacy of treatment on a regular basis. The combination of acarbose and orlistat should be avoided as both produce gastrointestinal side effects.

Combining insulin with oral agents has some advantages, both theoretical and practical. Enthusiasm for combinations varies widely however and one body of opinion suggests that once insulin therapy is initiated then patients should be given the benefit of having to take fewer tablets. No trial data are available for clinical outcomes and so therapy continues to be based on glycaemic performance and patient preference. A logical combination is that of insulin and metformin, especially late in the course of the disease when $\beta$-cell function may be markedly impaired (Fig. 3).

# Complications of treatment

## Hypoglycaemia

In the Diabetes Control and Complications Trial (DCCT), intensive treatment in type 1 diabetes was accompanied by a threefold increase in rate of hypoglycaemia ($p < 0.001$): 27 per cent of intensively treated experienced at least one episode of severe hypoglycaemia during the first year compared to 10 per cent in the conventionally

treated group.[29] However, the high rates of hypoglycaemia in type 1 diabetes in the DCCT are not relevant to type 2 diabetes. The UKPDS intensively treated group showed a 2.3 per cent annual incidence of severe (requiring help from another person) hypoglycaemia in those on insulin and a much lower percentage rate for those on oral agents (Fig. 4).[1]

Although the increased potential for hypoglycaemic episodes with intensive treatment may limit the degree of control attainable, this should not deter clinicians and patients from attempting to achieve tighter control. Appropriate oral therapy can minimise hypoglycaemia (glibenclamide causes more hypoglycaemia than chlorpropamide and metformin less than any sulphonylurea) and patients should be reassured that disabling hypoglycaemic episodes are not common. There is no inherent reason why clinicians should be prepared for some hypoglycaemia episodes in type 1 diabetes and not in type 2 – the aim of therapy is the same, namely to avoid complications by appropriate glycaemic management.

## Treatment of hypoglycaemia

All patients on hypoglycaemic agents, but especially those patients taking glibenclamide or insulin, need to be advised to carry glucose. When treating an acute episode of hypoglycaemia, it is important that the ingestion of oral glucose is followed by a long-acting carbohydrate snack in order to prevent hypoglycaemia recurring.

Patients experiencing recurrent hypoglycaemia should be advised to reduce their insulin (or oral hypoglycaemic) dose rather than to increase their food intake.

# Cardiovascular risk factors

Diabetes is associated with a 2–4 fold increase in cardiovascular mortality[30] which accounts for 50–60 per cent of deaths in the diabetic population.[31] Not only is coronary artery disease more common in type 2 diabetes, but it is associated with an increase in acute mortality following myocardial infarction[30] and a higher rate of reinfarction. Silent ischaemia is more common and carries a worse prognosis in diabetes than in the normal population. Other forms of large blood vessel disease – accelerated atherosclerosis – also occur earlier and more intensively in type 2 diabetes and active management of the additional risk factors for cardiovascular disease in diabetic patients is essential.

All patients with diabetes need education aimed at helping them optimize their diet, achieve and maintain an ideal body weight and encourage them to take some form of regular exercise. In addition all those with diabetes should be strongly advised against smoking and helped to achieve stopping, if necessary. Smoking cessation is associated with a 40–50 per cent reduction in the risk of recurrence of acute ischaemic syndrome or coronary death in patients with coronary artery disease. Five years after smoking cessation, the additional risk from smoking has reverted to zero.[32]

The use of aspirin should be recommended in patients with evidence of macrovascular disease and considered in those with microalbuminuria or proteinuria, hypertension, dyslipidaemia and cigarette smoking. People with diabetes derive at least as great a benefit from aspirin in terms of risk reduction of myocardial infarction and stroke as do the non-diabetic population.[33]

Strokes account for 15 per cent of all deaths in type 2 diabetes and the majority are thrombotic, not haemorrhagic.[34] There is no increase in the incidence of haemorrhagic stroke, gastrointestinal haemorrhage, retinal nor vitreous haemorrhage in diabetic patients treated with aspirin.[35] The risk of gastrointestinal bleeding can be further minimized by using enteric-coated aspirin and prescribing low doses.

There is compelling evidence for the use of β-blockers as secondary prevention in diabetes. β-blockade confers a reduction in relative risk of mortality following myocardial infarction of between 39 per cent and 63 per cent in diabetic patients,[36] a greater benefit than derived by non-diabetic patients. They have also been shown to be beneficial in all subjects in the treatment of myocardial infarction complicated by heart failure, reducing the mortality by 30 per cent and incidence of recurrent heart failure by 21 per cent.[37] Although β-blockers pose a theoretical risk of deterioration in glycaemic control and blunting of counterregulatory response to hypoglycaemia, these are rarely a problem in clinical practice. Critical limb ischaemia is an absolute contraindication to the use of β-blockers but peripheral vascular disease *per se* is not, even in the presence of intermittent claudication.[38]

## Lipids

The hallmark dyslipidaemia of type 2 diabetes is hypertriglyceridaemia, which is often raised in association with hyperglycaemia. It is thought to be an independent risk factor for ischaemic heart disease. Hypercholesterolaemia is no more frequent than in the normal population, but the risks associated with raised cholesterol are much higher.[39] The European Atherosclerosis Society guidelines suggest much lower thresholds for intervention in hyperlipidaemia when diabetes coexists simply because the major risk in diabetes for morbidity and mortality is ischaemic heart disease. However although their table giving guidelines for intervention thresholds, is helpful in the mid-age ranges, it is not useful in younger age groups in whom a longer term view needs to be taken. The tables fail to take into account family history of coronary heart disease, make no distinction between ex- and current smokers

and underestimate the influence of hypertension if the blood pressure value is obtained while on antihypertensive treatment. The tables are falsely reassuring in younger patients in whom familial hypercholesterolaemia is likely.

Once ischaemic heart disease is apparent, thresholds for intervention should be lowered. The strongest indicator of risk for myocardial infarction is having previously had an ischaemic episode, and so the aim should be to lower cholesterol below 5.0 mmol/l and triglycerides below 2.0 mmol/l.

The first line of treatment is to advise patients to adopt a healthier lifestyle by: modifying dietary fat intake, taking regular exercise, which increases HDL-cholesterol (high-density lipoprotein) levels in addition to promoting weight loss, and giving up smoking.

The pharmacological agent used depends on the major abnormality detected: predominant hypercholesterolaemia should be treated with statins and hypertriglyceridaemia with fibrates but in isolated hypertriglyceridaemia, glycaemia should be optimized prior to pharmacotherapy. Combined hyperlipidaemia treatment depends on the predominant abnormality. The optimal outcome from these treatments has not yet been assessed in a prospective trial, though one is now under way.[39]

## Hormone replacement therapy (HRT)

Orally administered oestradiol has favourable effects on the lipid profile: it increases HDL concentrations by approximately 20 per cent[40,41] in diabetic women (a figure comparable with non-diabetic women), with no significant increase in triglycerides.[41] In short term studies, oestrogen replacement has also been shown to reduce HbA$_{1c}$, fasting plasma glucose, C-peptide levels[41] and plasminogen activator inhibitor-1 antigen concentrations.[40] Despite the fact that postmenopausal diabetic women are at increased risk of developing ischaemic heart disease, compared to their non-diabetic counterparts, they are currently only half as likely to be on HRT.[42] Even though HRT exerts beneficial effects on HDL and LDL (low-density lipoprotein) cholesterol levels, current evidence does not show a role for HRT in the secondary prevention of cardiovascular disease in the general population over the short term; although there is no need to discontinue HRT in a woman already on it.[43] Although longer term prospective studies with combined oestrogen and progesterone preparations in diabetic women are lacking, based on present knowledge, HRT should be offered to postmenopausal diabetic women after discussion of the pros and cons and in the absence of any contraindications.

## Blood pressure control

Hypertension is common in patients with type 2 diabetes: about 40 per cent are hypertensive at the age of 45 rising to 60 per cent by the age of 75.[44] The UKPDS showed clear benefits of tight blood pressure control in terms of reducing complications (Table 3); the median blood pressure achieved in the tight control group was 144/82 compared to 154/87 in the conventional group. There was no difference in the benefit conferred by captopril and atenolol which suggests that reducing the blood pressure is more important than which particular drug is used. The study also demonstrated the need for polypharmacy in order to control hypertension: by nine years 29 per cent of those allocated to tight blood pressure control required at least three antihypertensive agents.[42]

First line antihypertensive agents include low dose diuretics, cardio-selective β-blockers and angiotensin-converting enzyme (ACE) inhibitors. The choice of agent depends on the clinical situation: patients with microalbuminuria or left ventricular failure derive additional benefits from ACE inhibitors, while those with ischaemic heart disease benefit from treatment with β-blockers. The use of diuretics and calcium channel blockers are recommended in Afro-Caribbean patients as β-blockers and ACE inhibitors are less efficacious in this group.

There is no evidence that cardio-selective β-blockers decrease β-cell function in type 2 diabetes nor is there any evidence that they increase the risk of hypoglycaemic unawareness.

Second line agents include α-blockers, calcium channel blockers and angiotensinogen 2 receptor agonists. When more than one agent is needed, logical combinations should be used such as: a diuretic and an ACE inhibitor, a diuretic and a β-blocker, a β-blocker and a calcium channel blocker. The UKPDS demonstrated no threshold at which intensifying antihypertensive treatment ceases to have beneficial

effects and, unlike aiming for tight glycaemic goals, the risks of over-treatment are minimal.

## Monitoring glycaemic control

Home blood glucose monitoring using meter recordings is essential for all those taking insulin therapy (Table 4). There is no other rational way of adjusting insulin dosage and the education of the patient in the appropriate recording of data and changing of insulin is essential.

Fasting plasma glucose is a cheap and efficient way of monitoring the generality of control in type 2 diabetes. It is worth checking HbA₁c as well on a periodic basis as this will assess basal and post-prandial glycaemia. In view of the progressive decline in β-cell function it is essential to monitor diabetes on a regular basis in order to increase therapy appropriately.

## Screening for complications

Type 2 diabetes is associated with macrovascular and microvascular long-term complications. Screening for complications necessitates annual assessment of various clinical parameters (Table 5).

**Table 3** Relative risk for the development of complications with tight blood pressure control in the UKPDS

| Clinical endpoint | Relative risk | p value |
|---|---|---|
| Any diabetes related endpoint | 0.76 | 0.0046 |
| Diabetes related death | 0.68 | 0.019 |
| Stroke | 0.56 | 0.013 |
| Microvascular disease | 0.63 | 0.0092 |
| Retinal photocoagulation | 0.66 | 0.004 |
| Deterioration in visual acuity* | 0.53 | 0.0036 |

* Deterioration in visual acuity by 3 lines using a ETDRS chart (or 2 lines on a Snellen chart). This suggests that tight blood pressure control prevents maculopathy in addition to retinopathy.

**Table 4** Rules for monitoring glycaemia

| Recommendations for monitoring | Comments |
|---|---|
| Use electronic meter | Colour-matching strips are inaccurate |
| Measure preprandial glucose | Postprandial glucose excursions are subject to wide changes and data therefore are inconsistent from day to day |
| Record data | Emphasize that without records it is impossible to assess trends |
| Assess trends | Over a one or two week period |
| Fix hypoglycaemia | If hypoglycaemia was unexpected or unexplained, then reduce dose of insulin at time of day responsible |
| Fix hyperglycaemia | Increase insulin by 10% at time of day likely to improve the problem |
| Continue to assess trends | … but wait a few days for new trends to emerge before re-adjusting dosages |

**Table 5** Clinical screening for complications in type 2 diabetes

| Complication | Clinical assessment |
|---|---|
| Cardiovascular disease | Blood pressure* <br> ECG <br> Echocardiogram to assess left ventricular function |
| Retinopathy | Fundoscopy (dilated pupils)* <br> Fluorescein angiography |
| Maculopathy | Visual acuity, with and without pinhole correction* |
| Peripheral vascular disease | Peripheral pulses* <br> Doppler studies <br> Ankle-brachial pressure index |
| Nephropathy | Plasma creatinine (plot 1/creatinine)* <br> Urine dipstix for protein* <br> Urinary albumin : creatinine ratio* <br> Creatinine clearance |
| Peripheral neuropathy | Vibration sensation* <br> – 128 Hz tuning fork <br> – biothesiometer <br> Sensorimotor: ankle jerks* <br> Pinprick sensation* <br> Protective sensation: 10 g monofilament* |
| Autonomic neuropathy | Lying and standing blood pressure <br> ECG: R-R interval on deep inspiration <br> ECG: R-R interval on Valsalva manoeuvre |

* These tests should be carried out on an annual basis unless more frequent assessment is indicated clinically. Other tests should be performed when clinically indicated.

# Special situations

## Pregnancy

### Pre-conceptual care

Not only are oral hypoglycaemic agents unlikely to achieve good glycaemic control in the face of increasing insulin resistance during pregnancy, but they also cross the placenta and are therefore potentially teratogenic. Sulphonylureas stimulate the fetal $\beta$-cells directly, exacerbating fetal hyperinsulinaemia and macrosomia. Women with type 2 diabetes trying to conceive should switch from oral hypoglycaemic agents to insulin therapy and optimise their glycaemic control. In addition to stopping smoking and avoiding alcohol, they should start taking folic acid (5 mg/day) until the end of the first trimester.

### Insulin requirements during pregnancy

Insulin requirements rise from the second half of the second trimester due to the effects of human placental lactogen and progesterone in decreasing insulin sensitivity and increasing glucose intolerance. A woman's insulin requirement may double by the end of the second trimester, but will return to prepregnancy levels immediately after delivery.[46]

## Breast feeding

Women who breast feed need to increase their carbohydrate intake but also usually need to decrease their daily insulin dose by about 25 per cent.[46] Oral hypoglycaemic drugs are contraindicated in breast-feeding women who should remain on insulin until they stop breast-feeding.

## Polycystic ovary syndrome and metformin

Metformin has been shown to increase insulin sensitivity (assessed by the euglycaemic clamp method)[47] and follicle-stimulating hormone (FSH), and to decrease testosterone, dehydroepiandrosterone sulphate, androstenedione and luteinizing hormone in women with polycystic ovary syndrome.[48] In some women, metformin restores a regular menstrual cycle and results in a progesterone level within the ovulatory range with a proportion of women achieving a spontaneous pregnancy.[49]

Metformin has been used extensively in South Africa in pregnant women with type 2 diabetes with no evidence of excess congenital abnormality or increased perinatal mortality.[50]

## Perioperative management in people with type 2 diabetes mellitus

Preoperatively it is important to optimize glycaemic and blood pressure control and to advise those who smoke to stop. Exogenous oestrogen therapy (combined oral contraceptive pill or HRT) should be withdrawn six weeks prior to surgery in order to avoid the associated risk of thromboembolism. In addition to the assessment of cardiovascular and renal function, clinical evidence of peripheral neuropathy and peripheral vasular disease should be sought, as their presence poses an increased risk of foot ulceration due to postoperative immobilisation. Fundoscopy should be carried out to exclude proliferative retinopathy if there is the possibility of anticoagulation being required postoperatively.

Long-acting oral hypoglycaemic drugs, for example, chlorpropamide, should be stopped five days beforehand and shorter acting agents substituted, for example, gliclazide. It is probably wise to discontinue metformin therapy perioperatively in view of the risks of dehydration and pre-renal uraemia. For similar reasons, care should be taken in patients undergoing radiological procedures with contrast media, if dehydration is a possibility.

The aims of perioperative management are to avoid metabolic decompensation in order to optimize wound healing and response to infection while minimizing the risk of hypoglycaemia. In addition to patients with type 1 diabetes, patients with type 2 diabetes with poor glycaemic control and those undergoing cardiac surgery also need insulin therapy perioperatively. Patients undergoing cardiac surgery need insulin regardless of their glycaemic control because this type of surgery is particularly stressful, with hypothermia and inotropic drugs causing rapid alterations in metabolic state. The usual morning dose of insulin and/or oral hypoglycaemic agents should be omitted and patients should be started on an intravenous sliding scale of insulin with hourly glucose measurements carried out using a glucose meter (Table 6). Fluid balance should be maintained by administration of intravenous fluids with appropriate potassium supplementation and urea and electrolytes monitored on a daily basis. The aim should be to switch back to the patient's usual regime, that is, subcutaneous insulin or oral hypoglycaemic agents as soon as they are eating, stopping the insulin infusion an hour after subcutaneous insulin has been given.

## Driving

In the UK, the regulations regarding fitness to drive are updated frequently and the advice of the Driver and Vehicle Licensing Agency (DVLA) should be sought if there is any doubt surrounding a patient's fitness to drive. Patients with diabetes treated by diet alone need not notify the DVLA nor their motor insurance company unless they hold a group 2 entitlement licence. All patients taking oral hypoglycaemic agents or insulin have an obligation to inform the DVLA and their insurance companies on starting treatment. No one with insulin treated diabetes is permitted to drive a heavy goods vehicle, a passenger carriage vehicle or pilot any type of aeroplane. Patients should also inform the DVLA in the event of recurrent hypoglycaemic episodes, loss of hypoglycaemia awareness or reduced visual acuity or visual field defects (as specified in the guidelines 'Medical aspects of fitness to drive').

# Emergencies

## Hyperosmolar non ketotic coma (HONK)

Patients with true type 2 diabetes do not present with diabetic ketoacidosis as their basal insulin secretion is adequate to suppress lipolysis. HONK is the extreme end of the spectrum of decompensated type 2 diabetes, is most commonly seen in the elderly, and carries a mortality rate of 30–35 per cent. About 60 per cent of those presenting with HONK are people in whom diabetes is previously undiagnosed.

# References

1. **UKPDS Group.** Intensive blood-glucose control with sulphonylureas or insulin compared with conventional treatment and risk of complications in patients with type 2 diabetes (UKPDS 35). *Lancet*, 1998; **352**: 837–54.

2. **Stratton IM** *et al.* Association of glycaemia with macrovascular and microvascular complications of type 2 diabetes (UKPDS 35): prospective observational study. *British Medical Journal*, 321: 405–12.

3. **Trovati M** *et al.* Influence of physical training on blood glucose control, glucose tolerance, insulin secretion, and insulin action in non-insulin-dependent diabetic patients. *Diabetes Care*, 1984; **7**: 416–20.

4. **Horton E.** Exercise and physical training: effects on insulin sensitivity and glucose metabolism. *Diabetes/Metabolism Reviews*, 1986; **2**(1&2): 1–17.

5. **UKPDS Group.** UK Prospective Diabetes Study 16: Overview of six years' therapy of type 2 diabetes – a progressive disease. *Diabetes*, 1995; **44**: 1249–58.

6. **Levy JC, Atkinson AB, Bell PM, McCance DR, Hadden DR.** Beta-cell deterioration determines the onset and rate of progression of secondary dietary failure in type 2 diabetes mellitus: the 10-year follow-up of the Belfast Diet Study. *Diabetic Medicine*, 1998; **15**: 290–6.

7. **University Group Diabetes Program.** A study of the effects of hypoglycaemic agents on vascular complications in patients with adult onset diabetes. 2. Mortality results. *Diabetes*, 1970; **19**(suppl. 2): 747–83.

8. **Wolffenbuttel BH, Graal MB.** New treatments for type 2 diabetes mellitus. *Postgraduate Medical Journal*, 1996; **72**: 657–62.

9. **Goldberg R.** A randomized placebo-controlled trial of repaglinide in the treatment of type 2 diabetes. *Diabetes Care*, 1998; **21**: 1897–903.

10. **Moses R.** Effect of repaglinide addition to metformin monotherapy on glycaemic control in patients with type 2 diabetes. *Diabetes Care*, 1999; **22**: 119–24.

11. **UKPDS Group.** UK Prospective Diabetes Study 26: sulphonylurea failure in non-insulin dependent diabetic patients over 6 years. *Diabetic Medicine*, 1998; **15**: 297–303.

12. **Johansen K.** Efficacy of metformin in the treatment of NIDDM. *Diabetes Care*, 1999; **22**: 33–7.

13. **UKPDS Group.** Effect of intensive blood-glucose control with metformin on complications in overweight patients with type 2 diabetes (UKPDS 34). *Lancet*, 1998; **352**: 854–65.

14. **Bailey C, Turner R.** Metformin. *New England Journal of Medicine*, 1996; **334**: 574–9.

15. **Lalau J** *et al.* Role of metformin accumulation in metformin-associated lactic acidosis. *Diabetes Care*, 1995; **18**: 779–84.

16. **Lalau JD** *et al.* Bicarbonate haemodialysis: an adequate treatment for lactic acidosis in diabetics treated by metformin. *Intensive Care Medicine*, 1987; **13**: 383–7.

17. **Campbell I.** Metformin and glibenclamide: comparative risks. *British Medical Journal*, 1984; **289**: 289.

18. **Lebovitz HE.** Current therapies for diabetes. In: Hirsch I, Riddle M, series eds. *Endocrinology and Metabolism Clinics of North America*, Vassello J, ed., vol 26, Philadelphia: WB Saunders, 1997: 539–51.

19. **Coniff R** *et al.* Reduction of glycosylated hemoglobin and postprandial hyperglycaemia by acarbose in patients with NIDDM. *Diabetes Care*, 1995; **18**: 817–24.

20. **Hollander AES** *et al.* Role of orlistat in the treatment of obese patients with type 2 diabetes. *Diabetes Care*, 1998; **21**: 1288–94.

21. **Orskov C.** Glucagon-like peptide-1, a new hormone of the entero-insular axis. *Diabetologia*, 1992; **35**(August): 701–11.

22. **Nauck MA, Kleine N, Orskov C, Holst JJ, Willms B, Creutzfeldt W.** Normalization of fasting hyperglycaemia by exogenous glucagon-like peptide-1 [7–36 amide] or [7–37] in type 2 (non-insulin-dependent) diabetic patients. *Diabetologia*, 1993; **36**: 741–4.

23. **Gutniak M, Orskov C, Holst JJ, Ahren B, Efendic S.** Antidiabetogenic effect of glucagon-like peptide-1 [7–36 amide] in normal subjects and patients with diabetes. *New England Journal of Medicine*, 1992; **326**: 1316–22.

24. **Turton MD** *et al.* A role for glucagon-like-peptide-1 in the central regulation of feeding. *Nature*, 1996; **379**: 69–72.

25. **Clark A, Charge SB, Badman MK, MacArthur DA, de-Koning EJAD.** Islet amyloid polypeptide: actions and role in the pathogenesis of diabetes. *Biochemical Society Transactions*, 1996; **24**: 594–9.

26. **Kong M** *et al.* Infusion of pramlintide, a human amylin analogue, delays gastric emptying in men with IDDM. *Diabetologia*, 1997; **40**: 182–8.

27. **Kolterman** *et al.* Receptor and postreceptor defects contribute to the insulin resistance in noninsulin-dependent diabetes mellitus. *Journal of Clinical Investigation*, 1981; **68**: 957–69.

28. **Stout RW.** Insulin and atheroma. *Diabetes Care*, 1990; **13**: 631–54.

29. **DCCT Research Group.** Epidemiology of severe hypoglycaemia in the Diabetes Control and Complications Trial. *American Journal of Medicine*, 1991; **90**: 450–9.

30. **Panzram G.** Mortality and survival in type 2 (non-insulin-dependent) diabetes mellitus. *Diabetologia*, 1987; **30**: 123–31.

31. **Morrish NJ, Stevens LK, Head J, Fuller JH, Jarrett RJ, Keen H.** A prospective study of mortality among middle-aged diabetic patients (The London Cohort of the WHO Multinational Study of Vascular Disease in Diabetics) II: associated risk factors. *Diabetologia*, 1990; **33**: 542–8.

32. **Julien J.** Cardiac complications in non-insulin dependent diabetes. *Journal of Diabetes and its Complications*, 1997; **11**: 123–30.

33. **Antiplatelet Trialists' Collaboration.** Collaborative overview of randomised trials of antiplatelet therapy-1: prevention of death, myocardial infarction, and stroke by prolonged antiplatelet therapy in various categories of patients. *British Medical Journal*, 1994; **308**: 78–97.

34. **Bell D.** Stroke in the diabetic patient. *Diabetes Care*, 1994; **17**: 213–9.

35. **Davis MD** *et al.* Risk factors for high-risk proliferative retinopathy and severe visual loss. Early Treatment Diabetic Retinopathy Study. Report 18. *Investigative Ophthalmology and Visual Science*, 1998; **39**: 233–52.

36. **Gundersen T, Kjekshus J.** Timolol treatment after myocardial infarction in diabetic patients. *Diabetes Care*, 1983; **6**: 285–90.

37. **Vantrimpont P** *et al.* Additive beneficial effects of beta-blockers to angiotensin-converting enzyme inhibitors in the Survival and Ventricular Enlargement (SAVE) Study. *Journal of American College of Cardiology*, 1997; **29**: 229–36.

38. **Solomon SA, Ramsay LE, Yeo WW, Parnell L, Morris-Jones W.** β-blockade and intermittent claudication: placebo controlled trial of atenolol and nifedipine and their combination. *British Medical Journal*, 1991; **303**: 1100–4.

39. **Holman R.** Lipids in diabetes study. *Diabetes*, 1999; **48**: S1; A1588.

40. **Andersson B** *et al.* Oestrogen replacement therapy decreases hyperandrogenicity and improves glucose homeostasis and plasma lipids in post-menopausal women with noninsulin-dependent diabetes. *Journal of Clinical Endocrinology and Metabolism*, 1997; **82**: 638–43.

41. **Brussard HE, Gevers Leuven JA, Frolich M, Kluft C, Krans HMJ.** Short-term oestrogen replacement therapy improves insulin resistance, lipids and fibrinolysis in postmenopausal women with NIDDM. *Diabetologia*, 1997; **40**: 843–9.

42. **Robinson JG, Folsom AR, Nabulsi AA** *et al.* Can postmenopausal hormone replacement improve plasma lipids in women with diabetes? *Diabetes Care*, 1996; **19**: 480–5.

43. **Hulley S** *et al.* Randomized trial of estrogen plus progestin for secondary prevention of coronary heart disease in postmenopausal women. Heart and Estrogen/progestin Replacement Study (HERS) Research Group. *Journal of the American Medical Association*, 1998; **280**: 605–13.

44. **HDS I.** Prevalence of hypertension in newly presenting type 2 diabetic patients and the association with risk factors for cardiovascular and diabetic complications. *Journal of Hypertension*, 1993; **11**: 309–17.

45. **UKPDS Group**. Tight blood pressure control and risk of macrovascular and microvascular complications in type 2 diabetes: UKPDS 38. *British Medical Journal*, 1998; **317**: 703–13.

46. **Alban Davies H, Clark JDA, Dalton KJ, Edwards OM**. Insulin requirements of diabetic women who breast feed. *British Medical Journal*, 1989; **298**: 1357–8.

47. **Diamanti-Kandarakis E, Kouli C, Tsianateli T, Bergiele A**. Therapeutic effects of metformin on insulin resistance and hyperandrogenism in polycystic ovary syndrome. *European Journal of Endocrinology*, 1998; **138**: 253–4.

48. **Velaquez EM, Mendoza S, Hamer T, Sosa F, Glueck CJ**. Metformin therapy in polcystic ovary syndrome reduces hyperinsulinaemia, insulin resistance, hyperandrogenemia, and systolic blood pressure, while facilitating normal menses and pregnancy. *Metabolism*, 1994; **43**: 647–54.

49. **Velazquez E, Acosta A, Mendoza SG**. Menstrual cyclicity after metformin therapy in polycystic ovary syndrome. *Obstetrics and Gynaecology*, 1997; **90**: 392–5.

50. **Coetzee EJ, Jackson WP**. Oral hypoglycaemics in the first trimester and fetal outcome. *South African Medical Journal*, 1984; **65**: 635–7.

# Index